MAKING CONFLICT WORK

MAKING CONFLICT WORK

Harnessing the Power of Disagreement

**PETER T. COLEMAN
AND ROBERT FERGUSON**

HOUGHTON MIFFLIN HARCOURT
BOSTON   NEW YORK
2014

For information about permission to reproduce selections from this book, write to Permissions, Houghton Mifflin Harcourt Publishing Company, 215 Park Avenue South, New York, New York 10003.

www.hmhco.com

Library of Congress Cataloging-in-Publication Data
Coleman, Peter T., date.
Making conflict work : harnessing the power of disagreement /
Peter T. Coleman and Robert Ferguson.
pages cm
ISBN 978-0-544-14839-0 (hardback)
1. Conflict management. 2. Interpersonal relations. 3. Interpersonal conflict.
4. Organizational behavior. I. Ferguson, Robert, date. II. Title.
HD42.C6424 2014
658.4'053—dc   232014011691

Book design by Victoria Hartman

Printed in the United States of America
DOC 10 9 8 7 6 5 4 3 2 1

CONTENTS

MAKING CONFLICT WORK

INTRODUCTION

HOW WELL DO you manage conflict with your boss or other superiors at work, or with the more difficult employees you need to supervise?

Belligerent bosses, petulant employees, demanding and disrespectful clients, former peers you now supervise, psychopathological CEOs. No matter how old you are, how long you have been in the work world, how many conflict-management trainings you have attended (or slept through), or how many best-selling books on difficult conversations you have read, problems with characters like these — up and down the food chain at work — are exhausting and can feel impossible. What can you do when your boss holds all the cards and enjoys being a jerk? Or when an employee you really depend on is constantly whining and being difficult? Or when vitally important clients insist on being demeaning?

When Sam* heard that the reorganization of his company had him reporting to a woman thirty years younger than him, he went quietly to his

---

* We conducted dozens of personal interviews for this book. During the interviews, we heard regularly about concerns over privacy and the possibility of making colleagues (or former colleagues) uncomfortable — or fears of reprisal. Or we heard about policies restricting employees at any level from speaking on the record about sensitive internal matters. Many interviewees agreed to speak with us on condition of anonymity. This book is about real people, attempting to work through real situations. Except for public figures, some story details and circumstances have been changed to protect confidentiality, and most individuals are identified by pseudonyms, and their organizations are kept anonymous by request.

office and stewed. He liked and respected Isabella; the sting he felt was not personal. But he had come up through the ranks of manufacturing in the eighties and nineties and had the battle scars to prove it. Now he'd be taking orders from someone a few years out of an MBA program. He tried to avoid contact with her and quickly acquiesced to her at the first hint of a difference of opinion. It made their working relationship excruciating for both of them.

Tammy responded differently. When her friend Susan became her supervisor at the nongovernmental organization they worked for, Tammy mumbled, "She's one of *them* now." Tammy believed that all people in positions of power grew to like it and abuse it. Although her former friend tried repeatedly to collaborate with her, Tammy treated her as a defector. Eventually Susan had to fire Tammy for a series of disciplinary problems and insubordination. Tammy pushed Susan to be confrontational and punitive and so confirmed her own bias about those in power.

Like many executives, Carlos, the new CEO of a $300 million textile firm, knew that his company's move toward global business required them to transform their transfer-pricing model, a method of profit allocation that helped to minimize their tax burden. The current system for setting transfer prices often benefited individual manufacturing sites but in effect punished the company for overseas sales. Carlos had to initiate a major change in transfer pricing, which would likely encounter stiff resistance.

Carlos started by asking Tony, his chief financial officer, to design a transfer-pricing model and suggested he get input from others. Tony was extremely bright and knowledgeable; he quickly developed a very good model. But he did it by himself. Feeling the urgency of the situation, Tony rolled out the new pricing model to the company. It was soon mired in conflict, as managers throughout the organization haggled over details. There was more resistance than expected — much more. Carlos had asked Tony to use a more participatory process for the development of the model but had not insisted.

"We ended up having to start over because my leadership had been weak," Carlos reflected. "Tony and I had been equals for years. He's got a sharp mind and a strong will. It had never been within my power to give him orders. But this time I should have directed him. I should have insisted he act more collaboratively on this initiative. Instead I watched Tony roll out a model created in a one-man vacuum. It was a great model, but I knew the process was wrong and I didn't follow my instincts."

When Richard took over as division head of a large communications technology company, his direct reports (and their reports) soon learned that stifling ideas might hurt innovation and problem solving, but sharing ideas could lead to career extinction.

Ernie, a quiet but thoughtful young accountant, got the point quickly. Richard invited him to participate in a "diagonal slice group." Specifically designed as a forum for top leadership to listen to employees from various functions at all levels of the organization, it was advertised as an open, nonthreatening environment where an administrative assistant's opinion carried as much value as a chief engineer's. When Ernie asked an innocent question about budgeting during one of the group's early meetings, Richard interjected with "Let me tell you why that's a *stupid* question." Ernie decided then and there never to question Richard again.

A pattern of such comments from Richard eventually led to fewer and fewer questions being raised—and no disagreement. From *anyone*. After a few months, his arrogant behavior had eliminated all candid, constructive feedback, but he concluded that he was doing such a great job leading and communicating that he had achieved "near total alignment" within the division. This delusion lasted until new ideas and products dried up and sales followed.

This is a book about conflict, power, and change. It chronicles the challenges and opportunities we face when we find ourselves in conflict with those in authority—bosses, executives, regulators, police officers, professors, and parents, to name a few—and with those we have authority over. It also addresses what to do in those precarious situations in which power shifts occur and we face new conflicts with former peers we now supervise, or with former supervisees who have now become the boss.

Conflict is a lot like fire. When it sparks, it can intensify, spread, and lead to pain, loss, and irreparable damage. It can distract, distance, derail, and occasionally destroy opportunities and relationships. It makes most people anxious, and as a result it is often mishandled and made worse. It can waste time and lessen productivity, impair teamwork and morale, increase counterproductive behaviors like stealing and sabotage, and poison the physical and mental health of employees. So conflict can burn.

Power is often likened to energy, which physicists define as the capacity to do work—to get things done. But for all our efforts to acquire power, both having it and not having it are riddled with traps, constraints, consequences, and misunderstandings. Having power and authority in relationships often comes with high expectations, demands, duties, and responsibilities that can be surprisingly constricting. Ask any new parent or president or CEO. And not having it is much worse.

When conflict and power mix, the results can be explosive.

Unfortunately, conflict and power tend to travel together. When people find themselves in conflict, they immediately—almost automatically—become aware of the balance of power in the situation or relationship: "Hey, you work for *me,* so back off!" Or: "Wow, he is much bigger and drunker than I thought he was before I told him to shut up. Bad idea." Or: "If you say one more insulting word to me, I will rally my fleet of attorneys to devote the rest of their careers to making you wish you had never met me." Conflict puts power differences into focus.

Similarly, power shifts and disparities in power often create conflict. Class conflicts, race conflicts, gender conflicts, generational conflicts—just about any intergroup conflict is essentially about power. When disadvantaged minority groups organize to demand their rights, it's about power. When unions strike, it's about power. At work, when people are demoted in rank, it creates conflict. Promotions too tend to stir envy and resentment, which often show up as conflict sooner or later.

Understanding how conflict and power affect each other is vital to effective conflict management, but talking about power differences openly is still taboo in most places in society. It is almost wholly absent from discussions over work conflicts, negotiation planning, and even conflict-management trainings, despite the fact that most workplace conflicts are not between equals and ignoring power dynamics is absurd. It's especially costly in today's work environments, where 25–40 percent of managers' time is spent mired in conflict with aggrieved board members, supervisors, clients, peers, and subordinates.[1]

We have seen this power taboo in organizations we work with across the globe.

The United Nations is an excellent case in point. To fulfill its mission of promoting international cooperation and peace, UN leadership and staff needed to understand and apply constructive conflict-resolution methods in their work. The UN's human resources (HR) department contacted our International Center for Cooperation and Conflict Resolution at Columbia University (usually referred to as the ICCCR) and asked for help developing a program of training for UN personnel, based on a model of collaborative negotiation originally created by ICCCR's founder, Morton Deutsch.

The training offered skill building and employed role-playing techniques that allowed the participants to negotiate three work-conflict scenarios, all based on actual UN incidents. The first scenario involved a multicultural conflict within a work team at the UN. The second was a conflict between two coworkers involving tensions over responsibilities and sharing credit for their joint tasks. So far, so good. The training, and especially the role-playing, brought familiar conflicts to life in a way that clearly illustrated basic challenges and win-win negotiation principles. It also allowed participants to practice and refine their skills before returning to the "real world" of their office or post.

During the third scenario, however, the training screeched to a halt.

This scenario involved a conflict between a superior and a subordinate at the UN, a very common occurrence. Almost without exception this case overwhelmed the collaborative skills of the savviest participants and proved discouraging to the instructors as well. Participants playing the boss would quickly leap into command-and-control mode, seeking to protect their authority and reputation and impose their will. They struggled to listen or stopped listening altogether. Empathy fled the scene. Negotiations morphed into competitive power struggles.

The participants playing the subordinate would attempt a strange combination of submissiveness and inflexibility as they tried to prevent going from less power to powerless. They appeared helpless and passive but would also automatically reject even the most reasonable solutions. Both parties quickly established their positions and dug in. Until, of course, the boss "won." Power and its peculiar effects on conflict derailed the training.

Ironically, it was never a simple case of domination by the boss. Typically, even though both parties in the case had interests to negotiate, 90 percent of the time in the session was devoted to listening to the employee's grievances alone, until the boss dismissed the employee's concerns in favor of "what needs to be done." The stickiness of a vertical conflict in the hierarchical world of the UN proved too difficult for most of the participants to navigate.

The world may now be flat, but most organizations are not. We encountered this problem during training sessions with every level of the UN professional staff and in cultures around the world. But HR at the UN had never mentioned it and was not prepared to address it.

The dynamic at the UN is typical. Research has shown consistently that high-power parties in conflict tend to behave in a domineering and exploitative manner—like Richard in the opening example, who believed that the lack of disagreement in his meetings was simply evidence of his fine leadership. In a variety of studies of U.S. trade negotiators, lab studies with MBA students, and survey studies with managers and supervisors, higher-power parties were found to prefer command-and-control, take-it-or-leave-it (or take-it-or-suffer) approaches to conflict and negotiation.² In contrast, lower-power parties in conflict tend either to behave submissively or to adopt counterdominance strategies such as acting ingratiatingly cooperative, knavishly evasive, or ideologically aggressive—like at the UN. And when power shifts and changes happen in relationships—as with Sam and Tammy—it can be terribly destabilizing for all involved.

This book is based on the premise that power and authority differences between disputants radically change the nature of effective conflict management. Constructive methods of conflict resolution—integrative, win-win approaches to negotiation, bargaining, problem solving, and mediation, which you may have read about in such bestsellers as *Getting to Yes* (Fisher, Ury, and Patton), *Crucial Conversations* (Patterson, Grenny, McMillan, and Switzler), and *Difficult Conversations* (Stone, Patton, and Heen)—are excellent when facing disputes or conflicts with peers. But conflicts up and down the chain of command are a different game completely; when the rules change, so must our strategies and tactics. Conflict-prone professional environments and political networks require leaders, managers, and employees to have a wide array of conflict-management strategies and tactics and to be able to employ them artfully and effectively. This is what we call *conflict intelligence*.

Work conflicts often have an emotional core which is well known to managers and employees but neglected by trainers and consultants. Although conflicts in business and industry are often practical matters—calculated strategy games—they still involve human beings. Even in the rational world of organizations, emotions often trump reason in conflict. Those without power feel zapped of motivation, thwarted, and even occasionally driven to subtle forms of retaliation and sabotage. Scholars suggest that the lack of detailed attention to emotions and relationships is the biggest gap in our understanding of conflict today.

We aim to offer a practical tutorial in managing conflicts across power differences effectively and channeling the considerable energies from conflict in organizations toward achieving important goals. Grounded in more than fifteen years of empirical research conducted in our lab at Columbia University and tested in organizations around the globe, this book offers groundbreaking, evidence-based insights into the strategies and skills necessary for managing even the most demanding work conflicts. In addition to integrating some of the most robust and influential empirical research in the field of conflict resolution, we draw on interviews and case studies with managers, administrators, and executives.

Peter T. Coleman is an internationally recognized expert in conflict resolution, a professor of psychology and education at both Teachers College and the Earth Institute at Columbia University, and director of the ICCCR and the Advanced Consortium on Cooperation, Conflict, and Complexity (AC4) there. He has conducted decades of research on social power and constructive conflict, has published widely in the area, and is also a New York State certified mediator and experienced consultant. Robert Ferguson has been a practicing psychologist and executive coach for more than twenty years, helping executives, managers, and entrepreneurs resolve conflicts and effectively influence individuals and teams. Together, we combine rigorous university scholarship with in-the-trenches insights, to provide the ideas, steps, and skill-building exercises for transforming work conflicts from crises into opportunities.

It's true that in general the research on work conflict tells a bleak story. But conflict can also help create more effective, creative, and innovative organizations.[3] Constructive conflict negotiation has been found to improve the quality of leadership, decision making, and resource and risk management within organizations. It can even boost bottom-line performance and build stronger employee relationships.

So what determines whether conflict at work causes dissatisfaction and burnout as opposed to strengthened performance, innovation, and enhanced relationships? This is a major challenge for anyone who has ever worked in an organization with two or more people, be it in a diner, a school, a department of sanitation, or a multinational corporation.

Our goal is to show you what you can do to make conflict work for you, not against you. We'll explain how to shed inhibitive habits of mind and action and learn to become more agile and adaptive in addressing the many different kinds of conflict you face daily at work, and what to do when even being adaptive doesn't get you a productive resolution.

When you find yourself in conflict with someone at work who has power over you, you will likely be inclined to capitulate, giving in or appeasing the other person to keep your job. Just as tricky are disputes and disagreements between you and your subordinates. Often, those in high power lose. That's right, *they lose* — they don't get what they really need, they waste time, spend a lot of energy listening to the angry demands of subordinates, and fail to create value in conflict. Why? They have a hammer, so they use it. Their default reaction when in conflict is demand and control. This impairs a leader's capacity to lead effectively. Managers and employees who have honed their conflict intelligence respond differently.

Consider Rafael, the CEO of a medium-size manufacturing company, faced with the Great Recession of 2009. In order to tighten his company's budget, he set up several task teams made of middle managers. He knew that while cutting resources was guaranteed to stimulate conflict, not doing so could be fatal in a shrinking economy.

First, he worked with his executive team to identify several cost-cutting goals. Then he put together six teams and told them to look for $28 million to cut and to complete the project in three months. Once he presented the business case for the cuts, established numeric goals, and gave the teams adequate resources, he stepped away. He simply asked for a weekly summary, but resisted giving more specific instructions.

"I had the power to make dictatorial decisions," he said. "I could have claimed it was necessary because of the economic crisis. But I didn't want to do that. There may be fewer overt conflicts in a dictatorship, but the hidden conflicts and the passive-aggressive resistance are terrible. I have learned that you have to be adaptive on tough decisions that stir up conflict. I don't want to make all the decisions, but I know I have to set boundaries and provide enough time and other resources if I expect others to take responsibility."

The teams accomplished their tasks in nine weeks instead of the allotted twelve. And they exceeded the $28 million goal by $2 million.

"To be honest," admits Rafael, "I wanted twenty-five but gave twenty-eight as the stretch goal. And I said I wanted to see the savings in twenty-four months. We saw it in fifteen. I had confidence that the teams could find the right cuts, but more importantly, I needed them to feel committed to these tough decisions. To get that commitment I gave them a ballpark to run around in so they could be part of the game."

When Ruth first became head of an independent K-5 school, she felt inspired. Her dream had been to work at a child-centered school. She assumed everything about the school's curriculum, governance, and philosophy would be focused on the psychology and learning needs of young children. A few weeks into the job, she realized she was wrong. Although the school's approach was ostensibly child-centered, the fundamental power premise of the staff was that the teachers know best and should not be questioned. Too many of the teachers mistook their love of and devotion to their young students for expertise. It was as if they had an unwritten, sentimental commandment:

> THOU SHALT NOT QUESTION A TEACHER
> WHO OBVIOUSLY LOVES HER STUDENTS.

Because of this community-wide belief, the teachers had more power than the parents, the administrators, and the children. Ruth began to confront this belief early on. "You say you want a child-centered school," she announced at an early faculty meeting. "Of course that does not mean you let the children make the decisions, but it does mean that teachers are held to a professional standard concerning best practices."

She encountered tough resistance, but she was not intimidated by conflict. She argued, listened, educated, cajoled, charmed, collaborated, and at times coerced. "You cannot say you want one thing and do something contrary," she often commented. Eventually it became evident that she was not simply trying to take power away from the teachers. As paradoxical as it may sound, she was trying to increase and decrease their power simultaneously. She replaced the short-term power of resistance and stubbornness with a shared sense of power based on strategy, results, and professional development. She eventually altered the power structure of the school radically.

Now, years later, the very people whose authority she challenged say things like "When you work for Ruth, you end up giving your best because you know she's giving hers. You feel stretched and frustrated for a while, but in time you see yourself as a more competent and proud professional."

Nelson Mandela, one of our world's great leaders, was a man of many contradictions. Born the son of a village community leader, he developed an abiding respect for authority. Yet he spent decades of his life fighting doggedly against pro-apartheid state authorities in South Africa. Having had consensus-based decision making modeled for him by his father, Gadla Henry Mphakanyiswa, a local chief and councilor to the monarch, he learned to listen, facilitate, collaborate, and unite. But having trained as a boxer and a trial lawyer, he also developed as a tenacious fighter, spending hours every day training his body and mind to be strong, disciplined, and overpowering.

Years later Mandela became a leader of the African National Congress (ANC) and shared their core value of nonviolence. He was a master at methods of noncooperation and civil disobedience, organizing scores of nationwide mass marches and stay-at-home protests. But when these strategies failed and were met with brutal violence on the streets from government forces, he went underground for two years to start a militant wing of his party and studied military strategy, munitions, sabotage, and guerilla warfare. Yet Mandela had the foresight to target the use of violence against things, not people; he realized that the destruction of objects like energy grids, bridges, and communications towers—things that could make the country ungovernable—would be less alienating and less consequential to South Africans and the international community than human violence.

Mandela was later incarcerated on Robben Island and served as a political prisoner for twenty-seven years. While in prison, he developed the fine arts of jujitsu tactics, learning to leverage his low position of power by using the rules and laws of the authorities to bring about their own undoing. He studied the prison handbook and committed the rules to memory and then would cite them chapter and verse and use them to control the actions of the more violent guards. He also quietly built relationships of rapport with many of his guards, learning of their personal circumstances and the names of their children. When he was eventually approached by the Afrikaner government who instigated negotiations over the terms of his release, Mandela bargained tenaciously, even choosing to stay at the table when he learned that the government was simultaneously attempting to derail his party, the ANC, by providing their enemies in the Inkatha Freedom Party with weapons. Later, when elected president of South Africa in 1990, Mandela displayed the compassion, grace, and benevolence of a truly great human being—reaching out to unite all of the people of his fractured and damaged nation.

Mandela employed all of these seemingly contradictory competencies and strategies—as convener and boxer, nonviolent activist and violent militant, empowered prisoner and embattled president—over the course of his decades-long struggle against apartheid and journey toward a united, democratic, multiethnic South Africa. He needed all of these tools to adapt to a rapidly changing world and to change the world for the better. He needed them to lead. As President Obama said at Mandela's memorial, "Nothing he accomplished was inevitable."

Let's revisit Sam, the forty-year veteran at the manufacturing firm who was told to report to the newly appointed Isabella. As you may recall, Sam did everything he could to avoid or appease Isabella at first. But to Isabella's credit, she sensed how challenging the change was to Sam. She reached out to him, making it obvious that although she had a new title, she needed his knowledge and experience to help the entire team succeed. Instead of overruling his decisions or telling him what to do, she listened carefully and discussed many issues in depth. In time, Sam came to appreciate Isabella's efforts and reengaged, displaying and sharing his forty years of institutional knowledge and business acumen. These were welcomed resources to Isabella, who made sure that Sam was remunerated for his expertise. In fact, they made such a great pair that their unit excelled and was formally recognized.

Leaders, managers, and employees of all stripes can benefit from proven strategies and skills for navigating the hazardous challenges of conflict up, down, and across the organization. In a time when many organizations strive to be "flatter," or more democratic, and leadership strives to be "transformational," by appealing to workers' loftier goals and values, too many organizations still get stuck in hierarchical conflicts that inhibit candor and creativity, foster resentment, and falsely lead executives to believe that their organization is "perfectly aligned." These conflicts often impair information flow, problem solving, innovation, organizational adaptation, morale, and even survival. Today, most organizations need to flex and respond to rapidly changing environments. This requires the sharing of information, ideas, and opinions — from the bottom up and the top down. This takes a climate of trust, creativity, and respect — and a minimum of intimidation. It takes adaptation.

Making Conflict Work answers the plight of leaders at every level. We offer a map for navigating conflict and power at work, describe the various conflict-power traps identified in research, and provide seven basic strategies for channeling the lively but sometimes treacherous conflagrations of power and conflict on the job: benevolence, support, dominance, appeasement, autonomy, adaptivity, and rebellion. Mastering these strategies is best achieved by assessing what determines your own responses and outcomes when conflict is involved. To that end, we provide self-assessment tools, exercises, checklists, and summary tables to guide managers, executives, administrators, teachers, mediators, negotiators, consultants, and attorneys through what otherwise could be a complex and intimidating topic.

1

The Nature of Conflict and Power

CONFLICT IS NOT an inherently bad thing. It is a natural, fundamental, and pervasive part of life. It is what happens when things are opposed—when different interests, claims, preferences, beliefs, feelings, values, ideas, or truths collide.

Because conflict elicits anxiety, it can bring about extreme reactions from people. They can become overly obsessed with conflict and seek it out all the time, or they can become highly fearful and avoid it at all costs. They may feel a need to approach it in an overly formal or rigid manner, or respond with spontaneity and sloppiness. Some people feel desperate to get conflict over with as quickly as possible, while others hold on to it and ruminate about grievances long past. For some, conflict is a game or task to be approached with strategy and cunning. For others, it is a profoundly personal, emotional experience.

Despite its poor reputation, under the right circumstances, conflict can be functional and positive. When it goes well, the people involved tend to feel satisfied, can learn or innovate, and may even grow closer as a consequence.

Conflict can also be destructive and isolating. When it goes poorly, people can feel dissatisfied, frustrated, or wronged and become resentful and alienated. At work, it can lower job and team satisfaction and increase rigidity of thought, psychosomatic complaints, and burnout.[1]

Higher levels of conflict in marriages have been found to compromise immune systems, elevate coronary calcium levels (a risk factor for heart disease), and slow the healing of wounds and infections.[2] When conflict grinds on and begins to feel unsolvable, it can bring misery.

For decades, the Holy Grail of conflict research has been the answer to one question: Why do some conflicts go horribly wrong while others go quite well? This is what some of the world's most influential thinkers, like Sun Tzu, Aristotle, Marx, Freud, Kurt Lewin, Mary Parker Follett, Mahatma Gandhi, Martin Luther King Jr., Nelson Mandela, and Morton Deutsch, spent their lives contemplating.

The answer, generally speaking, is some combination of two things: the people and the place. Our personalities, histories, sensitivities, temperaments, gender, training, cultural upbringing, language, levels of impulse control, and other characteristics — these qualities combine to affect how we generally tend to respond to conflict. The circumstances of a specific place — cultural norms and rules, laws, the presence of authorities or other third parties, the prevalence of violence, availability of weapons, codes of honor, temperature, and so on — also impact how a conflict will unfold there. But what really matters is how these two things, people and place, interact. For instance, think of how you might react to a conflict with a traffic policeman in your hometown versus a border-patrol officer at a checkpoint in the West Bank in Palestine. And compare that with how one of your more impulsive, volatile colleagues might respond to the same situations. What will determine the direction of the conflict is how the natures of the people involved interact with the specifics of the situation.

Over many decades, social scientists have been busy at work in their labs and in the field conducting research on those aspects of people and environments that determine whether conflicts go well or poorly. We have learned a lot about the nature of conflict itself, and we've found that a few factors matter most in determining the nature and outcome of a conflict. Our lab ran a study with 149 expert conflict mediators to identify what they saw as the most important differences in conflicts that affect their conflict-management strategies and outcomes. We surveyed the mediators and asked them to describe their last conflict mediation in detail—regardless of whether it went well or poorly—and then to tell us what they did, why, and how it turned out. After analyzing their responses, we found that conflict processes and outcomes are most affected by the following three main components.

Conflict Intensity Level: Technically, *intensity* is the level of energy required to address a conflict. Conflicts can range from easy to tolerate or manage, to seemingly impossible. This basic quality captures a host of other related factors, including the amount of history between the parties, the level of emotion, the length of the conflict, its complexity, the importance of the concerns and issues involved, and whether the identities of the people involved (including race, class, and gender) were implicated in the conflict. Lower-intensity conflicts elicit less anxiety, irrationality, and extreme behavior, and evidence fewer contentious responses from disputants. As a consequence, they require less energy.

Conflict Structure: This refers to the actual, objective goals associated with a conflict (not how they are perceived). Conflicts can range from consisting of purely cooperative, win-win (also known as integrative) goals, where the disputants share the same underlying concerns, to those with purely competitive, win-lose (also known as zero-sum) goals, where the only way for Disputant A to achieve his or her goals is for Disputant B to lose. For example, two parents may dispute over the time of a curfew for their adolescent son, but fundamentally both share a common concern for his health and safety. However, if a divorcing couple is battling over who gets their shared assets, then the structure of their conflict is more competitive. When conflicts are more competitive, they tend to elicit more strong-arm, contentious, and domineering responses and to escalate more easily and move into escalatory spirals that result in more highly destructive patterns.

Conflict Transparency: This is essentially the degree to which a conflict is explicit or openly expressed. A lack of transparency in personal relationships and professional transactions is often a source of conflict. Generally, the more transparent or explicit a conflict, the easier it is to address constructively through discussion, negotiation, and mediation. However, under some circumstances, such as when the disputants themselves are unclear about what is bothering them, when the timing of sharing one's concerns is bad, or when the social or political repercussions of expressing a conflict are dire, transparency can be less of an advantage.

What we learned about the effects of these three components of conflict in our study was intriguing. The intensity of the conflict was the biggest predictor of the types of behaviors between the parties: the higher the intensity of the conflict, the more unfriendly and disrespectful their behavior. The degree to which the disputants shared common goals was the biggest predictor of whether they'd reach an agreement. The more explicit the issues in the conflict, the more the disputants viewed the mediation process as fair and the more likely they were to find a resolution.

Since conflicts that are low intensity, cooperative, and overt tend to be much easier to manage and more likely to result in positive outcomes than those that are high intensity, competitive, and covert, our most basic goals should be to better understand how to keep conflicts from moving in the latter direction and how to defuse the ones that do.

This might entail moving the conflict from covert to overt, so that you and the other disputants can better understand it and perhaps identify areas of misunderstanding, common ground, or possible compromise. This requires the capacity for self-reflection and contemplation, so that the disputants can gain a better sense of what is at stake, what their priorities are, and why they are reacting in the way they are. It also requires capacity for other-orientation and respectful inquiry, so that the disputants might better gauge the underlying concerns of the others involved and learn why they may wish to keep them hidden.

You may also need to move a conflict from high intensity to lower intensity so that threat, fear, anxiety, and impulsive reactions recede and a sense of possibility, hope, and reason returns. This often begins with space: allowing yourself and the disputants some time and space away from the demands of the conflict in order to regroup. Chapters 4–10 outline a myriad of ways to lower (and raise) the intensity of conflict.

To make a conflict less competitive, it helps to identify potential areas of common ground so that the disputants can recognize their shared interests and move the dynamic toward the constructive.

One of the most important things we have learned from the systematic study of conflict over seven decades is that conflict leaves its mark. Conflicts, even trivial ones, tend to have a lasting impact on us. They affect how we feel about ourselves, how we feel about the others involved, and how we feel about the place in which the conflict occurred. They are formative.

Morton Deutsch, one of the founders of the field of conflict resolution, discovered something important in his lab at Columbia University about forty years ago. He and his students had been conducting a series of laboratory studies on conflict for about a decade—using a trucking board game he invented called the Acme-Bolt Trucking Game—when he started to see something intriguing in the pattern of data across the studies. He noticed that certain conditions of conflict would perpetuate themselves. If they began the studies with the players in a cooperative mode (with shared goals or similar backgrounds or open forms of communication or a shared history of cooperation), then it was very likely that they would cooperate in the conflict and continue to do so until they resolved their differences constructively—with both of them winning. If the same participants played again, the same thing would happen. If, on the other hand, they started with the players in a competitive mode, then they would approach the conflicts in the game competitively as win-lose conflicts that would tend to escalate and lead to victory for one or a competitive stalemate. This pattern would repeat itself as well when the players played again. Deutsch called this his "Crude Law of Social Relations"—that cooperative conflict engenders more cooperation in the future, and competitive conflict, more competition.

This means that how we approach and resolve our conflicts initially—cooperatively or competitively—often has implications for the future, beyond the current event. The bottom line with conflict is sim-

ple: we want to minimize destructive conflict (where one or both disputants are dissatisfied or disgruntled) and maximize constructive conflict
(where all parties are sufficiently satisfied or at least not dissatisfied)
whenever possible.

Right (you may be thinking); this all makes perfect sense. But I've
heard much of this before, and the *real* problem is how I do this when
the conflict is with my (a) brutal boss, (b) most peevish employee, (c)
most demanding client, (d) supercilious trustee, (e) needy union rep, or
(f) all the other unhappy campers I deal with at work. How do I navigate
those constructively?

We have heard these concerns for years in courses and workshops
with managers, executives, and other employees around the world in
government, multinational organizations, private companies, universities, and the military. We consistently hear the same questions and comments:

> "What if you disagree with your boss and you know she hates con-
> flict?"

> "When I disagree with one of my employees, I do everything I can to
> make it a healthy give-and-take discussion. I want them to work with
> me, not just for me. Even so, my subordinates seem reluctant to tell
> me things or to offer their opinions."

> "My boss says he wants a candid exchange of ideas, but we all know
> what outcome he really wants from the beginning, so why stick my
> neck out?"

> "I was promoted and had to manage my old friends; one of them
> couldn't handle it. It was awful."

> "My manager is a bully. How can I use these conflict-resolution
> techniques when he's yelling at me or telling me to shut up?"

"Technically I am at the same level as the other team leaders, but in every meeting they try to overpower me by being argumentative and sarcastic."

Probably the number-one thing that aggravates and complicates conflict dynamics at work is power. Having it, not having it, hoarding it, sharing too much of it, bestowing it, abusing it, fighting it, channeling it, enhancing access to it by others, or wielding it over them. Power differences between people are a common source of conflict, and conflict makes people acutely aware of power differences.

This is a primary reason we had for writing this book. The effects of power on conflict management and of conflict on power dynamics have been largely neglected and marginalized in both the scholarship on conflict and especially in the practice and training side of conflict management. This gap is glaring given the fact that the vast majority of conflicts happen between people and groups with differences in power, authority, and status.

We wrote this book to help people better understand, cultivate, and more effectively leverage power for constructive conflict management.

Power means different things to different people. We prefer a rather straightforward definition derived from the work of the management visionary Mary Parker Follett. Follett was an American social worker by trade and is one of the great unsung heroes of conflict resolution and management theory. In the 1920s, she worked with labor-management conflicts in business and industry, was an advisor to President Theodore Roosevelt, and was one of the first women invited to address the London School of Economics. Follett offered a view on power and authority in organizations that was a radical departure from the prevailing emphasis on power through control and coercion. She defined power simply as "the ability to make things happen." Building on this, we define power as "the ability to cause or prevent actions and to make things happen, and the discretion to act or not act."

In conflicts, *relative power* is key: our ability, relative to the ability of the other stakeholders, to cause or prevent things from happening. Can you veto or obstruct my goals and desires? Can you help me achieve them or prevent me from harm, and can I, in turn, do the same for you?

The accuracy of our assessments of relative power is affected by several factors, including, most importantly, how we think about this thing we call power.

Our Assumptions about Power

In a series of studies conducted in our lab and elsewhere, we have found that a major factor in interpersonal relations and performance at work are the implicit theories we hold about abstract things like leadership, followership, intelligence, and power. These four constructs are central to everything that goes on in work organizations, but people think about them in very different ways, and these differences affect their attitudes, feelings, and actions.

We all operate on a set of unconscious assumptions or theories about constructs like power and rely actively on them when making sense of the world. These implicit theories guide the way we process and comprehend information about events, ourselves, and others.

For example, a basic assumption underlying many managers' views of organizational power is that it is a fixed-pie, or scarce, resource—that there is only so much of it to go around. If I delegate authority to you, I lose some power and control. This *fixed-pie theory* has been found in our research to automatically set up a competition for power between supervisors and employees (and even more so between peers). This win-lose perspective leads to more politicking, power hoarding, and a reliance on strategies of domination in conflict, which increase the need for constant scrutiny and control of subordinates.

Alternatively, some managers view power unconsciously as something that can be grown and increased in cooperation with others. They believe that by working together with their employees they can all gain more power and influence. This more cooperative and incremental theory of power, called an *incrementalist theory,* has been found in our research to be associated with managers who are more likely to share power and information with employees and support employee empowerment initiatives.

Which power theory do you hold? Fixed-pie? Incrementalist? A bit of both?

When it comes to power differences in conflict, your basic assumptions matter. The more you hold a fixed-pie theory of power, the more likely you are to take a competitive approach to power politics and conflict. The more you hold an incrementalist theory, the more likely you are to empower your peers and supervisees whenever possible and share your power and resources. You'll be more likely to try a more cooperative, win-win approach when appropriate.

The challenge for most of us is that we are unaware of the assumptions we hold that drive our responses to power and conflict. Simply being mindful of these different assumptions and theories can help control or enhance them.

The sources, types, and means of power are as infinite as our imagination. Whoever thought that one way to win a world-championship heavyweight boxing match was to constantly goad your opponent in public and then allow him to pummel you with punches until he was too exhausted to defend himself (until Muhammad Ali pulled this "rope-a-dope" strategy against George Foreman in Zaire in 1974)? Or that one way to end a war was to organize the spouses and concubines of the warriors to withhold sex from them until the violence ceased (as with Aristophanes' Lysistrata and later Leymah Gbowee in Liberia)? Or that one way to win an election as governor of a state was to promote yourself as a ridiculous comic-book hero who has no knowledge of or particular interest in governing (Jesse Ventura in Minnesota in 1998)? Power is everywhere, waiting to be identified, created, and mobilized.

Scholars have identified some particularly important distinctions to consider when facing or leveraging power in situations of conflict. Here, we describe what we see as three major factors—the approach taken, the resources drawn upon, and the levels of power engaged—that have direct implications for the strategies we outline in the remainder of this book.

Approaches to Power

Power over, power with, power apart from, and *power under* others are four distinct approaches to power in conflict, each with its unique values, costs, and consequences. We benefit most when we understand and are skilled in all four.

American political scientist Robert Dahl proposed that power involves "an ability to get another person to do something that he or she would not otherwise have done." We call this approach to power *power over.* It is linked with the capacity to overcome the resistance of the other and emphasizes the controlling and potentially coercive aspects of power, viewing it as both a mechanism for maintaining order, efficiency, and authority and, when abused, a problem to be contained.

Understanding *power over* is immensely important. Managers need to be able to maintain a reasonable degree of order and efficiency at work, and coercive power can be a necessary or practical tool when you find yourself in a conflict with unjust or unresponsive others or in situations where subordinates are hostile or unmotivated to comply with reasonable demands. Accordingly, this approach will be discussed in detail in chapter 6, on dominance.

However, employing a predominantly controlling approach to power at work can have negative consequences. It can produce alienation and resistance in those subjected to it. This, in turn, can limit your ability to use other types of power that are based on trust and increase the need for continuous scrutiny and regulation of subordinates. If your goal is to achieve compliance *and* commitment to the job from your subordinates, then sole reliance on a *power-over* strategy will prove costly.

Alternatively, the management guru Mary Parker Follett argued in the

1920s that even though power in work organizations is usually conceived of as *power over* others, it should also be possible to develop *power with* others.[3] She envisioned this type of power as jointly developed: coactive and noncoercive.

Power with is based on an incrementalist theory, which views power as an expandable resource that can bring about constructive and satisfying outcomes for all. It tends to motivate people to search out one another's abilities and competencies and to encourage and appreciate their contributions, and to exchange resources that will help both parties be more productive.[4] As you can imagine, this creates a very different type of response and climate than *power over*.

Follett suggested that one of the most effective ways of restricting the use of coercive power strategies at work was to develop the ideas, capacity, and conditions that foster *power with*. This presents employees and managers with an alternative approach to managing conflict. In this way, Follett was able to rise above the contentious and violent power struggles between labor and management that had threatened the survival of many organizations during the 1920s. She did so by encouraging both groups to see the value of working together to improve their mutual situation.

Research on cooperation and power has largely supported Follett's thinking. Researchers have found that when managers and employees view their tasks, rewards, and outcome goals as shared or cooperative, it increases the likelihood of the constructive use of power between higher- and lower-power persons. Cooperative goals at work, when compared to competitive and independent goals, have been found to induce higher expectations of assistance, more assistance, greater support, more persuasion and less coercion, and more trusting and friendly attitudes between superiors and subordinates.[5] The tactics inherent in this approach are discussed in detail in chapters 4 and 5, on benevolence and support.

The *power-with* approach in organizations has its own pathologies and detractors. An overreliance on *power with* can result in what hardliners call a well-intentioned pipe dream: an idealistic vision of something ultimately unattainable. Given the ruthless jungle of the marketplace and of most organizational environments, they argue, the possibilities for mutual enhancement through cooperative power are limited. At its extreme, *power with* can lead to inefficiencies, irresponsible leadership practices, chronic consensus seeking, and nepotism at work.[6]

A third approach to power is *power apart from* others. This is essentially the power that comes from independence or from a lack of dependence on others, the ability to make things happen unilaterally. This will be very familiar to those of you who have adolescent children who increasingly employ the strategy of slamming and locking their bedroom door when in conflict, or who artfully ignore every word or caution their parents utter.

Power apart from has been a particularly popular strategy in business negotiations. For instance, the theory of power dependence in negotiations states, "The power of A over B is equal to and based upon the dependence of B on A."[7] This means the less you need me in a negotiation, the more power you have. Laboratory research has generally supported this model, finding that negotiators who hold more attractive BATNAs (best alternatives to a negotiated agreement, or the possibility of achieving desired outcomes through alternative means[8]) or who are able to increase the other party's dependence are less dependent on their negotiation partners and thus possess greater power relative to them.[9] The more independent someone is in negotiations and conflict, the more options, leverage, and therefore *power apart from* others they have. We elaborate on this approach in chapter 8, on selective autonomy.

However, the use of *power apart from,* unlike the previous two forms, is usually limited to those work or business situations in which the need to work with or through others is low, dwindling, or absent. These situations are much less common in today's work world, where our increasing interdependence is more and more obvious and robust. *Power apart from* tends to be a particularly suspect tactic in cultures that value collectivism and teamwork. Nevertheless, this approach to power is a good one to keep tucked away for the right occasion.

Finally, there is the often-dreaded and rarely cited approach of *power under*. This is an approach to power that involves obtaining assistance and support from others, often through a dependence relationship.[10] In chapters 5 and 7, on support and appeasement, we outline a variety of tactics used by lower-power parties for "borrowing" power.

Dependence relationships can serve the needs of those in low power, but they can take many forms, from benign and supportive (as in many mentor-mentee relationships) to oppressive and abusive (as with dictatorial leaders). The negative physical and psychological impact of prolonged experiences of dependence and powerlessness by adults has been shown to be dire and can lead to a tendency to become more rigid, critical, controlling of others in lower power, and, ultimately, more irrational and violent.[11]

Resources for Power

Whether you're employing *power over, with, apart from,* or *under,* there are two basic types of resources for power that you can use: hard and soft. Harvard Professor Joseph Nye has written extensively in the realm of U.S. foreign affairs and trade negotiations about the distinction between *hard power* and *soft power*. Hard-power tactics, be they military, economic, technological, or legal, essentially coerce or incentivize others to do things through the threat of punishment or the promise of reward, typically against their will. It is therefore commonly associated with the *power-over* approach. Soft power, on the other hand, suggests the ability to attract and co-opt others—rather than force or coerce—drawing on cultural, moral, inspirational, and social sources. It is getting others to want the outcomes you want. Nye writes, "Seduction is always more effective than coercion, and many values like democracy, human rights, and individual opportunities are deeply seductive."[12]

This distinction translates easily to conflict in the workplace. At work, formal authority and the power to hire and fire, reward and punish, and even threaten and humiliate others are typical forms of hard power employed in negotiations and conflict. Alternatively, developing a reputation as the go-to problem solver or an IT wiz or as having high emotional intelligence, compassion, or a clear moral compass can give you a lot of soft power. Wielding this type of influence can serve to prevent, mitigate, and resolve conflict.

Smart power employs a strategic combination of both hard and soft power to achieve desired outcomes.[13] Chester Crocker, former assistant secretary of state under President Reagan, describes it in the international realm as "involving the strategic use of diplomacy, persuasion, capacity building, and the projection of power and influence in ways that are cost-effective and have political and social legitimacy."[14]

The art and science of combining hardball tactics with softer, resistance-removing forms of influence like trust, inspiration, persuasiveness, and personal relationships to negotiate and resolve conflicts effectively has been largely absent from research and discussions of conflict management in business, industry, and nonprofit organizations until now.

Levels of Power

Power dynamics in conflict can be thought of as operating at two distinct levels: one determining the nature of the interactions between players on a field, and one determining the nature of the field itself.[15] *Secondary power* refers to the exercise of power in the conventional sense—the ability to get one's goals met in a relationship. *Primary power,* referred to by sociologists as the *deep structure of power,* signifies something more fundamental and pervasive: the ability to shape our sense of what is good and bad, important and unimportant, valuable and worthless. Primary power refers to the ability to affect those basic activities (such as laws, ideology, morality, symbolism, the media, policies, agendas, and decision-making processes) that shape the playing field. Secondary power involves the many strategies and tactics used while playing on the field to influence others.

At work, people often find themselves thrown into a conflict game in which the playing field has been skewed to the benefit of one of the parties. From this perspective, power does not reside solely within the A-B (*power over, power with, power apart from, power under*) relationship. Instead, A and B are embedded within a set of rules and norms that have been previously established. A manager can give orders and expect them to be followed, because the role of a manager has been historically established to include notions of order giving. The various strategies that managers may use to obtain their employees' compliance or commitment are forms of secondary power, but primary power makes those options possible.

The distinction between primary and secondary power is consequential and will play a direct role in our discussion of the various strategies, in particular when circumstances call for radical *change or revolution*.

At this point, you should have a working understanding of the pieces of our puzzle: the two types of conflict (constructive and destructive), the three levers for conflict management (intensity, structure, and transparency), the four approaches to power (*power over, power with, power apart from,* and *power under*), and the two sources (hard and soft) and levels of power (primary and secondary). Together, they provide us with a set of options that readies us for the constructive management of most work conflicts. In the chapters that follow, we will employ these distinctions to elaborate more thoroughly on the seven strategies for addressing power and conflict at work.

For now, the bottom line with power in conflict at work is simple: whenever possible, we want to maximize our use of effective power when in conflict. What do we mean by *effective power*? Simply the ability to make the things we want to happen, happen.

Having all the resources in the world and a sophisticated knowledge of influence strategies and control over defining the playing field does not necessarily translate to effective power. History is replete with powerful groups and individuals who hoarded, abused, or squandered their power to no meaningful effect. Exercising good judgment and employing power so that it is appropriate in type and magnitude to the situation are key factors for wielding effective power.[16] They will also directly impact the very foundations for conflict at work, your *emotional reservoirs*.

2

Power-Conflict Traps

THE VAST MAJORITY of conflicts we face are not one-time exchanges with strangers but encounters with people with whom we have some type of ongoing relationship. The emotional context of these relationships—whether they are mostly positive, mostly negative, or mixed—largely determines the nature of our experiences of the conflicts we face.

A few years ago, Jared R. Curhan and his colleagues at the MIT Sloan School of Management and UC Berkeley set out to map what is really important to people when they negotiate disputes.[1] The researchers found that four things are most important to negotiators:

- Their *feelings* about the instrumental outcomes
- Their *feelings* about themselves in the negotiation
- Their *feelings* about the negotiation process
- Their *feelings* about their relationship with the other negotiator

In short, emotions rule.

Of course, these findings challenged the traditional rationalist assumptions that have dominated the negotiation field for decades, which presented conflict negotiations as robotic, strategic, purely economically motivated interactions best practiced by rational, unemotional actors.

Even though we have known since the early work of Nobel laureate Herbert Simon and James March in the 1950s that humans are crummy rational decision makers, the field of negotiations has clung to rational models too long. Many practical techniques of conflict management offer recommendations like "If you become emotional during conflict, wait until it passes before you act," or "Rise above your emotions and try to get a *rational* perspective on the situation." This advice may be useful when emotions are a passing anomaly or inconvenience in conflicts, but not when emotions are enmeshed within the conflict—not when they *are* the rationale.

We are not merely poor rationalists affected by our emotions. The role of emotions in conflict turns out to be much deeper than that; in fact, they establish the basis for our experience and understanding.

This discovery comes from the work of researchers like John Gottman, who studies marital conflict and divorce in his Love Lab in Washington State (described in Malcolm Gladwell's book *Blink*); Marcial Losada, who studied conflict within strategy teams in business and industry in his Capture Lab at the University of Michigan; Barbara Fredrickson, who studies positivity in her Positive Emotions and Psychophysiology Lab at the University of North Carolina at Chapel Hill; and Katharina Kugler and Peter T. Coleman, who study moral conflicts in their Intractable Conflict Labs at the Ludwig Maximilian University in Munich, Germany, and Columbia University in New York. Their mathematical-modeling approach to conflict research has shown that, in many ways, emotions trump reason.

These researchers and others like them are finding increasingly that emotions set the stage for conflict. First, surprisingly, and despite the volumes of negotiation research that suggest positive emotions are good and negative emotions are bad in conflict, this research has found that negative conflictual encounters are in fact good and necessary. Under the right circumstances, negative interactions between romantic partners, colleagues, and others in conflict can actually help the people in conflict learn important things about the other person, their relationship, and themselves (like the fact that they can be jerks).

The second thing that emotion researchers have identified is what they call the *negativity effect*. This is the simple fact that negative experiences and emotions tend to have a significantly larger and more lasting impact on people than positive ones do.

This is important because of the third thing researchers have learned: *emotions pool.* Over time, our emotional experiences of other people, relationships, or particular situations gather and collect into neurological reservoirs of positive and negative emotions. In fact, our malleable, neural-plastic brains can become rewired through repeated interactions with people and places and so increase or decrease our propensities to experience them as positive or negative.[2] Think of what it might feel like to return to the bar where you first met your spouse, or the high school gymnasium where you blew those free throws in the waning seconds of the divisional championship game, or the corner candy store where you hung out and snuck cigarettes with your friends in high school. These places hold emotional memories for us. Similarly, other people and our relationships with them also carry pools of positivity and negativity—usually some combination of both.

These emotional reservoirs are the main consideration in most conflicts; they set the stage for destructive or constructive interpretations and interactions to unfold. If you overhear a colleague speaking to some of your coworkers about what a bum you are at a bar after work, how will you react? It depends, right? It depends on your past relations with him and whether you have experienced him as a warm and friendly smart-ass who enjoys giving you hell, or whether he has been a conniving backstabber with his eye on your job. It's the emotional context of your past experience that affects your reactions. In fact, research on emotions and decision making with patients suffering from severe brain injuries has found that when people lose the capacity to experience emotions, they also lose their ability to evaluate and make important decisions.[3] Emotions are not only relevant to our decisions in conflict; they are the basis for them.

It is very important that a sufficient reservoir of positive emotions be present in the context of relationships to buffer the potent effects of negative emotions during conflict. In fact, this is probably the most important finding from the emotion researchers—the central importance of the ratio of positivity to negativity in our relationships for predicting difficulties in social conflicts.

Losada has found that a 4:1 ratio of positive to negative emotions was associated with higher-performing work teams.[4] Gottman found that a ratio of 5:1 predicts stability and marital happiness (which makes sense because marriages are more about feelings and sentiment than most work relations).[5] That means that workers need to experience four positive encounters with their coworkers for every one negative encounter in order for them to be able to use the inevitable conflicts they will face together instructively. In marriages, it's five positive encounters for each negative experience. The studies show that with lesser ratios, say, an even 2:1 positive to negative, the power of the negative acts begin to overwhelm and spoil the relationship. In time, the reservoir for negativity becomes vast and the reservoir for positivity vanishes, setting the relationship up for disaster. Then, even minor skirmishes can trigger all-out wars.

This research doesn't suggest that cognitive processes associated with conflict analysis, negotiation planning, strategy, and integrative problem solving are not important to managing conflict constructively. They are. But focusing solely on them is a mistake. Emotions establish the scaffolding for our cognitive processing of information. Even in the rational world of organizations, emotions often trump reason in conflict. Especially in the long run.

Although our individual temperaments and specific hot-button issues play a role in influencing which type of emotional conflict traps we develop and become most susceptible to, studies have shown that it is largely the nature of the situations we face and our power relative to others in conflict that determine this.

While the stumbles of the very powerful are often more blatantly on display than those of us peons (we all know when the U.S. president or Donald Trump or Sarah Palin makes a misstep), they are not alone in their susceptibility to such snares. Everybody up and down the food chain—the boss, the boss's boss, the underling, and the peer—faces a unique set of conflict traps.

High-to-Low Power-Conflict Traps

Having power in its many forms is often mesmerizing, intoxicating, and addictive, and has been known to drive men and women to all forms of extremes. Having power in conflict is typically much better than not having it. Nevertheless, several pitfalls of being in high power in conflict can affect our perceptions, values, morals, and behavior. Here are the more common forms.

THE POWER-PSYCHOSIS TRAP

In the classic comedy *Bananas,* Woody Allen captures with poignant absurdity how people in power often go too far. In the film, the newly "elected" dictator of a fictitious Central American nation, President Esposito, announces to his citizens: "Hear me. I am your new president. From this day on, the official language of San Marcos will be Swedish. . . . In addition to that, all citizens will be required to change their underwear every half hour. Underwear will be worn on the outside so we can check. Furthermore, all children under 16 years old are now . . . 16 years old!" In hushed tones from the crowd, the protagonist, Fielding Mellish (Woody Allen), whispers to a friend, "What's the Spanish word for 'straitjacket'? The power has driven him mad."

Research has shown that the powerful tend to develop a very different psychological experience of the world than those in lower power. When in high power, individuals tend to begin to process information more abstractly, perceive other people in more instrumental terms, and become more goal focused, self-confident, and less inhibited than those in low power. In addition, wielding power has been shown to have a hampering influence on cognitive processes, which reduces the capacity for complex social reasoning, constrains moral judgment, and increases the use of stereotypes.[6]

In one particularly telling lab study, participants made to feel powerful (by being asked to think of a time when they were in authority) systematically underestimated the physical size of a target person, both when the target was presented in a photograph and face-to-face.[7] This suggests that the experience of powerfulness leads people to misperceive power-relevant cues in others (like physical size), distorting what they actually see.

The implications of this trap for conflict management are straightforward: the powerful should not trust their own eyes. There is a high probability that their reading of conflict situations will be highly biased, skewed in their favor, and inaccurate. So if anything important is on the line, check yourself and verify your understanding of events with others.

THE BULLETPROOF TRAP

Research has also documented how the powerful come to feel increasingly invulnerable to the consequences of their own actions. Take Bernie Madoff. In 1960, he established a penny-stock trader firm with five thousand dollars he earned working as a lifeguard and sprinkler installer. He borrowed fifty thousand dollars from his father-in-law to establish the Wall Street firm Bernard L. Madoff Investment Securities LLC. His business grew slowly with the help of his father-in-law, who referred his close circle of friends and their families. By Madoff's own account, the business began as a legitimate investment business but evolved into a corrupt Ponzi scheme in the 1990s (the FBI suggests it was the 1970s). Even as many on Wall Street became openly suspicious of his business practices and his firm underwent several fraud investigations, Madoff continued to defraud thousands of investors of billions of dollars. Today he's serving a 150-year sentence in a federal penitentiary for committing what's considered the largest financial fraud in U.S. history.

This is a dynamic of the powerful that scholars call "superoptimism." It is a form of hubris or arrogance in which power holders feel they can do or say whatever they want and so act on their urges and needs even if they violate the rules. If they aren't caught, they aren't punished. Their behavior is then reinforced by the reward of satisfying their urge or need without any (meaningful) punishment. Over time, they move on to more egregious violations, believing they can't be caught or punished. Until, of course, they are.

In conflict, the bulletproof trap translates into unnecessary and even frivolous risk taking, which can bring harm to you and your group (think of former U.S. Representative Anthony Weiner), as well as alienate other parties and stakeholders.

THE INVISIBLE-UNDERLING TRAP

People in high power have also been found to simply pay less attention to those in lower power.[8] In negotiations, high-power parties typically respond less to their counterpart's emotional displays than do low-power parties. High-power individuals are also less likely to adopt someone else's perspective or accept another person's background knowledge, and are less accurate judges of facial expressions. The powerful also recall less correct information about their subordinates and are less able to distinguish their unique characteristics.

The research suggests that those in power attend less to their subordinates for three reasons.[9] Those with lesser power are seen as having little impact on the power holder's goals, and are thus not worth their attention. Power often comes with additional responsibilities, which can make people distracted and less likely to pay attention to others. Those in power may also choose not to attend too closely to the less fortunate, because it stirs feelings of guilt and shame.

Having higher power seems to impair your capacity to appreciate what others see, think, and feel. When the less powerful become invisible and inaudible to those in authority, there is often a cost in morale and declining positivity, which can exacerbate conflict. When it happens commonly within an organization, it has a high cost, wasting critical information, expertise, and feedback.

THE POWER? WHAT POWER? TRAP

In negotiations, high-power bargainers are notoriously bad at analyzing and estimating the leverage and resources available to their counterpart in lower power. In a study of several high-level international negotiations over aid, trade, and resource disputes, scholars found that the more powerful countries' negotiators typically neglected to think about power differences at all.[10] If they did, they usually operated on the assumption that their superior aggregate power was sufficient to allow them to prevail in negotiations, and so they paid little attention to the specific types of leverage their lower-power adversaries might employ in the negotiations.

Weaker-power parties are often much more powerful than they appear to be at first glance, and more powerful parties are often weaker than they assume they are. The aggregate power of each side is usually a bad predictor of the outcomes of a particular negotiation.

THE SCREW-THE-RULES TRAP

One of the more intoxicating side effects of wielding power for extended periods of time is the tendency to start to believe that rules are for chumps.

This is particularly common in politics. Take the mayor of a medium-size city who had aspirations for national office and who regularly got people to act outside of city ordinances and without council approval. People were so intimidated by him (or expected some sort of favor) that he never got in trouble. More than once he told people, "If you don't like it, hit the door." He used city maintenance workers to work on his farm, to move furniture in his personal residence, and eventually to build the desk he took to D.C. when he won election to the U.S. House of Representatives. When a local strip club refused to give him a percent of their profits, he threatened to shut them down. It was as if he believed the resources of the city were his own—that power deserved entitlement.

In a fascinating (and slightly terrifying) series of studies conducted at Berkeley University in California, wealthier people were found to be more inclined to violate rules and break the law.[11] For instance, drivers of more-expensive cars (like BMWs and Mercedes) were three to four times more likely not to stop for pedestrians crossing a crosswalk than drivers of less expensive cars. Wealthier participants also took two times more candy from a pile set aside for children during a study, and were four times more likely to cheat in a dice game when money was on the line. The wealthy were significantly more likely to lie during negotiations and to endorse unethical behavior like stealing at work. This pattern of findings was consistent across more than thirty studies conducted with thousands of people, both liberals and conservatives, across the United States.

In these studies, wealthy people who were made to feel temporarily poor became more generous and altruistic, while poor people who were made to feel wealthy became more selfish and self-focused. These researchers at Berkeley suggest that "Generosity is for suckers" appears to be the ideology that springs from being wealthy.

This trap is double-edged. Rule breaking and a selfish disregard for others is both bad for you and, more obviously, bad for those with whom you dispute—albeit great for setting the stage for rebellion, discussed in chapter 10.

THE COMMAND-AND-CONTROL TRAP

People in high power tend to become very comfortable adopting a domineering and controlling conflict-resolution style and often lose the capacity to respond in other ways. Research has consistently shown that power holders fall easily into domination. Having power in negotiations is strongly associated with monopolizing speaking time and speaking out of turn.[12] Similarly, those with greater power are much more likely to express their private opinions and true attitudes, and they are much less affected by the expressed attitudes or persuasion attempts of others.[13]

In case studies of international negotiations, the high-power parties all adopted one of two strategies: "take it or leave it" or "take it or suffer." The researchers wrote, "The stronger parties regarded themselves as having more important things to do, since they were strong, and although they valued the bilateral relationship, they were often annoyed by their weaker partner's lesser concerns and narrow interests. No one showed special indulgence or generosity toward the weak targets."[14] Ultimately, many of the more powerful negotiators fared less well than their counterparts and failed to create value by acting in a more flexible manner.

When dominance starts to always feel right, it probably isn't.

THE BLIND-AMBITION TRAP

You remember Macbeth, Shakespeare's Scottish nobleman who was on an already impressive career path when his ambition got the best of him? So strong and blind was his drive for success (along with that of his lovely wife) that he risked his otherwise solid career by murdering the king. Not even a team of executive coaches (referred to by Shakespeare as "witches") could talk him out of it.

High-power individuals tend to become increasingly more optimistic, more confident about their choices, and more action oriented. This increase in optimism also affects attraction to risk, with high-power individuals showing greater risk preferences and making riskier choices than low-power individuals.[15] People in high power also tend to pursue their goals more actively and aggressively with little or no inhibition or empathy for the little guy.

Power can create a sense of license. People with blind ambition fail to notice what is happening around them. They narcissistically overlook the emotions, reactions, and interests of others. They ignore relationships, other than for their political or otherwise self-serving value. Leaders aren't the only ones who do this. When star athletes at an NCAA Division 1 basketball program were disciplined for fighting with "townies"—just months before the NBA draft—powerful alumni called to threaten parents of the non-university combatants. Besides the obvious stupidity of this behavior, it shows that power plus blind ambition can add up to cutthroat tactics.

THE VORTEX OF POWER—WHEN IT ALL WORKS TOGETHER

Ultimately, the research suggests that these many different psychological, social, and behavioral effects of power can work in concert in organizations to create a self-reinforcing tide of top-down domination that is very difficult to overcome.[16] In other words, a formidable conflict trap. The different psychological experiences of the powerful help power holders maintain control of the critical resources on which others depend. This provides the powerful with higher status at work and guarantees their continued access to important resources. Such a situation can seem intractable for those in lower power or anyone trying to transform a company toward a more decentralized, adaptive organization.

Low-to-High Power-Conflict Traps

Power, as we have discussed, is not some absolute quality or asset. Power is relative to the situation. You can have less power in one situation and more in another. A CEO can make a phone call and affect millions of dollars and many lives but still have to wait in line to use the restroom at a busy conference center. Some people experience low power in more situations than others, but most everyone gets to experience it at some point.

When people remain in low-power positions for extended periods of time, they too are susceptible to certain emotional conflict traps. Here, we describe several of the more common low-to-high power-conflict traps in brief.

THE KEEP-YOUR-HEAD-DOWN TRAP

Ed worked on the factory floor for twelve years; his father, more than twenty-five years. They had seen plenty of supervisors and managers come and go, some better than others. Both men felt that it did not matter much what they said to or asked for from the "higher-ups." If they followed all safety rules, showed up on time, did not abuse break time, and met their production quotas, they would be paid. Ed believed he could make some things happen at work, but there certainly was a limit. So when he was asked by the new boss what he wanted, he said he wanted more overtime work, maybe better ventilation, and longer breaks. He did not even consider education benefits, profit sharing, or a chance to make the rank of supervisor. He liked to keep his goals "realistic."

People with less power tend to have lower aspirations and expectations and think and plan in shorter time spans. Research has found that low-power individuals are subject to more social and material threats, especially the threat of losing favor among higher-ranking individuals, and they are more acutely aware of the constraints that these threats place upon their behavior.[17] Reduced power has also been associated with a more negative affect; greater attention to threat, punishment, and others' interests; more careful and controlled information processing; and more inhibited social behavior. Even when subordinates try to engage in overt acts of upward influence to improve their own situations and thus reduce the gap in power, they are likely to feel that their voices have fallen on deaf ears.

In negotiating contexts, those lower in power are less likely to initiate a negotiation and to make the first offer, even though making the first offer has been shown to lead reliably to the accumulation of more resources and thus more power. For example, studies have found that undergraduates who negotiated their starting salaries earned, on average, an additional $5,000 in their first year on the job.[18] Although a $5,000 difference may not seem like a huge sum, given a conservative rate of 3 percent in both raises and interest, by age sixty those who chose to negotiate would have $568,834 more!

THE BURDEN-OF-LOW-EXPECTATIONS TRAP

In the classic 1968 *Pygmalion in the Classroom* study, teachers were led (falsely) to believe that some of their students would show dramatic intellectual growth during the course of the year, while others would not. By the end of the year, those students that teachers expected to improve did in fact improve: their average increase in IQ was twice as large as the increase in IQ for the control group of students.[19] The study showed that teachers' expectations contributed significantly to this difference; teachers gave more attention and support to the students who they expected would blossom, and this encouragement helped them develop more rapidly than the control group.

The "Pygmalion effect" directly translates to adults in organizations. In one study, researchers assigned participants to manager and clerk roles in an organizational simulation and found that clerks rated managers as more competent than fellow clerks, even though they knew the roles were randomly assigned.[20]

Low expectations from superiors tend to inflict strong psychological constraints on those in low power, further limiting their aspirations, expectations, and behavior in conflict and contributing to the depth of their negativity reservoirs at work.

THE POWERLESSNESS-CORRUPTS TRAP

In 1971 psychologist Philip Zimbardo conducted an experiment on power and roles at Stanford University. He recruited twenty-four students to live as "guards" and "prisoners" in a mock prison constructed in the basement of the psychology building. The students playing guards were instructed to make the prisoners feel powerless. Soon the guards inflicted intentionally intimidating authority on the prisoners, whose anger erupted into a riot on day two. The experiment had to be stopped after just six days. Many have interpreted this controversial experiment as evidence that powerlessness evokes resentment and rage.[21] Under real-life conditions, where power differences are complex and real—affecting one's livelihood, career choices, or even one's sense of safety and freedom—resentment simmers, one degree at a time, slowly heating to a tipping point of sabotage or uprising.

Powerlessness can produce a strong sense of latent resentment and rage, impairing the capacity to engage constructively in conflict. This can result in serious health problems, heightened rigidity, violent acting out, or a strong drive to sabotage and undermine those in authority. Harvard Business professor Rosabeth Moss Kanter reminds us that it is not just power that corrupts. Relative powerlessness can also corrupt by increasing "pessimism, learned helplessness, and passive aggression."[22]

The lesson for low-power conflict management is one of the more challenging: although destructive, contentious, and coercive responses to such conflicts may feel right, we must ask ourselves if this response is viable and effective in the long run.

THE DIVIDE-AND-CONQUER TRAP

People and groups in low power who are being oppressed by high-power groups often find it easier to vent their frustration by targeting members of other low-power groups, and they therefore are more easily manipulated into being divided and conquered by those in power.

This was a classic strategy employed by many colonial powers attempting to disempower the indigenous ethnic groups that resided in their newly established and resource-rich African and Asian colonies. In South Africa, groups like the African National Congress and the Inkatha Freedom Party, who were natural allies against the pro-apartheid Afrikaner government of P. W. Botha, allowed themselves to become further divided and antagonistic to one another by the actions and rhetoric of the government, and so more easily controlled.[23]

The negativity and stress that comes with being low power in a protracted dispute takes its toll. However, the manner through which low-power groups process and manage their troubles can take many forms, and turning on one another is often the least productive.

THE EQUALITY-ILLUSION TRAP

Some low-power workers choose to deny or ignore differences in authority and status between themselves and their superiors. Although this can help alleviate some of the psychological stressors of having low rank, sometimes the reality of the top-down chain of command comes crashing in.

Ava was excited to receive Howard's offer to join a K–12 private school in the Pacific Northwest as head of grades nine through twelve. Ava anticipated a strong, equal working relationship. Although he had the official authority that came with the title of headmaster, Howard repeatedly talked about working together to accomplish goals.

One of Ava's goals was to strengthen the academic program; she wanted to empower teachers in each core subject to serve as curriculum coordinators so that all teachers could incorporate innovations at the same time. A few weeks into the school year she presented her idea to Howard and received a decidedly noncollaborative response: "No, I don't want to do that."

"Looking back," recalled Ava, "I was arguing like a lawyer, thinking he would join in the debate. I thought of us as colleagues with equal power who would eventually influence each other toward a solution. But he was more like a judge than a lawyer, and shut down the conversation." Determined, she waited several months, then convinced other administrators and teachers to suggest it to him. The following year Howard allowed Ava to assign teachers as curriculum coordinators, just as she had originally proposed.

Over a four-year period, the pattern repeated. Ava proposed and argued for her proposals, and either lost completely or had to rely on surrogates for influence. As she felt less and less powerful in relation to Howard, the frustration made her very unhappy, and she eventually resigned.

"I was naive about how Howard would use his power as headmaster. He tended to be very dominant during a conflict and used his power like a bully. But others were able to influence him. They would chat and banter and laugh at his inane jokes. It seemed so indirect and ingratiating, like they were bowing to the emperor. But my argumentative lawyerlike approach failed miserably. They were clearly more effective."

THE VICTIM-STATUS TRAP

People and groups in lower power in conflict can get comfortable with the attention and higher moral status bestowed on them from their peers and outside parties for being disadvantaged. This sense of victim status can contribute to a more self-righteous orientation to the conflict and higher rigidity and resistance to resolution.

There are many instances of this trap. We see it in divorce disputes where one or both parties feel wronged by their former spouse and so make extreme, even impossible, demands during the proceedings. We see it in strikes by labor unions whose members feel bullied or ignored by businesses or corporations and so allow a strike to drag on interminably in order to share the pain. We see it frequently in the international arena when the plight of a low-power group in conflict with elites gets media attention and, as a result, a broader base of support. The rise in support increases the group's aspirations and demands at the bargaining table considerably or encourages them to pull out of negotiations altogether. We see it in the workplace when someone takes no responsibility for an interpersonal problem, preferring to feel the superiority of victim thinking rather than resolve the conflict.

We are not suggesting that increasing the aspirations of low-power groups in conflict is a problem. On the contrary, most low-power groups would benefit from aiming higher. However, if the status incurred by being recognized as a victim in a dispute leads to recalcitrance and resistance to talks, it can become a costly trap.

THE VORTEX OF POWERLESSNESS—
WHEN IT ALL WORKS AGAINST YOU

Low-power disputants have it harder. While they may have a more accurate view of the conflict situations they face than high-power disputants do, the view is much more dim, tiresome, and pessimistic. Again, the research suggests that the many effects of low power can work in concert to create constraints that are difficult to overcome.[24] Together, the psychological experiences of the less powerful serve to keep them down and help power holders maintain control. A perfect swamp.

Equal-Power Traps

In general, equal-power conflict results in more constructive negotiations than unequal. Equal-power parties reach agreements more often, require fewer trials to do so, make larger concessions, and use fewer damaging tactics.[25] However, a few traps do await the not-so-savvy disputant equal in power to the other side in conflict.

THE DEADLOCK-OF-EQUALS TRAP

Lab studies and analyses of case studies of international negotiations have found that some conflicts between colleagues with relatively equal power result in more deadlocks, as neither party is inclined to capitulate.[26] These situations are also more likely to encourage open expressions of conflict and escalation than those of unequal power.

Lucy and Kala were two new staff members at a nonprofit training organization. When Lucy noticed Kala using outdated handouts, she commented on it. Kala explained that she was too busy and did not have time to gather and photocopy newer handouts. "If you want to do that for me, then I'll use the new ones." Lucy pointed out that the older handouts looked dated, incomplete, and reflected poorly on the organization. "I think the old ones are good enough," replied Kala. Although Lucy felt strongly about her perspective, she dropped the issue. "I disagreed with Kala, but there's nothing I can do about it because I don't have any supervisory power over her."

Of course, if it were only about handouts, it would hardly matter. But the same two staff members began to have other, bigger conflicts. Lucy wanted to improve the organization's method for evaluating the effectiveness of the training they offer to communities and organizations. She proposed several evaluation methods and wanted to start using them soon. Kala wanted a different approach. "We can't start evaluating our training until we can articulate our theory of change. Otherwise we would just be collecting disconnected statistics. What is our big picture?" While they both had valid points, they could not escape the lure of deadlock. Both were hoping their director would step in and "resolve" the conflict. Until then, they were trapped in equality; trapped in the false belief that someone with more power had to break the tie.

THE BATTLE-OF-THE-TITANS TRAP

People in positions of high power tend to be more experienced in dominating and thus employ it more readily. When they are in conflict with another equally high-power party, they often appear more concerned with maintaining their status relative to the other party than with reaching an agreement.[27]

When Patrick and Bill, the respective sales and manufacturing managers for a small but successful company, disagreed over something—anything—the game was on. Both loved to win a good fight, whether it was about a policy, a hire, a contract, a strategy, or pretty much anything else. Both automatically tried to dominate the other. Argumentative, relentlessly logical, and stubborn, both believed there was no such thing as a dead heat. And each ran his department with a dominant style.

In many ways it worked. The company was profitable every year, and growing. Each department chafed a bit under its manager's style, but nobody would have labeled the micromanagement as abusive. The CEO was pleased with the approach and results of both men. He liked that they were scrappy with each other, referring to it as "creative tension." He thought highly of them and often bragged about his "team of winners." He paid very little attention to anyone below the leadership level and asked very few questions of his managers about staff morale. "Outcomes speak for themselves," he was fond of saying. Both men were determined to keep it that way.

When a major contract caused trouble, conflict rippled through the organization. Millions of dollars were on the line, and most people's first instinct was to assign blame. To the CEO's credit, he said he did not want a blame game, he wanted a solution. "I want us to minimize our loss, and maybe even use this as an opportunity to do better in the long run with this customer." He assigned Patrick and Bill to work together to solve the problem.

But for Patrick and Bill, it was "game on." Both believed that not winning was worse than losing. So they fought and struggled with each other and eventually their contempt for one another became apparent to the client. It was hard to miss. In the end, they all lost.

THE FIGHT-FOR-TABLE-SCRAPS TRAP

Because low-power parties in conflict feel anxious yet powerless to affect each other's behavior, they tend to become particularly concerned with defending the little status they have.[28] They'll be damned if they're going to be shown up by another underling.

When Elizabeth was first hired as assistant professor of psychology at a large university, she was excited about collaborating on research with other young researchers. She had many inventive ideas for investigating the mental health of police and firefighters and hoped to establish a line of inquiry that took advantage of the career drive and original thinking of early career academics.

She set up meetings, e-mailed her thoughts about possible joint investigations, and invited colleagues to coauthor papers. But within a year she became discouraged. Turf battles, disagreements, egotism, and other annoyances taught Elizabeth that collaboration among equals was hard to realize. She and her equal-rank colleagues could not agree on direction, strategy, or career benefits of any single research project. Meanwhile, experienced professors were inviting her to join their research as a way of getting started and "getting the attention of the right people." Eventually she decided it was more important (or at least more doable) to cultivate her image with her superiors than to create innovative research with equals. Her goal became to achieve a higher level of career status and power *before* she tried to innovate.

When we settle into our power and authority relationships, it is important to realize that they usually come packed with certain emotional tendencies, values, and action-proclivities that may not serve anyone's best interests. In fact, the traps outlined here are mostly disadvantageous.

These power-conflict traps constitute the hills and valleys of what we like to call our "conflict landscape"—the emotional-relational terrain that we must travel daily at home, school, and work. The less aware we are of these tendencies and traps, the more susceptible we are to their lure and negative consequences.

Managing these traps effectively requires more than mere awareness; it also requires developing competencies and skills for resisting the pull of these tendencies and employing alternative behaviors in conflict that work *for* us, not against us. It is to these alternatives and skills that we turn next.

3

Conflict Intelligence

IF POWERLESSNESS in conflict is so toxic, and conflict traps are so pervasive up, down, and across the organizational ladder, then what's a leader, employee, manager, temp, CEO, staff member, consultant, or intern to do? How can we survive and thrive under such conditions?

When one of the authors, Peter, was in his mid-twenties, he went to work for a private, for-profit psychiatric hospital in New York City named Regent Hospital. Peter was hired as a low-level mental health associate (MHA) on an "Adolescent Unit" (twelve- to twenty-five-year-olds admitted for psychiatric disorders or drug addiction), which means he was hired to do whatever the professional staff told him to do. This was his first postcollege emersion in a hierarchical, highly political work organization.

Mental health hospitals have particularly complicated political structures, because in addition to the formal power of the administration (CEO, COO, human resource director, and so on), you have the MD psychiatrists (real power), the PhD psychologists (pretend power), the nursing staff (the really real power), the insurance companies (omnificence), union reps and patient advocates (some power), the patients and their families (less power), and then the remaining staff, such as the MHAs (zilch). Regent was part of a larger corporation that was known to meddle in hospital affairs as well. So when Peter first joined the hospital, he found himself treated mostly as a cog, often very confused, and too often in the middle of power struggles between others, which he didn't comprehend and on which he could have no effect. He was powerless and stressed.

Fate also had it that Peter arrived at Regent in the late 1980s, when the mental-health industry was changing dramatically in the United States. What had been previously a somewhat laissez-faire insurance climate for mental-health hospital treatment suddenly tightened up, requiring major changes in hospital policies and procedures. This meant that the patient regulations Peter was trained to implement—like automatic expulsions for patients who participated in on-unit sex, drug abuse, or violence—were reversed. Now, if patients acted out in such a manner while an inpatient, they would not be discharged but in fact would be held much longer in the unit, often against their will. This resulted in the hospital becoming an increasingly more dangerous and threatening environment (with a more violent population and occasional visits from NYPD SWAT teams), and a catastrophic increase in conflicts of all types. It also led to the rise of a new source of power in the hospital: violence and intimidation.

As you might imagine, mayhem ensued with the policy changes, and the already complicated balance of power in the hospital shifted radically and often. During crises, which were frequent, much of the power of the formal power holders (MDs and RNs) was deferred quickly to the larger, beefy MHAs and maintenance-staff personnel (but not the new guy, Peter), or to those with strong crisis-management and negotiation skills. After each crisis, the CEO, MDs, and RNs would attempt to resume control of the hospital, but their authority slowly withered and the influence of the crisis teams ascended. Everyone found this time to be challenging and stressful. Business-as-usual was gone, and the new normal was disorienting, unpredictable, and menacing.

But for Peter, this chaos wasn't the hardest part of the job. For him, the most difficult challenges came from the increasing estrangement and eventual hostilities stirred up between him and his MHA peers—whom he had grown quite close with under such duress—due to his ascent in the organization. These tensions were first triggered when he was promoted above his peers to supervisor, and eventually crescendoed when he was named marketing director of Regent Hospital. That was the worst.

In this chapter, we will provide an overview of our approach to conflict, power, and change at work. First we will lay out the logic of our approach and summarize some of the findings from our research. Then we will offer brief sketches of seven strategies for addressing power and conflict.

So imagine you are Peter, mid-twenties, earnest, and green, and you show up for your first day of work at the Regent Hospital, where, as the logo says: "Caring creates change." It is 7:00 A.M. and the head RN is clearly not happy with the idea of having to orient a new MHA today—a task she was not previously informed about—so she mumbles something like "Over my dead body" and suggests you sit in the "day room" for a bit while she gets her bearings.

You step out of the nurses' station into the day room, which is stale and already filled with patients, pain, and anxiety. You steel yourself, then head over to an empty chair and introduce yourself to a young woman in a bathrobe sitting next to you. You strike up a conversation and learn that the woman, Gloria, is from New York City and has been an inpatient for three months now. She seems happy to talk and goes on in some detail about what brought her here.

Suddenly you hear, "Excuse me! Excuse me, Mr. Coleman! Can you come here?!" You turn to see the head RN standing next to a pale fellow in a tight suit who appears to be glaring at you. You excuse yourself to Gloria, and then are ushered back into the nurses' station, where you find yourself being thoroughly chewed out by the tight suit for breaking protocol and discussing personal matters with the clients. The head RN looks on silently but sternly until the suit—the team psychologist—finishes his diatribe and exits.

Reeling, you turn to the head RN, who grins and says, "Welcome to Regent."

So, you might ask, *what the heck just happened, and what do I do now?*

In fact, what just happened is quite typical. Conflicts often seem to drop out of the sky without warning. When they detonate, we often feel startled and unprepared. Most of us remain speechless or become defensive, lash out, and say things we come to regret.

The basic logic of our approach is straightforward: conflict almost always happens in the context of the flow of a particular relationship or social situation (with its accompanying emotional reservoirs and traps).

At Regent that morning, the situation's setting was the adolescent unit of a psychiatric hospital and the relationship of particular relevance to the conflict was between the head RN and the psychologist. Peter just happened to be the pawn in their game.

In this emotional context, two things determine our responses to conflict: people and place. Our dominant conflict-response tendencies are the product of many personal influences: our personality and temperament, habits, cultural upbringing, gender, social intelligence, formal training, education level, socioeconomic status, parental and peer influences, popular media, and so on. These factors come together over time to shape our default response to conflict.

Peter was young, Irish-French-American, Catholic-school trained, male, born working class but college educated, and a child of an alcoholic who never met an insult he didn't like. In other words, he had something of a temper.

But these conflict tendencies do not operate in a vacuum. At their most basic level, they operate in the context of the emotional reservoir for the current situation or relationship.

At Regent, Peter found himself in a new, unfamiliar employment situation with new relations that, although filled with anxiety and ambiguity, were emotionally neutral enough to mitigate his dominant tendencies.

Many of us, when we find ourselves in a conflict, are able to momentarily assess the situation before responding. (This is essentially what

Peter did on his first day on the job at Regent.) There are three major aspects of conflict situations we focus on instinctually:

- **How important are the other disputants to me?** Do I need them to meet my needs now or in the future? Do I want to stay in this relationship going forward? Can I walk away from this situation without consequence?
- **Are they with me or against me (or both)?** Are they on my side? Do they share my goals and concerns? Are they likely to help or harm me? Should I trust them?
- **Am I more or less powerful than them, or are we equals?** Who is in charge here? Do they have power over me? Do I have power over them? How about in the long run—who is *really* in control?

Together, these three concerns can override our dominant responses and largely determine our reactions and responses to conflict situations—the strategies and tactics we employ—when we take the time to consider them. Think of them as the three most basic elements of conflict situations. We put these three concerns—relationships, shared goals, and power differences—together to create a model of the seven most basic types of situations faced in conflicts. These seven situations follow.

Compassionate Responsibility: These are conflict situations in which you find yourself in higher power in relation to the other disputant, share common goals or concerns, and feel that your relationship with them is important and needs to be well managed. This is characteristic of many constructive parent-child, supervisor-supervisee, and teacher-student relations.

Command and Control: In these conflict situations, you have higher relative power than the other and pure competing or contradictory goals or needs, but also have a high need to remain engaged with the other as you move forward. This is likely how the team psychologist saw the situation when he confronted Peter on his first day at Regent Hospital.

Cooperative Dependence: In these situations, you have low power relative to the other disputants, share cooperative or complementary goals, and have a high need to remain on good terms with them. This was Peter's experience of the situation at Regent with the head RN, after the psychologist chewed him out. He needed her, reported to her, and discovered that they shared a newfound disdain for the psychologist.

Unhappy Tolerance: Here, you find yourself in low power, with purely competitive goals, and yet with a high need to remain in the relationship with the other disputant. This is where Peter found himself while being publicly humiliated at the hands of the team psychologist that fine morning.

Independence: In situations like this, you find that you have a low to absent need to remain in the situation or relationship with the other disputant. In these types of situations, we find that little else matters — not power or competing goals. For example, had Peter been independently wealthy or particularly uninterested in the job at Regent, or had he had a better offer at another hospital that first morning on the job, he would have experienced the conflict with the psychologist in a dramatically different way.

Partnership: These are conflicts in which you are in relatively equal power with the other, share mostly cooperative goals, and maintain a high need to remain engaged with the other. These are very common situations at work with peers and coworkers.

Enemy Territory: Here, you also enjoy equal-power relations with the other disputant, but you have clear competing or contradictory goals and yet have a high need to remain actively engaged with them. These situations, when they persist, are usually a recipe for contentiousness, escalation, and stalemate.

Situation	Value of relationship	Shared or competing goals	Your power position
Compassionate responsibility	important	shared	higher
Command and control	important	competing	higher
Cooperative dependence	important	shared	lower
Unhappy tolerance	important	competing	lower
Independence	not important	not relevant	not relevant
Partnership	important	shared	equal
Enemy territory	important	competing	equal

These seven situations represent the more extreme combinations of relational importance, cooperation or competition, and power distribution. You'll often encounter less extreme situations, but these seven help us to anchor our understanding of the most common conflict circumstances we face, and having familiarity with them will help prepare you for the others.

The more extreme the situation, the more it will override your dominant personal tendencies in determining your responses to a conflict. Even though strong personalities will tend to respond to conflicts in the way their personalities dictate (think of Donald Trump), extremely strong situations will tend to override personality and dictate behaviors (think of Donald Trump in prison).

Mindsets for Conflict Management

Our research has found that these different situation types tend to trigger distinct conflict mindsets, which affect disputants' conflict-related perceptions, emotions, values, and behaviors. We have conducted a host of studies with working people to identify two things: (1) how these distinct situation types affect conflict mindsets, and (2) the most common and effective strategies and tactics associated with each of the seven situation types. We conducted focus groups, simulation research, surveys, and lab studies to get a clear and nuanced understanding of these different approaches.

Each of the seven situations tends to correspond with a particular mindset that is most appropriate for that conflict situation. These are, in brief:

Benevolence (Response to Situations of Compassionate Responsibility): This is the most commonly reported approach to work conflict from most U.S. managers (although we suspect it to be somewhat overly reported). It involves an active, cooperative, and conscientious approach to conflict management, in which the power holder values taking responsibility for the problem at hand, listening to the other side(s), and modeling constructive conflict-management behaviors, and reports feeling genuine concern for their lesser-power counterpart. It involves constructive behaviors, such as open dialogue, prosocial modeling, and joint problem solving. This mindset has been shown to be highly effective in generating constructive solutions to many conflicts but can be overused or backfire when it becomes chronic or is applied in inappropriate situations. We will have much more to say about this in chapter 4.

Support (Response to Situations of Cooperative Dependence): This response is very commonly reported by supervisees and underlings of all stripes. This is a mindset for conflict of appreciative support, in which people respectfully seek clarification of roles and responsibilities, attend more carefully to the concerns and actions of the high-power other, work hard to make amends if they suspect they responded inappropriately, and feel a sense of genuine concern for their superior in the conflict (as tense conflicts tend to be an anomaly in their relationship). In these situations, people tend to value the supportive leadership and expected benefits bestowed by those in higher power, feel some degree of anxiety and confusion regarding the conflict, but engage in respectful followership and assistance—seeking support from both the disputant as well as others in a position to offer it. Although common, this approach too has its pathologies and consequences associated with its overuse. We break this one down in chapter 5.

Dominance (Response to Command-and-Control Situations): This is a very commonly observed but less commonly reported approach to conflict by executives and managers. It was clearly the team psychologist's approach to Peter at Regent (that morning and thereafter). It entails a direct, confrontational, even at times harsh or threatening response to disputes, where there is typically a heightened concern for preserving one's own power and less concern for the other's outcomes. It is a more controlling, at times exploitive mindset for conflict where people value winning and maximizing only their own outcomes, feel a lack of empathy for the other parties, and may use tactics of force, control, and deceit to achieve their aspirations. Although the costs and consequences of this mindset are notoriously well known, we have found that it is not only common but also a very necessary strategy, and that its bad reputation often leads to its underutilization in situations that demand it. This will be the focus of our discussion in chapter 6.

Appeasement (Response to Situations of Unhappy Tolerance): This is a tough one, despised (but often practiced) by many in the U.S. workforce, but embraced by workers in more collectivist or authoritarian cultures.[1] It was also Peter's initial response to being hollered at by the team psychologist at Regent. This mindset tends to engender higher levels of stress and anger, a strong need to remain quiet and tolerate the situation, and a desire to rectify the problem as quickly as possible to simply make it go away. Here people feel the most anxiety and resentment, value avoiding harm as much as possible, seek opportunities for cover or escape, but also may engage in covert, coercive tactics, such as sabotage and work slowdowns. In our focus groups, participants didn't mention sabotage until we asked, and then eagerly and enthusiastically elaborated on their many ingenious methods of undermining superiors. Although a particularly challenging strategy, this approach, when mastered, can be critical for managing those in positions of higher authority effectively, and is the subject of chapter 7.

Autonomy (Response to Independence Situations): This approach also tends to be underreported but commonly employed. It is found mostly in response to situations and relations that people feel are of little short- or long-term importance. Due to the lack of significance of the conflict, people typically prefer to simply exit the dispute or relationship altogether. In other words, they feel that engaging directly in the conflict is not worth it; they can just as easily get their needs and goals met through other means. So they opt out. This approach is a way to avoid conflict or gain leverage in negotiations and conflict but can be viewed with great suspiciousness and contempt by those more actively engaged in the conflict or organization, and thus it should be used sparingly. We will discuss these contingencies in more detail in chapter 8.

Cooperation (Response to Partnership Situations): Purely cooperative, equal-power situations of conflict in which people's goals and fates are linked tend to induce good things: a perceived similarity in beliefs and attitudes, a readiness to be helpful, openness in communication, trusting and friendly attitudes, sensitivity to common interests, a de-emphasis of opposed interests, and an orientation to enhancing mutual power rather than power differences.[2] As decades of research have documented the effects of cooperative, equal-power situations on constructive conflict dynamics, and as most models of integrative or win-win negotiations stress this as a primary strategy, we will not devote a chapter to elaborating further on this approach (see *Getting to Yes, Getting Past No*,[3] and the many other useful books on win-win negotiations). However, we do need to stress that, despite the unquestioned value of this approach, it too can become pathologically chronic and have adverse consequences if applied too broadly. Cooperative approaches don't always work in asymmetrical-power conflicts.

Competition (Response to Enemy Territory): In contrast to partnerships, purely competitive, equal-power, high-importance conflict situations tend to induce people to engage in a win-lose fight for limited resources; use tactics of coercion, threat, or deception; employ poor communication; experience suspicious and hostile attitudes; and ultimately increase the importance, rigidity, and size of the issues in conflict. These effects of competitive situations have also been well documented (typically in contrast to cooperative situations and win-win approaches—see Morton Deutsch's *The Resolution of Conflict*), and win-lose strategies have also been specified in great detail (see Nobel laureate Thomas Shelling's *The Strategy of Conflict*[4]). Thus, again, we will defer to these and other authors of competitive bargaining and not elaborate on these tactics here.[5]

As you may suspect, each of the seven conflict mindsets has its particular utilities, benefits, costs, and consequences, depending on the psychological makeup of disputants, the mindsets of other parties, and the nature of the situations faced. However, when people find themselves in particular conflict situations for extended periods of time, they tend to develop a strong mindset consistent with the situation. Once an individual has developed an enduring propensity for a particular mindset (for example, dominance), it can become very difficult to change that perspective, even when it fails to satisfy his or her goals, the intensity of the conflict dissipates, or as social conditions change.

What Are Your Chronic Mindsets?

Take ten minutes to fill out and score the simple conflict-management self-assessment here (our Conflict Intelligence Assessment—Short Form, CIA—SF). Doing so will give you a preliminary sense of your main tendencies when addressing the multitude of conflicts you face (or will face) at work, including your areas of strength and areas that may need some attention. (A more detailed assessment is available online at www.MakingConflictWork.org.)

Answer the following questions about *how often you tend to use each behavior at work* by indicating the number of one of the answer choices provided. Respond to each question with your current or most recent job in mind.

0 = Does not apply	3 = Sometimes
1 = Never	4 = Often
2 = Rarely	5 = Most of the time

_____ **1.** When I am in conflict with someone I supervise, I talk through it with him or her privately to resolve it fairly.

_____ **2.** When I am in conflict with someone I supervise, I use my authority to make sure he or she does what the person is supposed to do.

_____ **3.** When I am in conflict with my boss, I become more attentive and listen carefully to make sure we understand each other.

_____ **4.** When I am in conflict with someone I supervise, I invite him or her to discuss the matter cooperatively and share my concerns respectfully.

_____ **5.** When I face conflicts at work, I choose to walk away.

_____ **6.** As a manager, when I have a conflict with an employee, I make him or her see things my way.

_____ **7.** If I get into a conflict at work, I disengage right away and figure out some other way to get what I need.

_____ **8.** When I am in conflict with my supervisor, I listen carefully to his or her concerns and then propose solutions that work for us both.

_____ **9.** I give in to my boss as quickly as I can in conflicts. I don't want trouble.

_____ 10. I don't engage in conflicts at work; they are never worth it.

_____ 11. When I am in conflict with people I supervise, I try to model how to behave responsibly.

_____ 12. I work hard to achieve mutual understanding during a conflict, even when the conflict is with my boss.

_____ 13. I appease my boss in conflicts just to keep my job.

_____ 14. When I get into a conflict with an employee who reports to me, I make it clear that his or her behavior has consequences.

_____ 15. When I am in a tense situation with my boss, I simply keep quiet and tolerate it until it is over.

_____ 16. When I get into disputes with my colleagues, I play to win.

_____ 17. When I get into conflicts with other employees, I do whatever it takes to win.

_____ 18. When I get into conflicts with my peers, I get very competitive.

_____ 19. When I get into conflicts with my colleagues, I suggest solutions that address what is important to all of us.

_____ 20. When I get into conflicts with other employees, I treat the problem as one that can be solved by both of us working together.

_____ 21. When I get into conflicts with my peers, I look for and build on areas of agreement between them and myself.

SCORING

BENEVOLENCE: Add scores for nos. 1, 4, 11 = _____
DOMINANCE: Add scores for nos. 2, 6, 14 = _____
SUPPORT: Add scores for nos. 3, 8, 12 = _____
APPEASEMENT: Add scores for nos. 9, 13, 15 = _____
AUTONOMY: Add scores for nos. 5, 7, 10 = _____
COOPERATION: Add scores for nos. 19, 20, 21 = _____
COMPETITION: Add scores for nos. 16, 17, 18 = _____

So, what does all this mean?

First, take a look at your different scores for the seven mindsets (3–4 is low, 12–15 is high). What does this tell you about yourself?

Here is a typical set of average scores for the CIA—SF, from studies we have conducted.

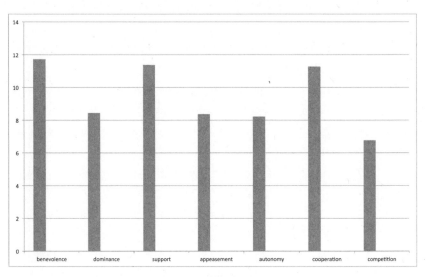

1= Never, 5 = Most of the time

Take a moment and reflect on how your scores on the different mindsets match with the averages of these studies. Anything interesting here? Any scores particularly high or low? Any surprises? Any areas you might benefit from increasing or decreasing?

Our research has shown that those of us who score above average (but not too high) on all seven of these mindsets are happier at work.

Moving from Mindsets to Strategies

In *The Art of War,* Sun Tzu wrote, "Thus it is that in war the victorious strategist only seeks battle after the victory has been won, whereas he who is destined to defeat first fights and afterwards looks for victory." Our research suggests that people who intentionally and strategically employ approaches to conflict that are consistent with the situation types they face fare better. In other words, people who choose a strategy of

- pragmatic benevolence in situations of compassionate responsibility;
- cultivated support in situations of cooperative dependence;
- constructive dominance in situations of command and control;
- strategic appeasement in situations of unhappy tolerance;
- selective autonomy in situations of independence;
- cooperation in partnership situations; and
- competition when in enemy territory . . .

. . . are more happy and satisfied with conflict and with work in general. They feel more of a sense of efficacy and control over their conflicts and their life. This is what we call adaptivity.

Adaptivity

When we respond to conflict situations in ways that don't fit, it feels wrong, aggravates others, and usually has negative consequences. More *adaptive* approaches to conflict—those that employ different strategies to meet the demands of different situations—lead to greater general satisfaction with conflict processes and outcomes over time. Each of the different strategies outlined in our model has its particular utilities, benefits, costs, and consequences, depending on the psychological makeup of people, the orientation of other parties, and the nature of the situations faced. Ultimately, what is particularly useful in evolving situations of conflict is the capacity for adaptivity: the ability to move freely between various mindsets and employ their related strategies and tactics to achieve your short- and long-term goals. This is the focus of chapter 9.

Two years into the job at Regent Hospital, Peter had found his rhythm. He had been able to respond effectively to the crises and the power shifts on the unit and had earned a reputation as a leader in stressful situations.

However, the hospital was still reeling from the transitions, and the various seats of power seemed stymied and at odds over how to respond to the changes. Of course, the pain of the change and indecision was felt most acutely by the staff and patients on the units.

At this point, Peter went "upstairs" and got his name on the calendar of the CEO. A week later, he met with him and shared his observations and concerns, including some thoughts for possible remedies. This meeting ultimately led to his promotion on the unit to senior MHA (where he was asked to supervise his former peers—all of whom had worked at the hospital longer than he had), and within months, to a job offer by the CEO to move over to community relations. A year later, Peter was made marketing director of the hospital.

Sounds pretty dreamy, right?

However, there were costs. Although Peter was developing an increasingly strong knack for adaptivity—by learning to negotiate effectively but differently with the MDs, administrators, corporate overlords, RNs, patient advocates, and members of the surrounding NYC community—he found it extremely challenging to manage, interface, and negotiate with his former MHA peers and friends. They simply were not having it. It was hard enough when he was first asked to supervise them: they clearly resented this but went along with it well enough. But when Peter was promoted into administration and then marketing, it seemed to cross a line. He was now a sellout, a company man, a mercenary who had abandoned the "healers" on the unit for money and status. His new titles carried absolutely no weight with his former colleagues and friends, and in time he lost touch with all but one. The negative reservoirs that had built up over time with his former friends and colleagues prevailed in the end. The lesson: the vast majority of conflicts are manageable, but some are not.

The Limits of Adaptivity

The adaptive approach to conflict management described here is a breakthrough model that has already helped hundreds if not thousands of students, employees, managers, and leaders around the world. We are proud and thrilled to share it.

However, adaptivity has two primary limitations. First, not all of the conflict strategies are equal when it comes to their susceptibility to escalation, destructiveness, and intractability. The use of dominance, competition, and appeasement can more easily set the conflict on a costly path of no return. Thus, they should be used sparingly if possible. The more cooperative strategies of benevolence, cooperation, and support — and even autonomy — tend to be ultimately less costly and more constructive and so should be considered one's default or baseline strategies, the strategies you usually try to return to.

Second, since its genesis, there has always been something about adaptivity that has bugged us. It is probably the closet radical, child of the sixties in us that has always been haunted by the thought *What if adapting is wrong?* What happens when you find yourself in a relationship, situation, or environment that is simply *wrong* — unethical, immoral, oppressive, illegal, or just stupid? Then what?

These situations may require more extreme measures. They may require the anti-adaptive response that we call *principled rebellion*. This is the final, bottom-line strategy that is the topic of chapter 10.

The Criteria for Conflict-Intelligent Behavior

At the end of the day, how will we know intelligent conflict behavior when we see it?

Consider the following criteria.

1. **It is mindful,** informed by a sufficient level of self-awareness of

the tendencies, traps, and emotional hot buttons that you tend to succumb to in conflict. Ideally, these are managed, avoided, or navigated effectively.

2. **It is strategic,** based on a fairly clear sense of what you want and need in the situation. It is proactive and informed by an accurate sense of which strategies and tactics are feasible and available to you at the time.

3. **It is emotionally aware,** based not on mere rational calculations but on a good understanding of the positivity-to-negativity ratio of the relations involved.

4. **It is adaptive,** responsive to the changing realities and demands of our social-political life. It involves specific behaviors that fit with the demands of the situation at the time.

5. **It is temporal,** informed by past and current needs and relations as well as best estimates of future needs, consequences, and relations. It understands conflicts as bumps and blips in the context of ongoing relationships.

6. **It is normative,** proving effective in the vast majority of personal and professional situations of conflict. But it does assume that the conflict falls within the bounds of legal, moral, legitimate behavior. If not, it might be necessary to break the rules, refuse to adapt, and fight the power.

It also works.

In the chapters that follow, we describe and illustrate in more detail each of the seven strategies necessary for increasing your conflict intelligence and for making conflict work.

4

Pragmatic Benevolence

GINGER L. GRAHAM became CEO of Advanced Cardiovascular Systems in 1993.[1] She took over as the company was floundering with morale problems, customer dissatisfaction, and hostile relationships between research & development and manufacturing. While people in power are supposed to have all the answers, she was honest enough to tell the employees she didn't know how to save the company. She needed them to step up and give her ideas. And she meant it. She paired each company executive with a coach from lower down the hierarchy of the organization. Her own coach worked on the loading dock. Over several months, she got an earful about how company leaders appeared distant and evasive. The executives being coached by subordinates discovered a long list of solvable problems they would not have uncovered had Graham not turned the power ladder upside down.

If you have power and you want subordinates to share ideas, effort, and grit, you have to share what you have in order to get what you want. The cost of inclusive participation is total control. Many managers and executives understand this about power and influence. Instead of clutching goods, information, decisions, and authority close to their chests, thinking they will lose it if they don't, they open it up, share it, and often end up with more..

• • •

The early management guru Mary Parker Follett saw power as something to share and expand, not as a zero-sum game. In the 1920s, organizations were dominated by competitive men (and workplace and labor-management conflicts were much more cutthroat and violent), making her ideas about power and conflict all the more revolutionary for the time. Today, her ideas still challenge us to approach power, conflict, and leadership differently.

Follett argued that even though power was usually conceived of as "power over" others, it is also possible to think of "power with" others. She viewed this type of power as collaborative and mutually beneficial.[2] In the world according to Follett, conflict is part of the normal flow of working together to achieve goals. Managers and leaders need to recognize the interdependence of coworkers and teams, she insisted, and need to understand that without conflict there is probably a lack of purposeful engagement.[3]

Decades of scientific research since Follett's observations, in marriages, families, schools, and other organizations, has overwhelmingly supported her thinking on cooperative power and conflict.[4] Evidence from the studies of benevolent leadership,[5] participatory leadership,[6] employee empowerment,[7] power sharing,[8] and conflict-positive organizations[9] have all converged on similar findings. Researchers have found that when people have a sense of efficacy and inclusion at work and view their tasks, rewards, and other outcome goals as shared or cooperative, it greatly increases the odds of the constructive use of power between them and of positive outcomes from conflict.

You may benefit from exercising pragmatic benevolence in conflict if:

- you need to maintain your relationship with the other party to reach your goals;
- the other party is generally with you, not against you;
- the other party is less powerful than you.

What Draws People to Benevolence?

The benevolence approach to conflict is attractive to leaders for several reasons, some healthier and more functional than others. Many leaders are genuinely concerned with the inclusion, success, and security of their employees, as well as of the larger community. Many business owners and leaders are appalled by news stories of corruption, abuses of power, and avarice and are truly motivated to make their organizations better places. Benevolent leadership has been found to mobilize a virtuous cycle of change in organizations through modeling and encouraging ethical decision making, stimulating positive emotion, and positively impacting the greater community.[10]

Harvard Professor David McClelland conducted years of research on power and leadership around the globe and found that as people mature, they often progress sequentially through stages of development in their approach to power and authority, ideally moving toward a benevolent stage he labeled *togetherness*. McClelland described this as "the most advanced stage of expressing the power drive in which the self drops out as a source of power and a person sees himself as an instrument of a higher authority which moves him to try to influence or serve others."[11] In other words, people eventually come to express their need for power by becoming part of a team, organization, group, or coalition. McClelland's research suggested that people who expressed this orientation to power were more fully actualized: more responsible in organizations, less ego-involved, more willing to seek expert help when appropriate, and more open with those close to them. Benevolence can also be a pragmatic strategy. When a leader has talented, motivated, knowledgeable subordinates who are committed to the success of the organization, the best way to get every drop of effort from them is to support and empower them—especially during disagreements. Involving subordinates in decision making fosters openness, honesty, candid feedback, and innovative thinking.[12]

Managing stress in the workplace by reducing worker frustration and hostility is also a draw for benevolence. Subordinates who are miserable because they feel bullied when they disagree with the boss might stop disagreeing aloud, but they are also likely to harbor resentments that are contagious to other workers. Working *with* as opposed to *against* subordinates in conflict keeps negative emotion at lower levels.

Some people choose benevolence simply because they have generally cooperative, nonauthoritarian personalities. Such people intuitively know that cooperation in conflict creates positive interactions, results in higher achievement and learning retention, promotes considerably more positive emotions between people, and results in greater physical and psychological health.[13]

Different work environments will be more and less conducive to superiors employing benevolence in conflict. National and industrial cultures that value and establish structures that encourage steep organizational hierarchies, strict authoritarianism, employee competition, and high-power distance or a preference for unequal work relations are likely to discourage benevolence in their managers and leaders. Alternatively, organizations that provide flatter, more decentralized decision-making structures and encourage more egalitarian, cooperative, and low-power-distance relations between staff and employees will be more supportive of benevolence.

Some of the motives behind benevolence are less healthy for individuals, teams, or organizations. If the main goal is to avoid conflict altogether, then this strategy can backfire. When leaders fixate on benevolence, they may set themselves up for exploitation. Often they get stuck in benevolence because they can't face the temporary unpleasantness associated with dominance, even when necessary. Or they have self-images that are so rooted in niceness that they can't make tough decisions or discipline others as needed. Or they work in a pathologically cooperative organization that doesn't allow for using power forcefully.

Self-Assessment: Are You a Conflict-Benevolent Leader?

Many leaders want to know if they are acting cooperatively enough when they disagree with subordinates — or if they are being too cooperative. The following questionnaire may help you get a sense of just how benevolent and cooperative you are in conflicts with lower-power others. To see how much you are attracted to benevolence, indicate the number that best describes your response to the following statements.

1 = Strongly disagree   4 = Agree

2 = Disagree   5 = Strongly agree

3 = Neutral

_____ 1. I believe in decisions made by groups, even when I don't get my way.

_____ 2. I listen to employees' opinions before coming to a decision.

_____ 3. I share my emotions during my personal discussions with subordinates.

_____ 4. I change established policies because of input from subordinates.

_____ 5. I provide subordinates with occasions to publicly challenge my leadership authority.

_____ 6. I patiently listen to my subordinates' grievances, no matter what the situation.

_____ 7. I allow exceptions to rules and policies in order to obtain a compromise with my subordinates.

_____ 8. I invite my direct reports and other subordinates to tell me what they truly think.

_____ 9. I welcome disagreement from my subordinates.

_____ 10. I play the role of mediator, arbitrating disputes between my employees.

_____ 11. I want to hear totally honest feedback and opinions from the people below me in the organization.

_____ 12. I develop and work hard to maintain very honest relationships with my subordinates.

_____ 13. My team decides on policies and action plans together.

_____ 14. To achieve my goals, I have to get the active cooperation of my subordinates.

_____ 15. I go to meals with my employees to improve and maintain positive emotional connections and rapport.

SCORING

Add up your scores. You may be asking yourself, Is a higher score better? That depends on the context of your job and your organization. While this approach to conflict is generally positive and effective, it does not always work, because it does not fit all situations.

Score	Meaning	Ask yourself . . .
<40	You are rarely, if ever, a conflict-benevolent leader.	Is it because the environment does not support this approach? Or are you underutilizing this strategy?
40–49	You are inclined toward this strategy.	Do you use it enough and in the right contexts?
50–59	You use this strategy quite a bit.	Do you use it too much or in the wrong contexts?
60+	You rely on this strategy in most circumstances.	You might be overusing it. Does the environment support this strategy as much as you use it? Are you using it effectively and in the right contexts? Do you need to improve your skills at discerning when to use other strategies for conflict?

Organizational Assessment:
Do You Work in a Benevolence-Oriented World?

Next, complete the following questionnaire. It will give you a sense of the extent to which your current work environment invites the benevolence strategy. Rate your response to each of the statements, using one of the following numbers.

1 = Strongly disagree   4 = Agree
2 = Disagree   5 = Strongly agree
3 = Neutral

_____ 1. It is typical in my organization to express personal concern for one's subordinates.

_____ 2. In the organization where I work, I don't have to feel afraid to say what I really think.

_____ 3. My organization supports group decision making.

_____ 4. I work in a very collegial environment, where people are trusting and cooperative.

_____ 5. I work for an organization that has a strong moral/ethical code.

_____ 6. My organization has a culture that supports open, constructive conflict.

_____ 7. My organization really values teamwork and relationships.

_____ 8. Where I work, honest feedback is normal at all levels of the organization.

_____ 9. Candor and openness are words that describe my organization's culture.

_____ 10. Encouraging subordinates to participate in major decisions is fostered where I work.

_____ 11. Respectfully disagreeing with your boss is acceptable where I work, no matter what the situation.

_____ **12.** My organization clearly makes a positive impact on the larger community.

_____ **13.** Soliciting opinions from lower-level employees is standard in my organization.

_____ **14.** The upper leadership of my organization models that debate and disagreement are completely acceptable at all levels.

_____ **15.** The organization where I work makes me feel like I'm serving a purpose higher than just making a living.

SCORING

Add up your score, which will fall between 15 and 75. The higher the score, the more it makes sense to use the benevolence strategy in your organization. Now compare your self-assessment score to the organizational assessment you just completed.

_____ Self-assessment score from the previous questionnaire

_____ Organizational-assessment score from the most recent questionnaire

Generally speaking, the more similar the scores, the more likely you are employing this strategy with discernment. Of course, the nuances of various conflict situations are such that you still have to distinguish when and with whom to use this strategy.

Six Good Reasons to Use Practical Benevolence in Conflict

1. **You care.** Leaders who exercise benevolence want their subordinates to find meaning in their work, enjoy their jobs, and feel they add value to the organization.[14]

2. **It works.** When people find shared meaning in their work, enjoy their jobs, and feel they are adding value, they work harder and perform tasks better, and they manage their differences more effectively.[15]

3. **You don't need enemies.** If you are in power and never cooperate with your subordinates, share power, or practice give-and-take during disagreements, they will work less, avoid you, leave you, hate you, or sabotage you. Subordinates who feel they work for an office dictator are less likely to trust their boss and more likely to feel uneasy and oppressed.[16] On the other hand, bosses who use a cooperative strategy when there is friction are more liked, more enthusiastically followed, and more tolerated for the occasional use of dominance.[17]

4. **You don't need to be right, and you don't have to win everything.** If you have confidence in yourself and your team, you can stand to be wrong, to gather better ideas from others, to give credit where it is due, and to lose a debate. President Abraham Lincoln knew this. He filled his cabinet with people he described as smarter than himself, including rivals, for the sake of the country.[18] The payoff: honesty and more informed decisions.

5. **You understand the leveraging effect of teamwork (2 + 2 can equal 20).** The more you develop a symbiotic team of dedicated professionals who are not afraid of constructive conflict, the more you and your organization will thrive. A benevolent leadership style produces and develops more talent inside organizations, resulting in superior long-term performance and employee loyalty.[19]

6. **You prefer to cooperate internally and use competition as a strategy toward your competitors.** Competition is great, if it is well aimed. An organization is like a sports team: cooperate internally so you can compete effectively externally.

The Consequences of Misusing Benevolence

As powerful as it is to share power, it does not always work. Sharing power with saboteurs is not a good choice. Some of your subordinates may not be mature or trustworthy enough to respond well to a benevolence approach. Some of them may be green or cynical about authority or so averse to constructive conflict that other strategies would more likely help you reach your goals. If you practice benevolence with subordinates who are manipulative, it may come back to bite you.

Furthermore, not everyone in low power wants to share power. They might be wary of the responsibility that comes with power and thus remain in low-power positions by choice. Ultimately, you cannot force someone to work with you during a conflict. You can only offer real opportunities for cooperative decision making and conflict resolution, and nurture trust. If someone is afraid of power and conflict, don't use benevolence until you can build that person's confidence through small positive experiences with both.

Power tends to intimidate; as the person with more power, it is your responsibility—more so than your subordinates'—to show that constructive conflicts can be a vital part of teamwork and that others can trust you not to abuse your power.

In some situations, sharing power and involving subordinates may lead to less effective decisions, especially if the leader has an expertise that is required for a specific decision.[20] Imagine a team spending valuable time on generating decision alternatives when the leader knows that the alternatives will not work for legal, regulatory, or other technical reasons.

In addition, group participation takes time and can delay decisions. The additional time needed for participatory decision making goes up with the amount of participation.[21] During a crisis, benevolence can cause panic. Subordinate: "Captain, the ship is under attack! What should we do?" Leader: "Let's get together and brainstorm possible solutions. But I want most of the ideas to come from the team, not me." No, sometimes a group needs the confident and quick decisions of a leader in charge. Even in noncrisis situations, group meetings that give space to divergent perspectives can burn up many hours of time better spent elsewhere.[22]

While leaders who practice benevolence during conflict are generally liked and trusted, if they don't help the team deliver results, the most motivated subordinates will lose faith. Sure, people matter. Sure, a team process matters. But results matter, too, and some leaders who excessively apply benevolence, or apply it when a quick dominant decision would work better, fail to achieve intended outcomes.

Finally, when conflicts get complex and involve multiple parties, no single strategy is likely to fit the overall situation. Benevolence is a powerful strategy for superior-subordinate conflicts, but a limited one if it's your only tool.

What Does Pragmatic Benevolence Look Like in Action?

The pragmatic-benevolence strategy fits with conflict situations characterized by compassionate responsibility, where you have more power than the other party, share common goals, and value the relationship. Cooperative egalitarianism is clearly the preferred mode for resolving conflict in this type of situation. In most cases it is the surest path to achieving tangible goals, and the best way to maintain positive emotions and strong relationships.

Benevolence works best when the conditions for compassionate responsibility have been established. It's much more effective in companies that prioritize the needs of their employees, like a number of small- and medium-size Turkish companies called "The Anatolian Tigers," who have been experimenting with infusing care and compassion into the workplace,[23] offering their employees free meals, tickets for cultural events and concerts, a library and a café where employees can meet and spend time together, educational benefits, and health coverage and scholarships for employees and their family members. The business owner who visits sick employees in the hospital, asks colleagues about family vacations, takes staff members to lunch just to catch up, and shows that disagreements from time to time are part of an ongoing community of caring relationships will be more likely to succeed with benevolence as a strategy.

Even under conditions of compassionate responsibility, a leader must still effectively navigate and leverage conflict. What does pragmatic benevolence look and sound like?

It sounds like Tom Storrs, former CFO of TK Holdings. When a manager expected an argument with Tom over a different way of assessing the cost of inventory in an overseas plant, Tom replied, "I don't care which cost system you use as long as you get good results. We have the same goal. You get to our common goal whatever way you want to." As Tom put it, "Other people bring things to discussions and decisions I haven't thought of, either because they've had different experiences or maybe they're better at something than I am. I'm willing to listen to people about what they want to do. I guess I don't have to fight with everybody."

Pragmatic benevolence looks like Neil Chethik, executive director of the nonprofit Carnegie Center for Literacy and Learning, who holds a retreat and asks his staff to give him feedback on his strengths and weaknesses as a leader, and to tell him which decisions he made that caused discomfort or disappointment. Because he was skilled at making staff members feel safe enough to be honest, it's likely that nobody left the retreat thinking, *Oh my god, we just spent two hours disagreeing with our boss.*

As an organizational culture, pragmatic benevolence looks like Jiffy-tite, a rapidly growing company that manufactures fittings for automotive fluid systems. Its president, Michael Rayhill, describes the culture this way: "We live by the golden rule. Treat others as you want them to treat you. I like to have my opinions considered, so in turn I need to listen to others. There is nothing anyone in this company cannot say to anyone else, at any level, as long as it is said respectfully. We want honesty. And we know honesty brings disagreements. That's a fair price to pay."

Stephen Knopik currently serves as CEO of Beall's, Inc., a billion-dollar-a-year retail apparel company with more than five hundred stores. Years ago Stephen learned the value of benevolent leadership from his mentor, Bob Beall, former CEO and grandson to the founder:

I reported to Bob for years, and once had to deliver awful news I thought would give him a heart attack. He's said a million times he does not want banks to have leverage over us. But we once defaulted on a covenant for purely technical reasons—nothing to do with our ability to pay—and I had to deliver the news. I felt like a teenager telling my dad I wrecked the car. He must have been steaming inside, but he barely displayed any anger or frustration. His just said, "Obviously I'm not happy about this, but let's figure out where we go from here." I never worried again about being totally honest with him.

Pragmatic benevolence involves a lot of listening, negotiating, non-hostile disagreements, measured reactions to bad news, focused problem solving, support, and candor. Power differences exist, but are de-emphasized. The leader who practices this strategy is unthreatened by the ideas, successes, and occasional mistakes of subordinates.

Ten Benevolence Tactics

1. EXPAND THE POWER PIE

Share power and responsibility so subordinates are unafraid to disagree, and so that you can prevent tension and hidden problems that come with powerlessness.

When Nyra started a health-care-strategy consulting firm in South Florida at age thirty, she was a self-described work addict: "I wanted to know everything about my industry and my clients, and I wanted everything we produced to be perfect. I ran my consulting firm like a small thriving law practice: I was the expert working seventy-hour weeks, assisted by a legion of hard-working assistants."

By many measures she was hugely successful, making plenty of money and a name for herself in the industry. "I thought of leadership as mostly about industry know-how, and I hoarded decisions and information," she said. But as the firm grew, so did her workload, which took its toll: "My marriage ended, when ironically it was my husband who gave me the courage to start my own company. My doctor told me I was killing myself. She said I could recover if I changed my life, but otherwise I'd end up with ulcers or a heart attack."

After nearly twenty years, she realized it was time to change how she worked.

Her first instinct after her doctor's warning was simple: work less. But that does not come easy to a work addict. She started by bringing an assistant, Darcy, to meetings with clients. She delegated more of the details when they returned to the office. But she hovered over the younger woman's work. One day Darcy asked Nyra to lunch so they could talk. Nyra responded that there was no time for lunch.

Her protégé disagreed. "Nyra," she said, "If you don't have time for lunch, you don't have time to change the way you work." At lunch, Darcy asked Nyra to stop checking on every detail. "You have given me more responsibility, but not much more decision-making authority. One without the other is very stressful. Please give me a chance to show that I can help run this business and help it grow."

Later that week Nyra sent Darcy to meet with a client alone. Nyra heard afterward from the client how impressed he was with the new account representative.

There were many more small disagreements between Nyra and some of her employees as she worked through her ambivalence about sharing power. But these disagreements were the very evidence that the tactic was working, as they revealed more of her staff's true opinions and underdeveloped skills. Gradually, Nyra sent high-potential team members to more meetings without her, surrendered portions of key projects, and continued to receive approving comments from clients.

Nyra learned over time that while giving away power did, at first, make her feel less in control, her company was able to do more for additional clients. The company became more powerful even as its leader shared some of her individual power.

2. BUILD UP THE EMOTIONAL BANK ACCOUNT

Cultivate congeniality, positive emotions, and prosocial attitudes within the group to prevent unnecessary conflicts and to ensure that necessary ones will be constructive.

With hospital executives she had known for years—some of whom were very powerful, egotistical men—Nyra could forcefully argue a point and navigate the tension because she had already earned their trust and respect. Chats over coffee or lunch about family and hobbies helped build a foundation of amiability that let both parties see each other as human. When they faced conflict over professional matters, the anger, anxiety, and hurt feelings all abated soon enough when the relationships were strong. *If I want my employees to be as forthright as these high-powered executives, I can't just share power, I have to create emotional safety through our relationships,* she deduced.

Reluctantly (because socializing with employees did not intuitively feel productive to a recovering work addict), she saved the last fifteen minutes of a staff meeting to solicit ideas for company social events. There was general interest, but ideas didn't exactly flow. Afterward, Darcy suggested to Nyra that she ask one of the other consultants, Nick, to head a committee to plan the events.

"He's got too much on his plate to head a committee. I'll do it," she replied.

"Let him decide if he has time," contended Darcy.

Nick was thrilled to lead the project.

Over the next year, the committee introduced several social events for the entire company—a trip to a professional football game, a family barbecue, a company volleyball game, and some weekend dinners. Most of her growing company of sixteen employees loved these events. Nyra learned to love them. And she noticed that they had their intended effect: more positive emotions, tighter bonds between employees, more conversations, a greater eagerness to work together, and an increased sense of "we-ness." She also noticed that staff discussions about projects, problems, and difficult clients were feistier, as staff members asserted their opinions with more energy.

People who like each other can afford to be honest because they have a reserve of positive emotion. Like a bank account, if there are frequent deposits that add value, occasional withdrawals are less significant. Interpersonal conflict is not an isolated event; it always happens in the context of how strong and positive a relationship is at that time. A weak or strained relationship is much more adversely affected by disagreement than a strong positive one.

3. BE SLOW TO SAY NO

Limit how often and how quickly you reject ideas from subordinates. When vetoing, use rational persuasion to convince others that the concessions are appropriate and fair.

James, a manufacturing executive, frequently disagrees with his VP of sales. Their discussions about pricing, contract terms, or customer complaints are sometimes fervent. James has the power to tell his VP exactly how to approach any situation, but he knows better.

"The few times I've vetoed his ideas, I carefully explained why, and he turned around and executed my instructions. He's a good soldier, always polite and professional," James reflected. "His success in sales is partly about his passionate commitment to a plan, and the strength of his customer relationships. I diminish all that when I come out and just say no."

James has learned how to bring out the negotiator in his headstrong VP. "He knows I don't like to be autocratic, so he takes a position and sticks to it, as if daring me to say no."

Recently they couldn't agree on the terms of a large contract. When the VP stubbornly clung to his first position, James almost said no. Instead, he responded, "Look, you have to be in front of this customer every week; you've built the face-to-face relationship. You've heard what I have to say. I trust your judgment, and though I disagree, this is your decision."

The VP paused. "Jim, you are the boss; I'll do whatever you want."

"If he wasn't going to get his way," James later recalled, "he wanted me to dictate the answer, just in case it didn't work out in the end. Instead, I wanted us to collaborate with creative thinking and negotiation so he would have a stake in the final decision. That's when we started negotiating. When he and I start combining our ideas instead of debating, we come up with a better solution and strategy."

Nyra learned the same lesson. Not all the ideas Nyra's staff offered were great. But in order to keep the ideas and decisions and innovations flowing, Nyra decided not to disagree too quickly.

When staff members offered ideas she knew would never work, she carefully explained the budgets, laws, and regulations that prohibited implementation. When a group came up with several ideas, some rather weak, she kept them talking until they could integrate the best aspects of all ideas so nobody walked away feeling stupid.

Her reluctance to negate innovative ideas soon paid off. When two staff members recommended a business opportunity, she was dubious. They wanted to send a proposal to a county health department in another state to help with regulatory guidance and planning. Nyra saw it as a long shot, since there was no prior relationship.

"You want to go in cold, without a connection, and propose to help a small client far away?"

"Yes, because we think it will introduce us to a valuable network that could lead to more work later."

"I'm doubtful, but if you want to chase it and it doesn't interfere with other projects, go for it," she said.

Indeed, they won the project; it was profitable and led to other promising opportunities.

4. TRUST YOUR TEAM TO TAKE CHARGE

Instead of telling subordinates what to do, help them make their own decisions. Develop an effective and disciplined organization that de-emphasizes individual authority in favor of group decisions and collective performance.

To prepare for the merger of two large energy companies, Kate had the authority to design her environmental compliance department as she saw fit. But she wanted all the honesty, creativity, and innovation she could get from her talented team. So she told the team to design the new department. She did it in steps.

First, she gave them the parameters her superiors had given her. The head count could not exceed fifty. She told them the primary functions for which they would be responsible. And they had to cut $250,000 from their current budget. The team met without her for weeks and made recommendations.

Second, they had a series of "challenge sessions." The rule: anybody could challenge any idea, regardless of a person's "rank." She challenged several team members' ideas; they challenged her back. They questioned her assumptions; she questioned theirs. All of this conflict was done in a civil tone and underscored with respect. The result was a synthesis of the entire team's thinking.

Third, as they refined the plan, the team developed contingencies. What if the final head count was lowered to less than fifty? They had alternative plans ready. What if the budget was cut again? They were prepared. Kate made no autocratic decisions of her own, although she passed along a few from above.

"My team is responsible for issues of environmental and human safety. I need my team fully engaged because the risks are high," she explained. "If I take the big decisions away from my team, as if I don't trust them, I don't have as much confidence in the outcomes for which we are responsible. I need to trust that they are candid and will give me their best thinking."

5. DON'T TAKE YES FOR AN ANSWER

Encourage and model earnest consultation and information sharing. Probe for candor with subordinates to avoid the suppression of creative ideas or divergent opinions.

When a client—a medium-size hospital—discovered it did not have enough capital to build an outpatient surgery center that Nyra had suggested as part of a strategic plan, the hospital CEO asked Nyra to come up with alternatives. She met with two of her top consultants, Nick and Jacob, to hear their ideas. Nyra offered several options first: cancel the project, delay it a few years, or build a smaller center. The two men quickly agreed that Nyra's ideas were good and offered to research costs and regulatory impacts.

"Now wait a minute, guys," said Nyra. "Why am I the only one coming up with ideas? You know this client and their situation; you must have thought about this."

"Well," said Nick anxiously, "We do have an idea we think is pretty good."

"Tell me," urged Nyra.

"We have a similar hospital client twelve miles away from the first. What if we suggested they partner on the outpatient surgery center? The regulatory work would be challenging, but if we could get the two CEOs behind a joint project, I think we could get it approved, they would both save money, and both would be more competitive with the university hospital."

"We've been sitting here for over thirty minutes. Why didn't you bring this up earlier? It might be the perfect solution."

Now it was Jacob's turn to speak up nervously. "Nyra, to be honest, it is not always clear you want our ideas."

"You think I want 'yes men' working for me?"

"Yes," said both men simultaneously. Then Jacob got even more honest. "Nyra, you seem to lead us to conclusions you've already arrived at."

That was a turning point for Nyra. In subsequent meetings, she started offering her ideas last, or not at all if the team generated sound opinions. She did her best to avoid biasing her employees' thinking. And she started responding to requests for advice with this question: "What would you do if I were not here and you couldn't get in touch with me and you had to make the decision yourselves?"

More often than not, the question led to sound thinking and good decisions.

Through this process, she identified her most talented team members: Darcy, Nick, and Jacob. Not coincidentally, they were also the most conflict competent: willing to disagree, push back, and negotiate instead of simply comply. She promoted them to principal consultants and asked them to serve as a management team. "I want to develop you further because you can deal with how intense I am, and the three of you are better suited to manage and develop the rest of the staff." They were eager for the challenge.

People in low power who are not convinced their honest perspective is really valued instinctively withhold their ideas. A leader has to do much more than say things like "My door is always open" or "I really want to know what you think" to get the goods from subordinates. The leader has to prove again and again through statements and actions that honesty is valued and that constructive disagreement goes unpunished.

6. FRAME THE CONFLICT AROUND OTHERS' SUCCESS

Practice give-and-take to find solutions to conflicts. Appeal to subordinates' own work and career goals so concessions feel less distasteful.

When James realized one of his managers, Meg, was stirring up unnecessary conflict with several of the customer service reps who reported to her, and sometimes snapping at her peers, he considered letting her go. But she had been with this manufacturing firm for twenty-five years, had extraordinary knowledge of the business and customers, and worked very hard. Meg had just started managing people a few years earlier, and while it had never gone smoothly, it was becoming a headache for several people.

She's just not cut out for management, thought James. But it felt wrong to let her go. Even worse, it felt impractical, like a bad business decision. She had brought such value for so long.

He started by listening to her. Meg was a very emotional person and would sometimes stop by his office at day's end to "chat." But the chats became long stories about how stressful it was to balance work and family and how hard the job had become as the company grew.

Eventually James directly asked her about the conflicts at work. She told him how demanding the purchasing manager was.

"Did you talk to him about your concerns?"

"No," she replied. James sensed that she was avoiding the direct confrontation. She was hoping that he would talk to the purchasing manager on her behalf. So he coached her on how to open the conversation without sounding confrontational and how to work through differences. A few days later, she said things were going better since her talk with the purchasing manager.

The following week it was one of the customer reps: "Too slow."

"Did you talk to her about your concerns?"

"Yes," said Meg. "She was very upset by my feedback."

James determined that Meg needed more coaching to be successful in her management position and that she was well worth the investment. He hired a coach who worked with her, and things improved further.

But soon after she finished working with the coach, the old problems reemerged. James concluded that she would need perpetual coaching, either with him or a professional coach, to maintain any semblance of good management and to refrain from needless conflicts. Not an option.

Still, he didn't want to simply take her position away. So he engaged her in a series of conversations about stress and happiness. She was quite animated about the difficulties of her job and the people she managed. He said it sounded like she felt more successful before she entered management. "It seems to me that the source of your stress is having so many people needing you for so many things," he said. Meg agreed but felt embarrassed. What would her colleagues think of her if she stepped down? James insisted there was no stepping down to do. "Let's think about how to use your talents in the best way to make you and the company most successful," he told her. They worked together and decided to hire someone from outside to supervise her group. They also agreed that the newly hired supervisor would work with her hand in hand in her new, revised role.

Meg probably never knew she was in conflict with James, her boss. All she knew is that he helped her out of a situation that made her feel like a failure, and that moved her back to success.

7. LET GO OF CONTROL AND THE NEED TO BE RIGHT

Create an environment in which subordinates have influence over how they fulfill their responsibilities, have a motivation to commit to the organization's priorities, and thus feel free to dissent.

In the energy industry, there is little turnover. That makes hiring decisions nearly irreversible, and thus very important.

When the director who reported to Kate wanted to promote an engineer named Lee, Kate disliked the idea. She had met with the other two candidates and ranked Lee third. She felt that although it was a technical position, it needed a well-rounded person with people skills and leadership courage.

"I think Lee is extremely smart, but not well rounded," she said.

The director disagreed. "I've observed him in his work at a sister plant. You mostly know him on paper and in interviews."

"Maybe, but I know of situations at the other plant where he backed down too easily. This position needs someone really assertive."

"You don't know all the factors. He was limited by administration much higher than him. His superiors were not as open-minded about disagreement as you are," he insisted. "I've talked to a lot of people about this guy, and I think he's the best choice."

She felt like she was right and her supervisee was wrong. But she also knew to be skeptical about such feelings. She wanted to take control by refusing to hire the candidate she ranked third. But she acknowledged that her subordinate made a good point about her having less exposure to this candidate. Moreover, she knew that he, the director, would work closely with this individual for years.

Rather than controlling the hiring decision or trying to be right, she yielded to the director because of how thoroughly he had done his homework and how respectfully tenacious he had been in his perspective. She let him make the decision.

Time told the story. Over the next year and a half, the engineer and the director worked very well together and delivered strong results even in difficult circumstances.

8. DON'T JUST TELL PEOPLE TO COOPERATE— MAKE IT INEVITABLE

Orchestrate project assignments that increase the prospect of solving problems jointly. A culture of cooperation brings fewer petty disagreements, and the substantive ones will more likely be constructive.

By the time James was promoted to president of the manufacturing firm, reporting directly to the owner, he had noticed a lot of internal competition. Salespeople chased every sale, regardless of profit, because they wanted their commissions. Everyone else in the company was on a simple profit-sharing plan and very busy, so they often argued with sales. Turf battles and examples of inefficient individualism existed everywhere. Over time, as he won the trust of the owner and his managers, James initiated changes. He knew better, though, than to simply give speeches about cooperation. Most people, he believed, want to collaborate, but need an organization set up properly.

He also knew not everyone was made for cooperation. As he got to know people, he identified the relentlessly self-serving individuals. Many employees were shocked—and relieved—when James terminated the salesman with the top numbers. Great at growing top-line sales, the man was a bully to colleagues and too often alienated clients. He was totally obsessed with his commissions at the expense of everyone else on the team.

James also changed the company culture over time. Every successful product launch was celebrated company-wide. James publicly praised individuals who proved they could work collectively and lauded teams that helped other teams. Anniversaries were celebrated, cooperative employees were supported when they had personal difficulties, and language was revised. "Hourly workers" became "manufacturing associates." "Departments" became "teams." "Employees" became "team members."

Then James changed the compensation plans. He eliminated all commissions and adopted a system in which everyone made more money only if sales grew profitably. Some features of the old compensation system pitted sales against engineering, and quality control against production. But with the new system, lack of cooperation took money out of everyone's pocket. Sales became more discriminating, working closely with engineering before pursuing a new opportunity. Production stopped treating quality control like an enemy and began treating that department more like a partner, which resulted in more satisfied customers.

Finally, James frequently invited and openly received straightforward feedback from all levels. He knew he was helping the company, but sometimes he heard that he was pushing things too fast or getting in the way of team decisions or ignoring a problem. This frank, constructive criticism, from the manufacturing associates to the owner, guided James to adjust his approach so that his change initiatives did not simply lead to excessive frustration or sabotage.

9. WHEN YOU SENSE A COVERT CONFLICT, SEND IN COLUMBO

Rather than suppress team conflicts, reveal and mediate them. Explore rumors, problems, and concerns. Express curiosity during exploration rather than authority or criticism.

As Nyra's team became more competent, the business grew. They opened a satellite office in another city, expanding into a larger geographical area. Team members took on projects and negotiations with top executives with little or no help from Nyra. They developed a good problem: too much business.

To address their growth, Nyra hired Ethan, a sixty-year-old executive with experience and expertise in the industry. In several interviews, he spoke about cooperation, shared goals, and teamwork.

Six months after Ethan joined the firm, however, Nyra sensed a hidden problem. Some things seemed fine—the work was flowing and the quality was high—but morale felt strained. She took each member of the management team out to lunch to bluntly ask what was wrong. Each assured her that everything was okay.

Surely, after all the times they had bravely disagreed with her and even confronted her, they wouldn't hold back now. Still, Nyra had a bad feeling.

When the direct approach didn't work, she decided it was time for detective work. One of her favorite old TV shows was *Columbo*. She liked the way the investigator appeared naive and even bungling, but was actually craftily gathering information to solve a crime. His indirectness was the secret to his success. She often emulated him while trying to figure out the needs of clients who were too proud or too defensive to openly admit their organization's problems. If she explored the client's needs *indirectly*, she was usually able to figure out the real problem that might have eluded her through straightforward questioning. So, instead of continuing to ask about the management team's conflicts directly, she let time pass. She dropped in on more meetings. She observed the team at social functions and inquired with clients as to how the work was proceeding.

An unpleasant picture emerged. The four-person management team never went to lunch together. Clients glowed when they talked about Darcy, Nick, and Jacob but damned Ethan with faint praise.

Still, Columbo knew better than to directly interrogate a suspect. So she set up an extended business trip with Ethan that included plenty of time driving between meetings with clients in different cities. They chatted about work, about the changing health-care industry, and about her team. Ethan turned out to be quietly arrogant. He subtly dominated discussions, not with a loud or blustery voice, but with an understated form of condescension. He frequently flexed the informal power of his expertise to inhibit discussion and disagreement. Over several days she came to see him as passive-aggressive and controlling.

A few days later she took Darcy to lunch and challenged her. "Why didn't you tell me what was going on?"

Darcy looked tense and sad. "We didn't want to let you down. We felt it was our responsibility to make it work."

Nyra tried to find ways to help the four of them work together. She empathized with Ethan, acknowledging that he was working with team members less experienced than himself. She acknowledged to the other three that he was difficult. She tried mediating their disagreements for months, but as Ethan showed more and more of his dominant personality, Nick gradually got more defensive and tense. One day Ethan and Nick had it out in the conference room, screaming at each other. Afterward, Ethan demanded Nyra put him in charge of the team.

Nyra was experiencing the limits of benevolence and saw clearly that she could lose one or more of her best people, with whom the strategy had worked beautifully.

Ethan was gone the next day.

Leaders who are overcontrolling or extremely conflict avoidant don't want to know about conflicts in the teams that report to them. If they do get involved, they use power to "resolve" the conflict but usually only manage to suppress it.

10. USE YOUR POWER TO REPAIR

After stressful disputes, it behooves leaders to decrease negative emotion through "repair conversations." These involve conciliatory statements about taking partial responsibility, making requests about similar situations in the future, and reviewing common goals and values. When warranted, sincere apologies can be very powerful at mending emotions and relationships.

Nyra expected things to return to normal with Ethan gone. But tension remained.

She had never been naive about power conflicts; she knew they often had residual consequences. An important lesson she had learned was the value of the postconflict repair conversation. Several times she had engaged clients in honest exchanges after a tense conflict and managed not only to save the relationship but, in some cases, to strengthen it. She noticed the conversation went better if the person with more power made the first move; that way the perceived risk was diminished for the person with less power. So she gathered the team.

"Let's talk about what happened," she began. "I hired a principal consultant to work with you as a peer and help us grow. My first mistake was not including you in the hiring decision. I also want to take responsibility for not paying close enough attention to the situation during Ethan's first several months. I got very focused on certain clients and didn't see the difficult situation you were in."

As they continued discussing, each person took partial responsibility for the mess — the team for not trusting Nyra enough to tell her what was happening, Nyra for disengaging and not picking up on it sooner — until they gradually reduced the negative emotions stimulated by the ongoing conflicts with Ethan. They also discussed how to prevent similar problems in the future as the firm expanded. The conversation was both analytical and heartfelt, and soon they returned to their preconflict trust and amicability.

Nyra was quite successful before she cultivated the honesty and talented contributions of her employees. Even when she was the expert served by assistants, she was known by her clientele for providing high levels of service and sound advice. But when she opened up the relationships with her assistants to allow for disagreement, candid feedback, and new ideas, she became even more successful. And healthier.

How to Master Benevolence: The Building Blocks

Benevolence works when it's applied in the right situation by someone who has the skills, patience, and confidence to navigate the complexities of shared power, strong emotion, and negotiation. It requires several of the interpersonal skills that a more competitive leader would need: self-confidence, assertiveness, vision and emotional regulation. But it calls for something else as well: the ability to transcend one's own ego. Leaders don't have to be gurus or saints, but those who effectively apply the benevolence strategy over time must be able to trust a collective process of dialogue, debate, and give-and-take. The benevolence strategy calls for a "we" identity more than an "I." The belief that group members can be intrinsically motivated by connection to a higher purpose and to each other underpins this strategy.[24]

It also calls for wisdom about the nature of conflict. A limitation of the phrase "conflict resolution" is its implication that the work begins when there is already a dispute. You can't resolve something until it exists. Benevolent leaders and supportive followers don't wait; they manage situations and relationships effectively to prevent unnecessary or destructive disagreements, and then they navigate necessary discord for the greater good of the group and the organization. People who understand conflicts also know that many are not single events but rather ongoing differences.

• PRAGMATIC BENEVOLENCE SUMMARY •

For Situations of Compassionate Responsibility: These are conflict situations in which you find yourself in higher power relative to the other disputant, share common goals or concerns, and feel that your relationship with him or her is important and needs to be well managed.

Strategy: To increase the lower-power party's awareness of your shared goals, of the importance of your mutually beneficial relationship, of your priorities, and of the many opportunities for you both to enhance your resources for power and influence, while modeling a constructive form of conflict management and organizational citizenship.

TACTICS

1. Expand the power pie.
2. Build up the emotional bank account.
3. Be slow to say no.
4. Trust your team to take charge.
5. Don't take yes for an answer.
6. Frame the conflict around others' success.
7. Let go of control and the need to be right.
8. Don't just tell people to cooperate — make it inevitable.
9. When you sense a covert conflict, send in Columbo.
10. Use your power to repair.

SKILL-DEVELOPMENT CHECKLIST

Check any skill you have already developed. Discuss your responses with someone you trust. This might be a consultant or executive coach, a close colleague, a friend who understands you and your organization, your boss, or even one of your subordinates.

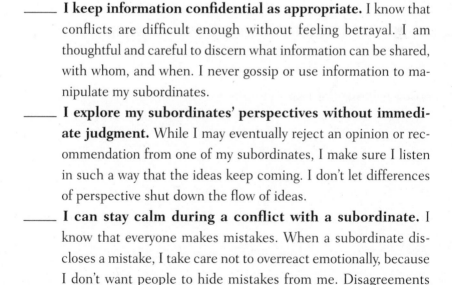

_____ **I keep information confidential as appropriate.** I know that conflicts are difficult enough without feeling betrayal. I am thoughtful and careful to discern what information can be shared, with whom, and when. I never gossip or use information to manipulate my subordinates.

_____ **I explore my subordinates' perspectives without immediate judgment.** While I may eventually reject an opinion or recommendation from one of my subordinates, I make sure I listen in such a way that the ideas keep coming. I don't let differences of perspective shut down the flow of ideas.

_____ **I can stay calm during a conflict with a subordinate.** I know that everyone makes mistakes. When a subordinate discloses a mistake, I take care not to overreact emotionally, because I don't want people to hide mistakes from me. Disagreements about how something should have been done are constructive rather than critical. My reports would not describe me as "freaking out" or "blowing up."

_____ **I practice candor and reward it.** I do not lie, avoid, or tiptoe around issues. My subordinates can count on me to be straightforward at all times, including when we are in conflict.

_____ **I communicate frequently and openly.** I demonstrate relevant and practical knowledge about what our organization does, but I do not come off as a know-it-all. I know people would not be honest with me, offer different perspectives, or ask "stupid" questions if I did that.

_____ **I practice fairness and do not show favoritism.** Since I want candor from my subordinates, I make sure I do not harm their trust by acting as if one person or group deserves more attention or advantage than another. I carefully consider fairness and how decisions will be interpreted. When I make unpopular decisions that might be interpreted as unfair, I am willing to discuss such decisions and face the issue of fairness head on.

_____ **I am approachable and accessible.** I give what I want to receive, so I am accessible even when busy. While I don't drop everything I am doing the second someone wants my attention, I make it relatively easy to get to me and to tell me something I may not agree with or like to hear.

_____ **I disclose things about myself, within reasonable limits of privacy.** I am not a cold brick wall, because if I were I would not get the information I want, including the creative tension that comes with innovation. I let people get to know me personally.

_____ **I advocate for my subordinates.** I build trust partly by advocating for my subordinates. While I do not make excuses for poor performance or mistakes, I stand up for my people to the organization when appropriate. This, in turn, sets the stage for them trusting me enough to tell me what they really think.

_____ **I follow through on promises.** I don't weaken trust by saying I am going to do something and then not do it.

DISCUSSION PROMPTS

Discuss the following questions with someone you trust to help you develop your skills at navigating disagreements effectively.

- How do you perceive me at meetings when the team is discussing an issue? Do I actively solicit others' ideas and opinions? If so, how? Do I subtly discourage open debate and honest perspective sharing? If so, how?
- Are any team members afraid to voice their true opinions to me? If so, what am I doing (or failing to do) that creates this reluctance?
- What actions can I take to make it clear that disagreements are safe and even encouraged on my team or within my organization? With which subordinate do I need to increase trust and openness so I can get more of his or her creative thinking, problem-solving ideas, and cooperative decision input?

5

<!-- ←———→ -->

Cultivated Support

THE DISNEY BROTHERS, Walt and Roy, were not afraid of conflict.

Walt is well known as a visionary leader who nurtured and encouraged creative talent. But the Walt Disney Company is the most successful entertainment company in history because of—not in spite of—the frequent conflicts between Walt and his older brother.

Roy was Walt's cofounder and managed all financial aspects of the company. Their tension flowed from their different roles and personalities. Walt was intense and thrived on risk, creativity, and big ideas. Roy was a down-to-earth, financially conservative pragmatist.[1]

But Walt had more power by virtue of his fame, creative genius, and personality. Clearly, he was king of the empire. If he insisted on something, he got it. They often argued about expenses, debt, investments, contracts, and innovations. But they usually listened to each other, even if sometimes they listened to the other screaming. Their conflicts were frequent and passionate but for the most part cooperative.[2]

Such is the nature of cooperative conflict. The parties do not agree on some issues, but they rarely dominate one another or capitulate. They discuss, argue, fight, and search for the proverbial win-win solution. The party with more power in such conflicts exercises pragmatic benevolence, sharing—but not relinquishing—power in order to maintain the relationship and elicit candor. The party with less power has to risk the possible wrath of standing up to the more powerful partner. Cooperative conflict thus requires trust, humility, and honesty.

Unless you are a member of a family company, you probably do not share the same type of bond as the Disney brothers' with your boss. Roy was extremely attentive to Walt. He was anxious on his brother's behalf. He was protective — even devoted. According to one of their attorneys, "There were tensions between the two brothers, but from my perspective, Roy Disney did whatever in the world he could to make life better, nicer, sweeter, etc., for his younger brother."[3] Still, Roy was willing to disagree with Walt rather than merely appease him or avoid tension.

The cultivated-support strategy outlined in this chapter is suitable for conflict situations typified by cooperative dependence, in which you have less power than the other party but share mostly cooperative or complementary goals, and the relationship is important to you. As a follower engaging this strategy, you are not tagging along mindlessly but rather working side by side with your leader and cultivating a high degree of trust and commitment by honestly expressing conflicting views when necessary to move toward your shared goals.

When possible and appropriate, cooperative conflict between benevolent leaders and supportive followers is likely to produce the best outcomes in terms of goal attainment, relationship enhancement, work satisfaction, and emotional well-being for all parties. When it works, everybody benefits.

But as this chapter will illustrate, this strategy does not just happen; it has to be cultivated.

Having less power than your boss is an obvious reality. But less obvious is how to leverage less power. Appeasing the boss in conflict, even strategic appeasement as we will discuss in chapter 7, is a temporary strategy at best. Opposing the boss, in the sense of trying to usurp or overturn him or her, is high risk. Supporting a leader — if indeed your boss is fair and sane and willing to share power — is an essential part of being an employee, but is not so easy, especially during conflict.

Mobilizing support during conflict does not mean simply backing the boss's position and giving in. Nor does it mean attacking or undermining your boss when you disagree. Cultivated support means soliciting, borrowing, and encouraging the sharing of power when you have less. Although you have less power, you are rarely ever powerless,[4] and it is often in your interest to cooperate with your boss toward shared goals, even if *some* of your goals are not shared.

The support strategy is not passive. It's a set of actions aimed at building a relationship that involves reciprocal influence and gain. And even if your boss is reluctant to share power, you can shepherd the relationship away from power *over* toward power *with*.

You may benefit from exercising cultivated support in conflict if:

- you need to maintain your relationship with the other party to reach your goals;
- the other party is with you, not against you;
- the other party is more powerful than you.

What Draws People to Support?

Many people are drawn toward this approach because it feels so much better than other low-power options. Driving home knowing you disagreed with your boss and actually talked it through and negotiated effectively feels so much better than driving home awash with anger, anxiety, and anguish. If you have a halfway cooperative boss who is not completely threatened by sharing power and talking things through, he or she will feel better driving home as well.

Another thing that pulls people in the direction of support is the collective feeling of the team. It feels good to feel good on your own, but it feels even better to feel good with others. You get attached to your coworkers. You care about them even if you never see them outside of work. You feel like an "us." When "we" can disagree with the boss and work through that conflict—when "we" negotiate rather than back down in fear—"we" have power. "We" are something larger than "me."

If you and your boss and your team can reach the stage where conflicts are not contests between each other but rather challenges to overcome *together,* the very nature of conflict changes. Instead of *me-against-you,* it becomes *us-against-a-problem.*

So why would anyone *not* want to be cooperative in a conflict situation with his or her boss?

For some, it's not in their nature. Experiencing less power than others do is alien to some because of ambition, neuroticism, or personal history. To cooperate when one's instinctive goal is to compete and dominate, well, that's asking too much. When life is all about winning, support feels like losing.

For others, the support strategy requires too much trust. Comfort with a support role requires what psychologists call a secure-attachment pattern, which comes from being raised by caretakers who responded appropriately and consistently enough to your needs as a child. Securely attached adults tend to have more trusting, positive views of themselves, their partners, and their relationships.[5] In contrast, more anxious adults seek high levels of approval and responsiveness from those in authority and tend to be less trusting and exhibit high levels of emotional expressiveness, worry, and impulsiveness in their relationships. They may find it impossible to trust anyone in authority or become wary of a specific authority figure who has not always been cooperative. *Maybe the boss's invitation to cooperate is a trap,* they might think. Others may simply find the support strategy much more difficult in practice than in theory.

The support strategy also may not fit with some organizational cultures. Sure, the values statement in the employee orientation handbook says "We value candid opinions and team cooperation," but if you don't see cooperation in action, you conclude—often accurately—that what this organization really calls for is watching your back. As with benevolence, organizations that have more decentralized decision-making and that reward more egalitarian, cooperative, and low-power distance relations between bosses and subordinates will be more conducive to achieving your goals through support.

Self-Assessment: Are You a Conflict Supporter?

To determine how oriented you are toward support when you face disagreements with someone in power, complete the questionnaire below. Rate your response to each of the following statements.

1 = Strongly disagree   4 = Agree
2 = Disagree   5 = Strongly agree
3 = Neutral

_____ 1. I experience conflicts with my superiors as an opportunity to learn and develop.

_____ 2. Disagreements with my boss work out okay no matter what they are about.

_____ 3. I worry about my manager's stress level and general well-being.

_____ 4. I ask for support from my boss and others when there is disagreement.

_____ 5. The first thing I do when I face a conflict with my supervisor is to ask for clarification of the problem.

_____ 6. I work hard to achieve mutual understanding during a conflict, especially when the conflict is with my boss.

_____ 7. I talk things out with my supervisor after a tense situation.

_____ 8. When in conflict with my boss, I am very attentive and listen carefully so we can make sure we understand each other.

_____ 9. My boss and I share many of the same goals and concerns.

_____ 10. My relationship with my boss is very important to me, and I work hard to keep it constructive.

_____ 11. I can influence my boss, no matter what the situation.

_____ 12. I give input to my supervisor when he or she has a decision to make.

_____ 13. I feel that I am a valuable part of this organization.

_____ 14. I am very honest with my manager.

_____ 15. I need my manager's cooperation to achieve my goals.

SCORING

Now add up your scores. As in the previous chapter, a higher score is generally better, but not always—the strategy has to fit the situation, especially the response of people with more power. Consider the following guidelines.

Score	Meaning	Ask yourself . . .
<40	You rarely, if ever, respond to conflict with a support strategy.	Is it because the environment does not support this approach? Or are you underutilizing this strategy?
40–49	You are inclined toward this strategy.	Do you use it enough and in the right contexts?
50–59	You use this strategy quite a bit.	Do you use it too much or in the wrong contexts?
60+	You rely on this strategy in most circumstances.	You might be overusing it. Does the environment encourage this strategy as much as you use it? Are you using it effectively and in the right contexts? Do you need to improve your skills at discerning when to use other strategies for conflict?

Organizational Assessment:
Do You Work in a Support-Friendly World?

Next, complete the questionnaire below. It will give you a sense of the extent to which your current work environment encourages the support strategy. Rate your response to each of the statements below.

1 = Strongly disagree   4 = Agree

2 = Disagree   5 = Strongly agree

3 = Neutral

_____ 1. My boss shows that he or she wants to know what I really think.

_____ 2. My direct boss tries hard to cultivate a positive relationship with me.

_____ 3. My job encourages my supervisor to share responsibility, decisions, and authority with me.

_____ 4. My current manager deserves a lot of respect.

_____ 5. Working for my current boss makes me want to support him or her.

_____ 6. My organization encourages my boss to try to talk it through and resolve disputes when he or she disagrees with me.

_____ 7. My job places a high value on teamwork and relationships.

_____ 8. My boss clearly is concerned for others, including his or her subordinates, when there is a disagreement.

_____ 9. When my current supervisor disagrees with one of my peers or me, he or she listens and explains things, rather than shutting down the conversation or giving a command.

_____ 10. It is very important to my organization that my boss behaves appropriately in situations where we disagree.

_____ 11. My supervisor deals with conflicts openly and constructively.

_____ 12. My boss believes conflict is healthy because it helps a team get honest and learn how to work together.

_____ **13.** Where I work, we feel comfortable expressing our opinions with mangers, even when we see things very differently.

_____ **14.** Where I currently work, I'm not worried about losing my job if I disagree with the people above me.

_____ **15.** In my current organization, we all feel safe from getting forced out, fired, or marginalized just because we disagree with the people in charge.

SCORING

Add up your score, which will fall between 15 and 75. The higher the score, the more it makes sense to use the support strategy in your organization. Now compare your self-assessment score to the organizational assessment you just completed.

_____ Self-assessment score from the previous questionnaire

_____ Organizational-assessment score from the most recent questionnaire

Similar scores generally indicate you are employing this strategy appropriately. Of course, the details and tone of various conflicts require that you differentiate when and with whom to use this strategy.

Six Good Reasons to Use Cultivated Support in Conflict

1. **Positive relationships work better.** When a team shares more positive emotion than negative emotion, it is more likely to perform better. These conditions provide us with a sense of psychological safety and flexibility that allows us to take more risks and innovate.[6]

2. **Negativity is less powerful with context.** It is harder to stay mad at someone with whom you share many other positive experiences. One reason to cultivate a support strategy is that you and

your superiors will calm down quicker, forgive more easily, and have fewer headaches.[7]

3. **You're building a long-term relationship.** Your affiliation with your boss will (hopefully) outlast an individual conflict, and by taking a calculated risk through sharing your best ideas and real feedback, you are investing in a deeper leader-follower relationship for the future.[8]

4. **All of us are smarter than any of us.** Teams offer an opportunity to leverage ideas, critical thinking, creativity, holistic thinking and problem solving. But nothing of value was ever created by a bunch of people sitting around agreeing on everything. Team members who passively wait for direction or carry out orders they believe will fail or who withhold their potentially valuable ideas play it safe at the cost of better outcomes for the team, the organization, and their own careers.[9]

5. **You are the CEO of your own development and chief marketing officer of your personal brand.** Your long-term development depends on you seizing opportunities to work with bosses who help you learn by utilizing your talent. Exchanging ideas (rather than simply receiving them) is part of your development and increases your probability of success. The best way to get others in your organization and beyond to think you are talented is to do exceptional work and then have your various bosses brag about you. Disagreeing cooperatively with your bosses in a way that helps them achieve organizational goals is one way to get others to promote you.[10]

6. **Power sharing is a two-way street.** Leaders also benefit when their subordinates take an active role in decision making. They are likely to feel less isolated and less pressure to fix everything themselves. When followers feel good about their leaders and leaders feel good about their followers, this creates a positive upward spiral of motivation and cooperation.[11]

The Consequences of Misusing Support

The efficacy of cultivated support, like the other strategies in this book, depends on degree, style, and context.

Initiating conflict too often with superiors can have costs. A cooperative boss can start to see it as naysaying or a power struggle, leading him or her to approach you with a more negative or competitive mindset. *How* you disagree with your boss also matters. Tactics like complaining, blustering, threatening to quit, and generally irritating and coercing your boss may win you a few battles, but they come at a high cost: they dissipate your "positivity reservoir" with your boss. If you anticipate a long relationship with your boss, or need him or her to promote you or recommend you in the future, avoid harsh or overly frequent methods of dissent and negotiation that will alienate him or her.

Think of the support strategy as a valuable resource that has to be carefully cultivated: developed, protected, measured, and sometimes repaired. It is much too valuable to be employed thoughtlessly or taken for granted.

What Does Cultivated Support Look Like in Action?

Most constructive follower-leader relationships are developed over time. Sharing power while in conflict is a negotiated dance through which the follower finds ways to influence the leader. People in the support mindset in conflict are aware of being in relatively low power with a generally benevolent party. They actively seek support and clarification of the dispute, carefully attend to the high-power person to gain insight into the issues, listen carefully, and make every attempt to cooperate. They also invest heavily in increasing their own soft power, developing skills and ideas that will be seen as valuable and worthwhile by those in power. Ideally, over time, the power holder in the relationship becomes comfortable with this approach. However, the process can be uneven and characterized by anxiety, resentment, and failed attempts at negotiation. But if both parties persist, and if they steer clear of perfectionism, a very effective pilot-copilot relationship can emerge.

Ten Tactics for Cultivated Support

1. MAKE IT POSITIVE

Cultivate a relationship with the power holder that is characterized by positivity and authenticity; explore similarities and shared goals.

All conflicts, mild or intense, occur in the context of relationships. While working for a benevolent leader is easier than working for a dominant one, the bond is not automatic. It still takes conscious investment to cultivate a human connection. Disagreements are much more likely to remain constructive and open to negotiation if the boss-subordinate relationship emphasizes positivity, authenticity, similarities, and a mutual commitment to the same goals.

Jeanne is soft-spoken. When she was hired as the controller for ACR Supply, a $25-million-a-year HVAC parts distributor with seventy-five employees, the person she replaced left suddenly, leaving nobody to train her. There were two bookkeepers at the time, but no other degreed accountants. For three months she put in extra hours learning procedures, policies, software, and numbers. She was so busy focusing on technical matters that she had little time to develop relationships.

Her former employer kept calling, begging her to come back. It was tempting. She was well respected there. She had a voice. *This new place is overwhelming,* she thought.

As she learned the new system, she saw ways to improve it. She saw waste, inaccuracy, and inefficiency but barely knew the boss and didn't want to stir the pot for no reason. *I'm not even sure I will stay here,* she thought to herself. *Why borrow trouble?*

Three months into her new job, she decided she had to open up. She asked for time with her boss, Troy, the owner and CEO. "I need to be honest with you. I'm torn," she told him. "There's still so much I haven't figured out here, and my old job is inviting me back." Troy's response was a turning point for Jeanne. "He really connected with me. He sat me down and told me at length how much he valued me. He said he had been trying to stay out of my way, but probably had not given me enough support. He pledged to be much more involved, helping me learn the systems and getting to know the people, and he hoped I would give it another month or so before deciding whether to leave."

Troy remembered that conversation as well. "I could see how talented she was and how well she fit our culture, but I wanted what was best for her."

Their relationship began to develop. Over the next several weeks, Jeanne and Troy got to know each other better. "We discovered our similarities," recalled Jeanne, "like the fact that we both raised sons, and how alike we thought about the world and about life. And we both made it clear that we wanted each other to succeed. I learned a lot about his priorities, and I became more committed to the company and wanted to see it thrive, and he insisted that any obstacles I encountered had to be addressed. As our relationship grew, he also said he wanted me to challenge him. He told me he liked me and respected my work and wanted to hear what I had to say about the company."

2. CAREFULLY CONSTRUCT THE INITIAL CONDITIONS

Odds are, as a conflict starts, so shall it end. A tone of cooperation, civility, and reason is more likely to lead to win-win outcomes. Harshness, argumentativeness, defensiveness, and criticism will end badly, with winners and losers — or just losers.

Adrianna is a branch chief in a federal agency; her job is to manage, support, and advocate for the scientists and engineers in her division. One of her two bosses, a division chief named Stefan, is seventy-two and approaching retirement. Adrianna likes Stefan and is quite candid with him. They are both proud of their Romanian backgrounds and often talk about their similar family histories and the world events that shaped their lives. Having family members who lived under Soviet rule, Stefan is proud to practice a democratic leadership style at work.

From Adrianna's perspective, though, he can be *too* open to influence. "Sometimes the last person who tries persuading him gets their way, especially if they're difficult," complains Adrianna. She has seen colleagues in low-power positions influence Stefan by acting indignant, stalling, walking out of a meeting in a huff, and generally making a nuisance of themselves until Stefan gives in so he can get other work done.

Over time Adrianna became one of the most influential people with Stefan, partly because she paid so much attention to the way each disagreement started. She intuitively knew that Stefan's state of mind and emotion was shaped in part by how she initially approached him when they differed on an issue. She also knew that there might be another difference of opinion in the near future, and that the tone of the previous negotiation would affect subsequent ones. She thus adopted more subtle, indirect, relationship-preserving approaches.

"Sometimes I start by telling him that my preference on a given issue is based on one of our previous discussions," explained Adrianna. On one occasion, she had an engineer who was not working near his potential, whom she wanted to transfer to a different project for which he was more suited. Others had tried to sway Stefan toward other solutions regarding this employee through harsh complaints and heavy-handed persuasion. So she reminded Stefan of some comments he had made in a meeting about this engineer's particular strengths, his attention to detail, his skills at microanalysis, and his ability to spot the smallest flaws in a technical project. And she explained she wanted to transfer him to a project that capitalized on those strengths. Stefan agreed. Expecting the engineer to resist, she went further, suggesting to Stefan that because it was originally his idea, perhaps he should deliver the news to the struggling engineer. When the engineer heard from his boss's boss that he was being assigned to a special project just right for him, he felt important and went without dissent. "So my subordinate was happy because the big boss transferred him to a special project, and the big boss was happy because he looked smart, and I'm happy because I met my goal *and* I think it is good for the organization."

3. CULTIVATE AN INFORMATION COALITION

Weaker parties enhance their power and are more effective in a conflict with a power holder when they establish support from a credible coalition.

As Jeanne got to know Troy, she noticed how he reacted to people. She learned about his priorities and how he wanted to hear ideas and feedback. When she had worked for Troy for a year, she felt she understood him well enough to disagree with him. She noticed the company paid a significant amount of money each year for a corporate chaplaincy service. A chaplain would visit each site weekly and was available for discussions as needed. She knew Troy was deeply religious and felt strongly about the program, but she also knew that there was an urgent need to cut expenses due to a downturn in the economy.

By then Jeanne had built many relationships in the company. She quickly won the respect and trust of many managers. She listened attentively to this informal coalition before discussing corporate chaplains with Troy. Many of the people she talked to felt that everyone who wanted a member of the clergy in their lives already had one through their place of worship. While it was convenient to have a chaplain stop by the workplace, only a few people in the company felt it was worth the money.

Still, she decided she needed a better feel for the popularity of the program before attempting to persuade Troy to cancel it. She asked if they could include an item on the employee culture survey, and Troy agreed. The results were clear: the expensive program did not have broad support. Troy agreed to downsize the program, reducing their fixed expenses considerably.

Informal networks in organizations serve many functions, offering advice, trust, support, organizational awareness, and more. But in Japan they take if further. Japanese companies have a practice called *douki-kai*. *Douki* means "the same year" or "at the same time," and *kai* means "group." The group develops an identity and a loyalty based on starting a new work life together. The Japanese love to establish *douki-kai* at graduation or when they start at a school or join a company in the same year. The group members create a bond and socialize together through their careers, even though some advance to management and executive levels and others do not. But the relationships of the *douki-kai* members provide an important sense of group identity as well as critical sources of information and influence up and down the chain of command at work. The people in Jeanne's network were not all hired at the same time, but she built her own *douki-kai* by getting to know people and listening to their perceptions of the company. Her informal network helped her serve the company and Troy by getting an accurate read on the greater good.

4. PRESENT PROBLEMS AS "OURS" RATHER THAN "YOURS"

People with less power are more influential with those in high power when they highlight mutual interests and define a conflict as a shared problem.

One of the best movies about teams ever made, *Apollo 13,* shows how a focused group of people can achieve more than any competent individual. When astronaut Jim Lovell (played by Tom Hanks) tells the engineers back on Earth about a problem, he instinctively makes it a collective problem. "Houston, *we* have a problem." On teams led by benevolent leaders, most problems are *our* problems. When a follower using the support strategy also frames problems and conflicts in terms of "we" rather than "I" or "you," the team is more likely to achieve its goals, whether they involve getting a spacecraft back to Earth or meeting quarterly earnings targets.

The federal agency where Adrianna works has a policy for research contracts with external partners. Private companies can pay the agency to do research. Stefan said yes to nearly all such proposals. He thought the division should do as much of this contracting as possible. But it caused problems for Adrianna. Her staff was overworked, and, worse, some of these contracts were just not interesting to the scientists and engineers who reported to her. As she put it, "It feels like we're sometimes chasing squirrels instead of focusing on our core mission."

Adrianna had complained to Stefan several times about the workload, but to no avail. She eventually sat down with him and made a case for their shared problems: these external projects dilute the focus of *our* technical staff, she told him. She talked about *our* vision and mission, to which Stefan often expressed his commitment. She talked about *our* staff and their talent, and about the limits on all of *our* time. And she appealed to Stefan as a scientist, reminding him of something he'd said in the past, that if you have to do research you don't find interesting, you don't get the best results. Some of the projects Stefan accepted, she explained, didn't fit the division's long-term vision; it would be better for the staff and the organization to say no.

The approach worked, but not the first time. After two or three such discussions, Stefan got Adrianna more involved in the process of evaluating proposals. He listened to her when she said, "This one does not fit our vision." Or "None of our people has any passion for this research question."

5. DON'T BRING ONE PROBLEM; BRING SEVERAL SOLUTIONS

Avoid the appearance of forced "either/or" choices or intractability. Provide the person in high power with multiple options.

This tactic allows leaders and followers to win something, even if they lose something. Negotiation is more fertile if there are more options for give-and-take.

As Jeanne prepared to discuss with Troy how to cut expenses without layoffs, she knew she ran the risk of falling into a series of tense debates. Spenders and savers are like oil and water. He was a shrewd business owner but had a better eye for new opportunities than cutting costs. She had a passion for saving money and managing the company's finances well. But she remembered one of his favorite sayings: "Don't bring me problems; bring me solutions." So she prepared a list of fifty ways to cut costs without hurting the business. She resolved from the beginning not to have to win on any given item. If he would agree to a reasonable number of her ideas, they could avoid layoffs.

Troy quickly acquiesced to several small items on her list, but the savings were nowhere near what were needed to keep all employees. Jeanne suggested reductions in the company's contributions to employees' retirement plans; Troy refused. She recommended canceling all overtime. "No." She offered the idea of canceling the company-sponsored beach vacation. "Maybe." She found a way to pay vendors on time but hold cash longer. "Only if we do it with our current bank," he said (but they wouldn't save money through their current bank).

"I didn't have to win on any one item, but I figured I had to push him to say yes to enough of my ideas that he could achieve his goal of avoiding layoffs," Jeanne explained. Instead of competing with him point by point, she reminded him again and again that to avoid layoffs they had to work together to find a combination of cuts.

"It wasn't him and me. It was us against layoffs," she said.

Eventually they made it. They canceled the beach vacation (and had a sand-filled family picnic behind the warehouse). They changed the language in the 401(k) program so the company could refrain from matching during any given year. They kept overtime but offered a voluntary reduction in hours. And where Jeanne pushed Troy the hardest, to change banks for a new program for paying vendors but holding cash, he finally said if it was up to him he would stay with the same bank, but that she could make the decision. She chose a program at a new bank and Troy backed her decision.

6. WAGE A PEACEFUL CAMPAIGN

Influence, especially for those with less power, is more likely to be achieved over time, through multiple cooperative attempts, than in one event.

A campaign involves repetition over time. The whiny child who keeps asking for ice cream while the parent gets increasingly annoyed is not waging a campaign. But when a strategic follower disagrees with his or her boss and wants to gradually cultivate alternative ideas in the leader's mind, and does so with sensitivity and transparency and with the good of the organization in mind—*that's* a campaign.

Monica worked in the central office of a national retailer of athletic shoes. She was instrumental in helping new franchisees succeed. A former college athlete with the assertiveness to raise three rambunctious, athletic sons, she knew a thing or two about going for a goal. But she also knew that in business, as in sports, it can take many repeated attempts to score.

Sometimes Monica disagreed with her boss, Dennis, the senior VP for business development, about some strategic issues. For example, she wanted to conduct focus groups with people who had not returned to the stores lately. She and others could guess why previous customers were not coming back, but she wanted to *know*. She found a researcher they had used in the past, but Dennis would not give her the money.

"He didn't say never; he just said he didn't think it was worth the money right now." So Monica, quite transparently, bounced the idea off prominent people in the company who could influence Dennis. And from time to time she brought it up to him again to remind him that better data could help increase return customers. "I don't annoy him with it. When I bring it up it's usually lined up with a project another group is doing to which the focus group would be a nice addition. I'm not sneaking around trying to find someone to point out to Dennis that I'm right. And I know he has a boss, too, so he has to watch his budget."

Dennis was not bothered or threatened by Monica's transparent campaign. In fact he appreciated it, probably because he used the same tactic. As he explained it:

> I report directly to our CEO, Jared. I've learned that if I have a great idea, I need to work it over time. Sometimes a few months, but sometimes years. So, we're getting ready to launch a big initiative. We're going to go after our apparel business in a big way. I started on this idea with Jared three years ago, and I'd just find occasions to

randomly say to him or other team members, "We need to find a way to expand apparel. . . . What do you think?" I threw out a lot of theoretical ideas for how to do it profitably. Jared is thinking about a million things. Sometimes a bold idea takes time because he's focused on other bold ideas.

Monica and Dennis waged peaceful campaigns of influence with their respective power holders but only on matters they considered important to the success of the organization.

7. FLEX YOUR INFLUENCE THROUGH YOUR FUNCTION

Expertise and specialization are potent forms of influence. People with less-formal authority are likely to be most influential when speaking from their area of recognized proficiency.

Influence and the likelihood of a successful outcome to conflict often rest on credibility. Wherever you have high credibility, you have more influence. That means you probably have some areas of your work where you have relatively less expertise, less of an impressive track record, thus less credibility and influence. In the long run, keep your focus on where you have the most influence, choosing your battles accordingly.

Jeanne had learned over time which disagreements were likely to end with her having more — or less — influence with her leader. After working for Troy for just a few months, she had his ears on all things financial. But in other areas of the business, her influence was less, or it grew more slowly.

When the leadership team was debating whether or not to expand to a ninth city, Jeanne was the only member of the team who thought it was not the right thing to do. "I was wrong," she later realized. "I'm not an entrepreneur. I am not a risk taker. I could never own a business and look for opportunities and jump in without certainty. So while I can be quite critical of how Troy spends money, and I have earned his respect for holding him and others accountable for spending, he has gained *my* respect for his intuitive ability to see an opportunity. My greatest influence and my best success in disagreeing with him come from the thing I do best: holding costs down. And I'm okay with being wrong. Especially if it's not about the expertise for which I most expect to be valued."

8. GET UNSTUCK ASAP

When someone with less power perceives an impasse with someone with more power, it is a matter of pragmatism to repair strained relations, compromise, temporarily accommodate, or search for options favorable to the more powerful party.

When you get stuck in a conflict with a boss who is mostly benevolent but who just happens to be a human being (meaning occasionally flawed), you may have to swallow your own pride to achieve your long-term goals.

Adrianna reports directly to Max, the associate division director. Max, like many benevolent leaders, has blind spots and sensitivities that make him obstinate in one context but quite cooperative in others. If you disagree with him one-on-one and have a good argument with sound logic and clear facts, he listens and will even back you up in conversations with his boss. But in public meetings he becomes strong willed and insecure.

In one meeting with the entire staff, Max made some strident statements about a problem in the division. Adrianna interrupted him—assertively but not harshly—to point out a fact he had gotten wrong. Max tried to suppress his anger, but he treated Adrianna differently for the rest of the meeting and the rest of the week. Other people noticed him avoiding her or making critical comments. A few days later she had a one-on-one meeting with Max that seemed tense and unproductive. The issue they disagreed on wasn't even brought up.

"I don't think I did anything wrong," she later reflected. "But I'm sure he thought I messed up his speech." They were at an impasse, and she knew it would go on for weeks, not just about this issue but others. She had a choice. "I could be right and stay stuck, or I could get unstuck by apologizing."

The following Monday she went to his office and put it this way: "I apologize for my part in the discussion at last week's meeting; I did not mean to cause you discomfort or stress."

Surprised, he replied, "Thank you."

An apology will sometimes dislodge you from an impasse with a more powerful leader. In other cases you may need to offer a compromise, a favor, a capitulation with hopes of a better outcome later, or in some cases, an authentic conversation about emotions or the relationship. But the goal is pragmatic: to preserve the relationship and to head off any deepening of the negativity reservoir for your relationship.

9. DO UNTO AUTHORITY AS YOU WOULD HAVE AUTHORITY DO UNTO YOU

For someone in low power to make the most of the support strategy, it is best to give what you want to receive. Cooperative conflict will engender more cooperation in the future, and competitive conflict, more competition.[12]

If Jeanne wants Troy to continue to solicit—or at least accept—her challenges, she serves her own cause by soliciting and accepting challenges from him.

"I try to get him as involved in finances as possible. He wants me to be the expert, but I want him to be an informed and involved leader. So over time he has learned more and comes to me with more questions about why certain expenses are higher or lower in a given month." One month she sent him a memo about a mistake from the previous month. A large company had issued a credit memo by mistake, and she did not catch it right away. Hence, the previous month's profits were inflated by fifty thousand dollars, which had to be repaid.

"He got back to me and asked, 'Is this a one-time mistake, or are we repeating it? How do we not let this happen again? Do we need to change something about our process?'

"I'm glad he's questioning me. Maybe there is something I didn't think of. He doesn't question me in a harsh way. After all, you don't know what you don't know, so if he is asking questions about something I am not aware of, that's a good thing. I trust him because I know his motives are good."

At other times Troy takes issue with some of Jeanne's decisions, or challenges her to do something differently. She sees it as her job to listen without defensiveness, be politely honest with him, and try to discuss and negotiate such disagreements cooperatively. "What goes around comes around," she says.

Troy likes her honesty. "I like that she disagrees with me and puts her ideas on the table. Otherwise we're only as smart as me, and that's not good enough. I listen to her because she is never harsh or confrontational. I trust that she wants the best for the business, and that's why she shares her ideas."

10. DISTINGUISH BETWEEN A LEADER'S WEAKNESSES AND FATAL FLAWS

Even the most benevolent, cooperative, and likable leader is human. Idiosyncrasies, blind spots, personal peeves, insecurities, and other common individual psychological differences call upon the lower-power party to discern between minor and major imperfections.

It's easy to find a bad boss; it's not so easy to find, keep, and disagree with a good leader with imperfections.

Wise followers consider their managers' weaknesses in context. Some flaws rarely matter: minor tardiness, the inoffensive joke that falls flat, infrequent anger, slight errors, occasional micromanagement. Some behaviors are always destructive: hostility, contempt, demeaning remarks, ethical breaches, broken promises, lies. But many faults are nuanced and contextual—even some potentially serious ones. How insensitive was that comment? Does my boss's behavior actually hurt my career and the organization, or is it merely unpleasant?

All-or-nothing thinkers beware: if you want to achieve your goals and those of your organization, you have to discern between what is vile and wrong and what is merely distasteful or stupid.

Dennis is basically a good boss, as Monica sees it, but no angel. He has been in this industry for a long time and has a lot of credibility. She respects a lot of what he does: his ability to work with vendors, his relationships with key players in the industry, his vision for the organization. She sees him as a decent and competent person.

"But he can be very abrasive," she points out. "He sometimes misbehaves under stress, like most people. But he's not an asshole, or I wouldn't stay."

Dennis has a rigorous international travel schedule. Sometimes after a stressful trip, he returns to the office and gives someone a hard time. He is a big man with a loud voice and does not have to yell to intimidate. Once, after returning from Europe exhausted, he chewed out Monica's subordinate for having too light a travel schedule. Monica pulled the young staff member aside and told him not to take it personally, that Dennis was tired. But Dennis did it a second time the same day, even more harshly.

Monica wanted to confront Dennis in the middle of the office, so everyone would see her stand up to him. She had some choice phrases ready to dress him down. But she stopped herself. *What is my goal? To create drama? No. To show Dennis I'm tougher than him? No. To embarrass him? No.* She realized that Dennis, although a decent person, lacked the awareness to handle his stress. She thought he could learn with feedback.

She waited until the end of the day, when everyone else was gone, and went to his office. She sat down across from Dennis and, without raising her voice, told him it was not his job to criticize her direct reports in front of the staff. If he had an issue with one of *her* subordinates, he should address it with her, she said. And she reminded him that the morale of the team was key to the company's success, and that he, Dennis, seemed to take it for granted when he was stressed out.

Dennis briefly became defensive, but Monica interrupted. "Dennis, you look worn out. Go get some sleep and consider what I've said. Let's talk in the morning."

The next morning, well rested, Dennis came into the office and apologized to the staff for how he handled the situation the day before.

The next time he returned from an overseas trip, Monica texted him before he reached the office, asking if he was tired. A meeting was scheduled with the entire staff, and she decided she would cancel if he was in a crappy mood. He knew she was really asking if he was in control of his emotions. "I'm fine," he texted back. And he was.

In these behind-the-scenes ways, paying close attention to the initial condition of a confrontation, Monica managed Dennis's flaws and gradually helped him become more aware of the effects of stress on his behavior.

It pays to have empathy for the powerful.

How to Master Cultivated Support: The Building Blocks

For the support strategy to work, it has to be built on real human relationships that go beyond role-playing or superficiality. The person with less power needs to use authentic relationship-building skills—interwoven with competent work and clear results—to demonstrate to the power holder the mutual benefits of their alliance. Understanding the personality, emotions, pressures, and the reality of your boss reduces your likelihood of appearing self-righteous or insensitive.

Emotional regulation is important in all types of conflicts, and dealing with tense situations, even with a benevolent leader, is no exception. You will not get your way all the time, and you will even encounter situations in which the outcome seems unfair or disappointing. Most people who use the support strategy report feeling somewhat nervous when in conflict with authority. It is okay and even healthy to experience whatever emotion you feel, but how you express those emotions in the workplace can be the foundation for the next tense situation.

Borrowing power to be used for the greater good is also a building block. You are not as powerful as your boss, but neither are you power-less. There are several ways to borrow power: through a supportive coali-tion, through your expertise, and through influence skills such as persua-sion, logic, and repetition. Just remember to return what you borrow; any power you gain when working for a cooperative boss needs to be rein-vested in the organization rather than usurped. Even a benevolent boss can feel threatened if you appear too competitive too often.

Walt and Roy, Jeanne and Troy, Adrianna and Stefan, Monica and Dennis—these relationships at their best work as coleadership alli-ances. They are characterized by trust, mutual commitment to a greater cause, cooperation, negotiation rather than control, and shared respect. At their worst, these leaders occasionally experienced hurt feelings, an-ger, and unhealthy conflicts. But over time, most of the disagreements between the members of these duets were worked out for the greater good. Both parties yield from time to time, but are willing to return to the table when things get tough. Both are willing to share power and truly consider the other's perspective.

In this type of relationship, conflict need not be a contest; it can be part of a negotiated process of achieving shared goals.

• CULTIVATED SUPPORT SUMMARY •

For Situations of Cooperative Dependence: In these situations, you have low power relative to the other disputants, share cooperative or complementary goals, and have a high need to remain on good terms with them.

Strategy: To increase the power holder's awareness of your shared goals and mutually beneficial relationship and to seek opportunities for you both to enhance your resources for power and influence, in a manner that is nonthreatening to the power holder.

TACTICS

1. Make it positive.
2. Carefully construct the initial conditions.
3. Cultivate an information coalition.
4. Present problems as "ours" rather than "yours."
5. Don't bring one problem; bring several solutions.
6. Wage a peaceful campaign.
7. Flex your influence through your function.
8. Get unstuck ASAP.
9. Do unto authority as you would have authority do unto you.
10. Distinguish between a leader's weaknesses and fatal flaws.

SKILL-DEVELOPMENT CHECKLIST

Check any skill you have already developed. Discuss your responses with someone you trust.

_____ **I am skilled at rational persuasion.** I can use logical arguments and factual evidence to influence people with more formal power than me. I use this skill to disagree without appearing too emotional or combative.

_____ **I am skilled at consultation.** I can suggest improvements to a plan or help plan an activity when someone in authority wants my assistance. I thus know how not to come across as contentious when I disagree; I can be seen as just trying to help.

_____ **I am skilled at reciprocity.** Without appearing manipulative, I often do favors for others, which motivates them, including those with formal power, to do things for me. This reduces defensiveness or control when we disagree.

_____ **I am skilled at cooperation.** I am known for helping and collaborating with others, which leads to others wanting to cooperate or negotiate with me, even when we don't see eye to eye.

_____ **I am skilled at building deep relationships.** Beyond being friendly, I really get to know others and frequently demonstrate my support, including for those in power. This allows me to appeal to the relationship and to ask for favors or support, even when we hold different perspectives.

_____ **I feel genuine empathy for many in authority.** I am well aware that with authority comes considerable responsibility and stress and that most leaders face strong constraints on their time, attention and influence. Life is not always a picnic on top.

_____ **I know how to make people feel positive.** Because I can make people feel good, I am more likely to influence them in a direction I prefer. Someone in power is less likely to assert dominance over me because of these positive feelings. I can also appeal to values and ideals of those with authority over me, which keeps things positive during some disagreements.

_____ **I have skills at exerting pressure in a way that does not alienate people in power.** I can artfully remind, push, request, and follow up on issues or promises without simply appearing as a nag. I use this to gradually influence someone in authority to keep a promise or see things as I see them.

_____ **I build coalitions.** I know how to get several people to agree with my perspective, so when I try to influence those in authority I am part of a group rather than someone only out for my own agenda.

_____ **I know how to create dependence.** I develop expertise or niches that make power holders dependent on me. When we do not agree, I can use this specialty knowledge or skills to negotiate, not just comply.

_____ **I know how to figure out others' interests.** Rather than simply advocating for my position during conflict, I take into consideration the power holder's needs and interests, and I find a way to practice a give-and-take discussion to get at least part of what I want.

DISCUSSION PROMPTS

Select someone you trust to discuss the cultivated-support strategy and how it fits your current situation.

- How often do I disagree with those above me in the organization? Do I do it too much? Do I overplay "the devil's advocate"? Or do I seem to keep my opinions and ideas to myself too often?
- How effectively do I disagree with superiors? Do I sound like I am trying to solve "our" problem, or do I sound like a complainer or contrarian?
- What actions can I take to be more influential with those above me? What can I do to build a richer relationship with my boss and other leaders so that they want to hear what I have to say, even when it is a different opinion than theirs?

6

Constructive Dominance

DOMINANCE — BY FAR the most common conflict-management strategy employed by power holders — can backfire against those who dominate and be disheartening for those who get dominated. Sure, there are bullies running nations, corporations, schools, and teams, and some of them are very efficient and productive. But dominance only works effectively under very narrow circumstances, and it often fails. Leaders may get "alignment," with everyone rowing in the same direction, but not innovation. They get subservience and compliance, but neither candor nor commitment. Winning through domination, in short, can lead to losing in the long run. Some leaders know this but have trouble limiting their use of it. Others struggle to dominate even when situations require it.

Muriel "Mickie" Siebert was the first woman to become a member of the New York Stock Exchange. Tough, fair, and innovative, she detested the greedy elements of Wall Street, preferring instead to take care of her customers, help women and young people learn financial literacy, and build relationships based on trust.[1]

She was also the first superintendent of banks in New York, serving from 1977 to 1982. When a reporter asked her if she thought a woman was capable of doing the job, Siebert replied, "Yes, the initials are S.O.B." And she proved it. She compelled some banks to merge for the good of customers, but she stood up to powerful state government influences and refused to support other mergers that were bad for small towns upstate. She once forced a bank president to cut his salary by six figures because she thought he should pay for his investment mistakes like his customers had to.[2]

Not a single New York bank failed on her watch, when many banks around the United States collapsed.

When Mickie returned to her own company after serving in government (during which time she had put her company in a blind trust), she discovered the firm had been badly mismanaged. When an arrogant executive challenged her, Siebert let her go. Then she laid down the law in the form of strict new rules for all employees, some of whom had delivered bad service or who had a propensity for acting rudely to customers. Mickie was willing to face any conflict that had to do with retaining, attracting, or protecting consumers.

But she wasn't stuck. Neither a manipulator nor a dictator, Mickie could be cooperative, warm, and trusting. When it was time to navigate a conflict forcefully, she did.

Dominance has a bad name in today's work world. It seems primitive and distasteful.

Leaders who frequently dominate in disagreements damage morale. They are called "brutal bosses" and often do more harm than good. But it does not have to be that way. If you use dominance wisely, it can be constructive for your organization.

Under certain conditions, dominance can be a necessary or practical tool, such as when you are in conflict with unjust and unresponsive adversaries or in situations where subordinates are hostile or unmotivated to comply with reasonable demands. It would be unrealistic to expect prison guards or riot police to use anything but dominating strategies under crisis conditions in their work.

You may benefit from exercising constructive dominance in conflict if:

- you need to maintain your relationship with the other party to reach your goals;

- the other party is clearly against you, at least for now;
- the other party is much less powerful than you.

The trick is to not overdo it or apply it in the wrong situation.

What Draws People to Dominance?

Many leaders dominate by default when faced with a disagreement. They play to win and seek victory at any cost. Some build their fame and fortune on this approach—George Patton, Margaret Thatcher, Shaquille O'Neal, and Donald Trump come to mind. Others probably choose dominance out of a sense of urgency or efficiency. Why waste hours listening and engaging in drawn-out discussions when you can assert your superior power and resolve a conflict with a few words? Others enjoy the rush of adrenaline that comes with commanding and controlling others and dislike the vulnerable feeling of losing control.

For some, dominance emanates from a life story. Lose enough, and some people get determined to *never* lose again. Some over-dominators are just passing the buck (or the abuse) they've been handed from above. Grow up in a family or subculture that overemphasizes strict obedience to authority, and dominance looks normal.

The belief that conflicts are all-or-nothing, win-or-lose contests is very common and creates an ultimatum to dominate: the only goal is to win.[3] The same goes for power: if power is seen as a fixed pie with only so much to go around, why share it or waste it by involving others in decisions? If someone thinks that not getting 100 percent of what she wants is the same as losing, she will do anything to win at all costs, leaving no room for cooperative strategies. The belief that getting things done matters more than the people involved also drives dominance. Many leaders who dominate in conflicts actually believe they are negotiating. Our tendency to dominate can even be traced to our biochemistry. Higher levels of testosterone have been linked reciprocally to dominance behaviors, with acts of dominance boosting testosterone and spikes in testosterone increasing dominance. A striking study conducted by Columbia University Business School Professor Dana Carney found that people who were instructed to stand or sit in "power positions"—stances that are open and expansive—even for a few minutes, demonstrated significant increases in their testosterone levels and in feelings of powerfulness and tolerance for risk.[4]

The structures that surround you at work can also encourage conflict dominance. Hypercompetitive, hierarchical organizations discourage cooperation, except among underlings. If your colleagues or superiors clearly expect you to dominate in top-down conflicts, the press of the system will be hard to resist.

Many situational contingencies call for dominance. You may find yourself needing to protect yourself or your subgroup from stressful or even destructive forces within your organization, with dominance the best or only tool for the job. You may be in conflict with another party who gives you no other viable choice.

But there are counterforces that hinder the strategic use of dominance even when it is reasonable or necessary. Nice people who don't like to be seen as controlling others may have trouble wielding power at someone else's expense. People with low self-esteem are often too deferent in conflicts. A company culture where managers are discouraged from dominating will make them think twice about doing so, even when the conflict calls for it. Often, dominance is seen as identical to abuse and bullying. One of the problems with traditional conflict-resolution methods is that they can call for *too much* cooperation and win-win negotiating. Good-hearted people feel better when benevolent cooperation works, but unfortunately, cooperation often fails. And any leader who can never dominate in a conflict is going to be ineffective.

Self-Assessment: Are You a Conflict Dominator?

Many leaders wonder (and worry) whether they are too dominant or too passive. The questionnaire below may help you get a sense of just how dominating you are in conflict. To see how much you are drawn toward dominance, choose the number that best describes your response to the statements below.

1 = Strongly disagree   4 = Agree
2 = Disagree   5 = Strongly agree
3 = Neutral

_____ 1. Being very competitive is the best way to get ahead.
_____ 2. When I disagree with a subordinate, I go ahead and make the decision without much discussion.
_____ 3. I don't like to get into disagreements with people who report to me.
_____ 4. Obedience is extremely important in an organization.
_____ 5. If employees did what they were told, organizations would have fewer problems.
_____ 6. Authority must be maintained or a company will fall into chaos.
_____ 7. As the person in charge, I have to know more about the objectives and procedures of my area than anyone else, or I will lack legitimate authority.
_____ 8. I've been told I can be intimidating.
_____ 9. I almost always win a good debate with an employee.
_____ 10. I don't really know what my subordinates are thinking. They probably hide information from me.
_____ 11. When you are the boss, you have to win an argument or you'll lose the respect of those around you.
_____ 12. Most people need to be told what to do.
_____ 13. Good leaders are forceful; they push people so the right things get done, regardless of how people feel about it.
_____ 14. I don't let discussions go very long; it's often a waste of valuable time.
_____ 15. My subordinates almost never disagree with me. We are extremely aligned.

SCORING

Add up your scores. Keep in mind that the specific content of your job and your organization, rather than your scores on this questionnaire, determine how much dominance is too much or not enough. But your scores offer a starting point for reflecting on your use of this strategy. Study the table below. If you have a very high score, there is a good chance you are overusing this strategy. But a low score may also be cause for concern.

Score	Meaning	Ask yourself . . .
<40	You rarely, if ever, dominate in a conflict with a subordinate.	Is it because the environment does not require or support this approach? Or are you underutilizing this strategy?
40–49	You are inclined toward this strategy.	Do you use it enough and in the right contexts?
50–59	You use this strategy quite a bit.	Do you use it too much or in the wrong contexts?
60+	You rely on this strategy in most circumstances.	There is a high probability that you overuse the dominance strategy. Does the environment really support this strategy as much as you use it? Are you using it effectively and in the right contexts? Do you need to improve your skills at discerning when to use other strategies for conflict?

Organizational Assessment: Do You Work in a Domineering Environment?

Now try this one. To get a sense of how much your current work environment pulls you toward dominance, rate your response to each of the following statements.

1 = Strongly disagree   4 = Agree
2 = Disagree   5 = Strongly agree
3 = Neutral

_____ 1. Conflict between bosses and subordinates is considered bad for morale around here; we are expected to come to an agreement quickly so we can move on.

_____ 2. Management in this organization keeps its distance from the other employees.

_____ 3. There have been several instances here in which a manager screamed at a subordinate.

_____ 4. If you are in a position of power in this organization, you are expected to make sure everyone knows you're in charge.

_____ 5. You are viewed negatively in this organization if you let your subordinates challenge you.

_____ 6. People in management don't trust subordinates around here.

_____ 7. Management is expected to minimize conflict in this organization; we are supposed to be aligned.

_____ 8. Where I work, someone has to lose power for someone else to gain it.

_____ 9. Most of the people who work here are reluctant to make a decision; they are very dependent on someone in charge.

_____ 10. You have to be careful around here because other people are trying to take away your power and authority.

_____ 11. The less power you have around here, the more likely you get blamed for things.

_____ 12. It's very competitive inside this organization, no matter what your job.

_____ 13. Subordinates don't trust management in this organization.

_____ 14. It is foolish where I work to openly disagree with someone in charge.

_____ 15. Those in charge where I work keep their distance from everyone else, unless there's a problem.

SCORING

Add up your score, which will fall between 15 and 75. The higher the score, the more your work environment or organizational culture pulls you toward dominance. Now compare your self-assessment score to the organizational assessment you just completed.

_____ Self-assessment score from the previous questionnaire
_____ Organizational-assessment score from the most recent questionnaire

The more similar the scores, the more likely you are employing dominance strategically (at least in general). Nonetheless, because of the potential for the dominance strategy to get overused and cause damage, if either your self-assessment score or your organizational assessment score is high, we encourage you to carefully reflect (and get some feedback) about whether or not your use of this strategy is working.

Six Good Reasons to Use Constructive Dominance in Conflict

1. **It's eat or get eaten.** You may find yourself in conflict with a difficult and disengaged employee. Many organizations have people who are intentionally working against success. Some have malicious motives, are stuck in a competitive or petty mindset, or are bitter and retaliatory. Dominating in a conflict may save the organization (and yourself) tiresome trouble.

2. **Your opponent has benign motives but incompatible goals.** Some people may have decent motives, but their goals are nonetheless incompatible with the organization or with your own. There may be insufficient common ground to cooperate. Domination doesn't have to be personal; sometimes it is necessary to achieve important goals.

3. **Time is of the essence.** Dominance is often quicker than coop-

eration (at least in the short run), and some situations simply demand it.

4. **Security and confidentiality are at stake.** Maybe you know something the other party does not know and you cannot share that information. Since cooperation involves a certain level of disclosure, security or confidentiality may necessitate dominance at times. Leadership sometimes requires us to appear in an unflattering light in order to act ethically or achieve vital goals.

5. **Dominance is your best BATNA.** Sometimes you try cooperative strategies and they fail miserably. Everyone needs a BATNA (best alternative to a negotiated agreement) in conflict. When a problem cannot be negotiated, occasionally the best alternative — or the only one — for those in authority is domination.

6. **It is mission critical.** Sometimes the mission of a team, project, or organization requires domination. The dramatic decisiveness of this approach can be necessary to signal strength and commitment to a goal or cause.

The Consequences of Misusing Dominance

Excessive dominance can have extreme consequences. Many people are reluctant to share their true thoughts with any boss, but who in their right mind would share creative ideas, dissension, or challenges to authority with a chronic dominator? Perpetual domination is also bad for morale; it makes people feel anxious, even depressed.

Domination can have consequences for a leader's career. One of the major reasons for executive career derailment is the inability to resolve conflicts with subordinates constructively.[5] Many conflict-dominant managers and executives see their careers stalled or ended prematurely. Dominators also risk losing their best employees. If someone has a good education, self-confidence, and talent that are valuable to an industry, he or she has options other than putting up with a drill sergeant for a boss.

Dominance is also expensive. It tends to elicit mere compliance from subordinates instead of deeper levels of commitment to the work.[6] But compliance with the expectations of a dominator only works when the boss is watching. This means that dominators must continually scrutinize and oversee their employees to make certain their demands are met. Outside of the watchful eye of their superior, the employees are much more likely to goof off, act out, or worse.

Dominance can create a culture of passivity. Take George Eastman. He brought photography to the masses with the invention of roll film and made a fortune leading Kodak. But he also left behind a rigid, hierarchical culture with strong incentives to avoid conflict, which threatened Kodak's ability to adapt to change. So when Tony M. Perez joined Kodak in 2003 as president and CEO, people seemed completely unable to openly disagree with him. "If I said it was raining, nobody would argue with me, even if it was sunny outside," he once commented.[7]

To reform Kodak's conflict-avoidant and complacent culture, Perez replaced many executives and created "The R Group" (R stands for Rebels) to restore skepticism, innovative thinking, and urgency to address the challenges faced by the company.[8] But after several false starts, as of this writing, Kodak has emerged from chapter 11 bankruptcy as a much smaller, weaker company, and many business analysts are predicting its demise. Cause of death: founder dominance.

What Does Constructive Dominance Look Like in Action?

Dominance can be a strategy based on reasonable motives, invoked when you have more power than others and when the conflict situation is more competitive than cooperative. It does not have to be a personality style, pathology, or destructive force. Nor is it inherently evil, brutish, or antisocial. It can be a useful and constructive strategy if it fits the context, is seen as legitimate, is delivered artfully, and serves the greater good. A dominance strategy can be satisfying and necessary for the well-being or effective functioning of a team or organization, even if one or more individuals is not satisfied in the short run. Every business owner or manager knows that an organization needs to maintain a good degree of order and efficiency or it will cease to exist.

Dominance is most likely to be constructive when it is used thoughtfully and intentionally. It needs to be considered in context, and with an eye to the long term. Four points are crucial here. First, nearly all conflict in organizations happens in the context of ongoing relationships. A relationship that is positively cultivated *over time* is more likely to benefit from one party asserting dominance over another than is a neglected or abusive relationship or a conflict with a stranger. Second, dominance should always be seen as a last or later resort after more-cooperative strategies fail. Third, constructive dominance requires exercising good judgment and ensuring its use is appropriate for the situation. And fourth, beware of all-or-nothing thinking and strategies. A dominance strategy that resolves the conflict in favor of the party with more power should not obliterate the loser. Winning a conflict may not be worth losing a relationship or gaining a reputation as an abusive dictator.

Ten Dominance Tactics

1. CLARIFY AUTHORITY

It is sometimes necessary to remind others that not everyone in the organization has the same options or the same latitude.

Jonathan is not a naturally dominant person in conflict. Although he's a former army officer turned entrepreneur and CEO, he is soft-spoken and seeks cooperation and consensus whenever possible. He is patient and quite willing to invest the extra time it takes to find a mutually satisfying outcome.

As a computer security expert in the U.S. Army, Jonathan would gently and humorously assert rank when there was not enough time for a full discussion. "We always have time to protect democracy, but right now we don't have time to practice it," he would tell someone of lower rank with a smile. This proved to be all he needed for ending minor disagreements without damaging the motivation of his highly skilled subordinates.

But he also learned the necessity and the value of clarifying authority more directly.

When he noticed some inappropriate shortcuts in a computer activity log, he brought it to the attention of the sergeant responsible.

"Not to worry, sir," the man replied. "I've worked with these systems for nearly five years. I know them inside out. I value efficiency, as I'm sure you do, and I know how to get the work done without wasting my time."

"Sounds reasonable enough," responded Jonathan. "All the same, because I'm new here, I'll be working with you side by side for the next few weeks. I'd like to better understand your work."

"With all due respect, sir, I don't need a babysitter. I know what I'm doing."

As Jonathan felt his skin heat up, he remembered a discussion he once had with a mentor. "It's one thing to disregard rank in some situations," the older man explained. "But it's not good for an organization to pretend that everyone has the same level of authority. Power sometimes needs to be clarified."

"Sergeant," Jonathan said in a quiet but firm voice. "I am not your babysitter. I am your boss. I am your commanding officer. I will be working very closely with you for the next few weeks, and you will provide any information I ask for, immediately and without commentary."

"But sir, the last commanding officer—"

"My predecessor is gone, and I am the CO. We will meet weekly at this time and go over the reports until further notice. Dismissed."

Later, as he built a successful company, he occasionally had to remind argumentative employees that *he* was in charge, not them.

2. CULTIVATE SOFT POWER TO BUFFER HARD

Leaders can use soft-power tactics such as persuasiveness and relationship building and focus on cultivating a trusting workplace culture to create a more positive context for future disagreements that may sometimes require hard power to resolve.

Hard power is the means to get people to do what you want them to do; *soft power* is the ability to get others to want the outcomes you want. Hard power is closely associated with asserting authority and controlling resources (for example, deciding rewards like bonuses and promotions, and consequences like disciplinary actions, demotions, or termination). Soft power, in contrast, is motivational by way of affiliation, attraction, and inspiration. Hard and soft power are both important to effective leadership.

In both the military and in business, Jonathan learned the value of soft power. While he was not a gregarious extrovert, he liked people and enjoyed getting to know them. He liked helping people and knew the value of reciprocity. When a member of his army staff wanted to debate a decision, Jonathan would listen to the other perspective if there was enough time or if the context involved technical expertise.

As a business leader, Jonathan spent even more time building relationships with customers, vendors, and employees. If someone worked extra hours, he noticed and was likely to encourage them to go home early on a subsequent day. He sought the opinions of his employees frequently, often withholding his own opinion to ensure that it did not prematurely taint theirs.

But Jonathan took soft power even further. He learned that it was not enough to carefully emphasize listening, persuasion, and cooperation in his own behavior; he needed to institutionalize it. He wanted to build a technology services company with a culture of trust and engagement that encouraged innovation, creative problem solving, and smart risk taking, where occasional dominance by the boss would be understood as a necessary exception to an overall pattern of cooperative candor.

He hired the best people he could find to establish a culture of competence and excellence. Together, they generated a code of ethics that made them feel psychologically and professionally safe. He modeled openness in his leadership style and encouraged others to follow suit. This combination of competence, sound ethics, and openness leads to trust.[9] This helped establish a culture where soft power could thrive and people could survive occasional bouts of hard power.

3. MONITOR AT MULTIPLE LEVELS

In some situations, even trusted, competent subordinates need to be monitored closely to develop their talent.

At a highly innovative nonprofit staffed with former valedictorians and other whiz kids, poor performance stands out. So does weak supervision. When Marsha, the nonprofit's director, learned that a six-month employee was doing a very poor job, she met with the employee's supervisor, Wendy, who was compassionate to a fault.

"Let's give her thirty days to show improvement," Wendy pleaded.

Marsha told her she'd need to see a well-defined plan with goals and criteria that included close monitoring. "While I don't intend to impose a decision here, I do want to know in detail how you handle this. You will have situations like this many more times in your career." Marsha monitored Wendy's monitoring of the underperforming employee. They met frequently, and Marsha politely but clearly asked for measurements of the employee's productivity and quality. After three weeks, when it was painfully obvious the employee was getting worse, Marsha asked Wendy her intentions for day thirty.

"I want to keep helping her," replied Wendy. "Another thirty days."

Marsha replied, "What I observe is that you have set specific and reasonable goals for the employee, and by your own measurements she is not coming close to reaching those goals, and yet you want to keep trying. Help me understand."

"I don't like how closely you are monitoring me. I feel like Big Brother is watching. Just let me handle it."

"You are monitoring her to give her a chance to save her job. I am monitoring you to develop you. I will still give you the thirty days we agreed to, but if she doesn't turn this around, you will need to make a decision. And I want to be closely informed about her progress or lack thereof."

On day thirty, Marsha asked to see the metrics. It was obvious the employee was not right for the organization.

"*Termination* is such a nasty word," said Wendy.

"It's hard to let people go," said Marsha. "But that's why I watched you so closely on this one. You are a great manager of highly motivated and talented people, but you also have to manage the problems. I think if I had not monitored you so closely, you would have let this go on and on."

"I hate to admit it, but I think you're right," Wendy said.

4. DELEGATE DOMINANCE

Some leaders establish a networked infrastructure of command and control in order to manage important issues efficiently.

Famed NFL coach Bill Parcells knew something important about oppressive, in-your-face conflict management: not to do it. Instead Parcells, two-time Super Bowl champion and pro football Hall of Famer, delegated dominance.

Working in professional football, there was no skirting the need to come on hard and strong with many of the hyper-testosterone, egomaniacal, three-hundred-pound superstars Parcells coached. But the system of coaching that he developed delegated and distributed such functions. Often his player team captains, such as the great linebacker Lawrence Taylor, would take up the role of lieutenant enforcer. Parcells would express his concerns privately with Taylor, who would then confront those team members who were slacking, acting out, or otherwise screwing up. Parcells would make a point of sitting down with every one of his fifty-plus players every week for a few minutes to check in and keep up morale and rapport. This combination of caring and outsourced confrontation worked exceptionally well in the NFL, as Parcells's stellar record indicates.

Mindful of this, Jonathan developed a process for his managers to give each other feedback so that they didn't need to rely on him so much.

This strategy paid off when a lower-level employee started causing work-flow problems.

The company had a copywriter on the marketing team named Jessie, who did high-quality work but was immature. His supervisor, Sarah, was one of the company's most valuable employees, but she hated conflict and found it hard to manage people.

In a leadership meeting Sarah disclosed with some frustration that Jessie was extraordinarily creative but slow, and thus left much of his noncreative work to her. She sometimes stayed late completing his paperwork and proofreading his writing.

Rather than insisting that Sarah confront her subordinate, Jonathan employed the peer structure. He turned to his sales manager, who was very good at holding difficult employees accountable, and asked, "Noah, what do you think?" Noah had learned to be sensitive with Sarah. With most people he expressed his opinion quite forcefully, but he spoke softly to Sarah. "If Jessie isn't getting the work done, it's better to stand up to him now rather than later. The problem will grow the longer it lasts." Then Jonathan turned to one of his most soft-spoken managers. She agreed with Noah: "I know you don't like conflict, Sarah, but Jessie will never learn unless you hold him accountable."

"I'll talk to him," Sarah said with faint determination.

5. DOMINATE AS AN OPENING GAMBIT

Negotiations sometimes go better if they start with a clear message that the leader will not be exploited or manipulated.

Kari prides herself on her collaborative leadership style. But she's not a softy. Working for a large chemical manufacturer, she was the first woman assigned to run a production plant for the company. The employees had repeatedly pressed to change from five eight-hour shifts per week to four ten-hour shifts. For years they had asked each successive plant manager for this change and each time had received a blunt no.

As the first day of her new job approached, Kari heard rumors that many of the workers thought she had been overpromoted, and they expected her to be soft. She knew they would ask about the shift-format change and was not preemptively opposed to it. She just didn't know how it would affect the business and safety concerns. But she also wanted to dispel any notion that she would be easy to push around. *I'll never succeed as a cooperative leader if I am perceived as weak,* she thought.

On her first day a group of employee representatives came to her office and stridently made their case for the four ten-hour shifts per week.

"No," replied Kari.

Shocked, they pressed harder.

"No," she repeated.

As weeks went by and most of the employees noticed how much more collaborative Kari was about most issues than previous plant managers were, the representatives returned.

"We don't understand why you seem so cooperative on most plant issues, but you said no so quickly to our proposal for restructuring the work week."

"Two reasons," Kari replied. "First, you were harsh and demanding, as if you were trying to run me over. You wanted me to listen, but you made no efforts to discuss it. Second, you didn't make a business case for your proposal. You just acted like I should give you what you want because you want it. Remember, I have a boss, too. Several, actually. I have to answer to them for the productivity and safety of this plant."

A few weeks later they returned with a thoughtful business case that addressed all pertinent issues. Kari presented it to the managers above her, who agreed to a pilot program, which went well. Eventually the new policy was adopted.

6. IMPOSE STRUCTURE ON GROUP DECISIONS

Use your influence over ground rules and decision agendas to guide people through confusion and conflict to optimal decisions.

As Jonathan became aware of new competition in the region, he wanted to find ways to attract and keep the best talent, and he wanted to remain profitable if competitors tried to compete on prices. After studying several profit-sharing models, he decided to get his senior staff involved: "We have new competitors in the area, and I want this company to stay on top. I hope all of you continue working here because you like it and because you're paid well. I've prepared a summary of several different ways to increase your pay based on performance, and I think we have to move on this soon or we'll have trouble recruiting the best engineers and salespeople as we continue to grow."

Then he handed the team a thick binder of information and left for a four-day business trip. When he returned, he discovered his team in disarray. They were asking themselves and each other anxious questions: "Is the company in trouble because of a major competitor? Will we make less money? Does this mean I have to compete with my coworkers to prove I'm worth my salary? Is Jonathan hiding something from us?"

Over the course of several days he tried to reassure the team and the entire company, but he couldn't extinguish their anxiety. Jonathan had given his team too much detailed information about profit-sharing models and too little information about how the group could choose a model that was advantageous to the company and its employees, leaving them feeling overwhelmed. So he called another meeting and narrowed the decision to two models he felt would be good for a company of their size. The team's job was to choose one and then to figure out the scorecards upon which profit sharing would be based. Nobody would make any less money, he emphasized, and everyone would make more money whenever the company was more profitable.

Over the next few days, the arguments ended, confidence returned, and rumors evaporated.

When control is used in the right context and in the right proportion to the situation, it instills confidence. We want someone to take charge in tense, important, or ambiguous situations. We need to know some of the basic parameters of a complex decision so we can wrap our minds around it.

7. BROADEN YOUR BASE OF POWER

Sometimes dominance requires an accumulation of power beyond a title.

When an entrepreneurial company started experiencing rapid growth, the owner hired Regina as HR director to help the organization become more corporate and professional. The existing HR person, Cindy, had been with the company for years and was used to wearing many hats, working countless hours, and, as Regina put it, "making things up as they went along."

When Regina noticed that the younger woman knew very little about HR, she suggested she attend a thirteen-week course on benefits and compensation. Cindy resisted: "You're complicating everything." But Regina insisted. Eight weeks into the course, Cindy stopped attending. Regina considered terminating Cindy for her lack of competence and insubordination but decided to talk to the owner first.

"She's been here from the beginning," the owner responded. "She's loyal and she's worked more hours than the rest of the staff combined. I don't want to lose her. Find a way to keep her."

Regina's positional power as Cindy's supervisor was not enough. She realized Cindy had legacy power, and the sense of entitlement that comes with it. Regina began documenting every conversation she had with Cindy and kept a careful record of errors, omissions, and knowledge gaps. At the same time, she had frequent talks with the owner about the long-term goals of the company. She finally convinced the owner that the expanding role of HR needed Cindy to further her education or she would become increasingly useless. The owner finally agreed.

Regina sent Cindy back to school, and Cindy again attended only half the course before complaining it was unnecessary and refusing to finish.

By this time Regina had earned more social capital with the owner. Regina told Cindy to complete the certification course or she would be let go.

Cindy went promptly to the owner, expecting support. She was shocked when the owner reluctantly and awkwardly said that Regina was in charge of HR and that Cindy would need to follow her direction.

When Cindy pushed back one more time about having to take a course, Regina gave her three days of administrative leave without pay to consider whether she wanted to continue working there.

Cindy returned stubbornly unchanged and was terminated.

8. DIAL UP DOMINANCE GRADUALLY

Even excellent employees sometimes need to be dominated in a conflict, especially if they grow increasingly resistant to change.

Scott was an excellent employee of a wholesale gourmet-food distribution company, but his new boss (and former peer), Rebecca, felt that the information technology department he managed needed to change. She met with him to discuss upgrading some technologies and outsourcing some aspects of IT that were not part of the core competencies of the business. She also felt IT needed some new blood, as the entire staff had never worked for another organization. Scott was not defensive but he disagreed. He felt his department was gradually evolving in the direction of greater efficiency and professionalism and felt Rebecca was pushing too hard.

Rebecca was reluctant to force Scott to change. But at the same time, she had consulted with IT directors from other companies in the industry and felt strongly she should not simply capitulate to Scott. She decided to negotiate.

As the months and meetings went by, her cooperative approach with Scott yielded only minimal changes for the better. So she dialed things up. She made a list of changes she wanted, and she indicated which ones she was willing to wait for and which ones needed to happen before specific deadlines.

Scott missed the first two deadlines. At his first performance review, Rebecca praised Scott at length for his knowledge of the company, the customers, the industry, and his skills with people. But she also let him know that she had become increasingly skeptical about his ability to lead IT over the next five years. She gave him ninety days to make certain well-defined changes in IT.

"Are you thinking of firing me?" he asked.

"No. I don't want this company to lose you. But I'm considering a change for you in the company. I want you to take the rest of the week to think about whether you can really commit to these changes or if we should move you somewhere else."

A few days later Scott returned to negotiate a change in his position. "I still disagree with some of the changes you want and the pace at which you want them, but I love this company and want to contribute in some way."

Scott was very successful in a different role, and Rebecca successfully restructured IT with the help of a consultant.

9. INSULATE THE GIFTED, OBNOXIOUS DOMINATORS (GODS)

It is sometimes necessary to create a layer of protection around someone who is incredibly talented but extremely difficult. The insulation protects other employees from the GOD, and also protects the GOD from distractions.

Steve Jobs was obsessively creative and manically visionary, revolutionizing the world of technology and design multiple times.[10] But he also bullied and humiliated people for their inferior ideas or for disagreeing with him. To Jobs, collaboration was not civil give-and-take—it was a battle for excellence. He was intolerant of imperfection. When distributors struggled to deliver enough chips on time, Jobs screamed at them.[11] If he didn't like an idea, he would tell its originator it was shit.[12]

As Jobs matured, he came to realize that he was exceptionally talented but abusive. On his second stint as Apple CEO, he wanted to contribute without harming the organization. He knew he could not control himself, so he made sure that Apple hired other executives who were effective at buffering his emotional excesses and his potential to harm others.

Leaders who understand the dominance strategy, without automatically pathologizing it or relegating it to moral inferiority, can see the talent behind an abrasive style. But it is a learning process.

A common misstep made by business owners and executives is to promote the best salesperson to sales manager. Jonathan fell headlong into this trap when he put Ken in charge of the sales staff. Ken was a selling machine. He was stellar at developing relationships with prospective clients, exceptionally skilled at explaining the company's services without sounding too technical, and, best of all, dazzling at closing sale after sale after sale.

At first Jonathan was reluctant to put Ken in a management position. Selling is a different skill than managing is. But Ken wanted it and was persuasive; he presented a thoughtful plan for helping the rest of the sales team excel.

The other salespeople will learn a lot from him, thought Jonathan, *even if he's not a perfect manager.*

But Ken never followed his own elegant plan for training, coaching, and encouraging the sales staff. Instead, he argued with them when they didn't do things exactly the way he did. He "inspired" them by badgering. He barked when people took a break from cold calls. Anyone who dared disagree with him was subjected to harsh reminders that he, Ken, was the boss, not them.

Jonathan intervened several times, pulling Ken aside to discuss techniques for conflict resolution, strategies for building on staff's strengths, and ways to incorporate different perspectives into a team approach.

But everything Jonathan suggested fell on deaf, narcissistic ears.

When two good salespeople quit in three weeks, Jonathan knew he had screwed up. He didn't want to lose any more salespeople, but he also didn't want to lose Ken, the GOD of sales numbers.

Jonathan made an executive decision. He told Ken he was too experienced to work with beginners, gave him a new title ("business development specialist"), and told him that he, Jonathan, would be managing him, instead of the soon-to-be-hired new sales manager. Ken went back on the road doing what he did best, closing sale after sale after sale.

10. PLAY HARDBALL

When cooperative methods fail, sometimes we must force the other party into making concessions.

Dominators have a number of hardball tactics they can turn to as a last resort, like issuing threats, playing good cop / bad cop with a partner, offering highball or lowball offers, using "the nibble" (inducing slight concessions from other parties that can be built on), playing chicken (committing publicly to positions that are irrevocable), as well as straight intimidation.[13]

When Kari discovered that one of four shifts at the chemical production plant she led was performing far below the other three, she sat down with the workers for a heart-to-heart. She shared the numbers and her perceptions and how the shift was viewed negatively by workers on the other shifts. But try as she might to engage them in a meaningful conversation, the shift leaders were arrogant and even clownish during the meeting. They spoke as if they were more powerful than her and could afford to ignore her concerns. And their stories indicated they felt like victims of bad management and unfair policies. Kari would have taken their perspective more seriously except that the other shift workers did not see things that way at all. She had been very successful in building cooperative relationships with the other three teams.

So she pointed out more firmly that they did not meet production goals.

"The goals are not realistic," they replied.

"But the other three shifts meet their goals every month and told me they think the goals are challenging but reasonable," she said.

At first she was intimidated by their arrogance and flippancy. But as she thought through the situation and consulted with others, she realized that some members of this shift were toxic to the plant. If she let it continue or acquiesced to their demands, their attitude could spread, hurting production and damaging her reputation and credibility. Whether she felt comfortable with it or not, she knew they were insisting on war.

She called another meeting.

"I have considered your complaints, and also consulted with representatives of other teams. I am going to start by splitting up your team and dividing you among the other shifts. If that doesn't help you change your way of thinking and your approach to your jobs, I will fire anyone who cannot make the change."

The group's main spokesman did her a favor. "I don't need this shit!" he exclaimed as he stormed out. "I quit!"

"Okay, so he made his choice," she said calmly. A few days later she fired someone else for insubordination.

Over the next few weeks, without the influence of the shift's dominant malcontents, the team showed that it was unnecessary to break them up. Team members worked together to prove to Kari they could cooperate and improve their performance, which they did under her leadership.

How to Master Constructive Dominance: The Building Blocks

When dominance works, when it resolves a competitive conflict with minimal damage to the players or the organization involved, it is because the leader using the dominance strategy is not addicted to it. It is a conscious choice made by someone with clear goals.

Effective leaders must have comfort with authority and control to dominate selectively during conflict. The person in power must also have negotiation skills that are a combination of pro-self and pro-organization. Furthermore, assertiveness (with aggression control) allows leaders to be forceful without crossing over into abuse. Finally, a leader must have an appreciation for complexity. Simplistic, all-or-nothing thinking about complicated situations is more likely to turn strategic dominance into retaliation or vilification.

Masterful dominators have a dimmer switch. They can keep the strategy in reserve until they exhaust more cooperative methods of resolving conflict. But such a master can also produce dominance behaviors in the right proportion and intensity as needed by the mission, the team, or the organization.

• CONSTRUCTIVE DOMINANCE SUMMARY •

For Situations of Command and Control: This refers to conflict situations in which you have higher relative power and strong competing or contradictory goals or needs, but those in which you also have a high need to remain engaged with your current adversary in the future.

Strategy: To increase the lower-power party's awareness of your authority and control, of their high level of dependence on you, and of your priorities, while decreasing their sense of their own unilateral power and decreasing your level of dependence on them.

TACTICS

1. Clarify authority.
2. Cultivate soft power to buffer hard.
3. Monitor at multiple levels.
4. Delegate dominance.
5. Dominate as an opening gambit.
6. Impose structure on group decisions.
7. Broaden your base of power.
8. Dial up dominance gradually.
9. Insulate the gifted, obnoxious dominators (GODs).
10. Play hardball.

SKILL-DEVELOPMENT CHECKLIST

Check any skill you have already developed. Discuss your responses with someone you trust.

_____ **I am capable of cooperation and rational presentation.** In most cases, before I resort to dominance, I try other methods of resolving disagreements, such as reasoning, listening, negotiating, and persuading. Dominance is rarely the first tool I pull out of my toolbox.

_____ **I listen and consult.** Even if some conflicts call for a dominance strategy, I do not operate in isolation. I have trusted colleagues with whom I have built strong relationships, and I seek consultation and insight before and after a difficult encounter.

_____ **I know how to assert myself.** I can take a stand, remain firm, and commit to a point of view. I can make myself clear and can articulate the consequences of someone not complying with my demands. I can stay steady and avoid flip-flopping or vagueness.

_____ **I can communicate clearly.** I have developed my skills for sending clear, unambiguous messages, even during stressful disagreements.

_____ **I can take pressure and can cope with highly stressful conflicts.** I can stay on message when someone is attacking me. I can repeat myself, making myself clear every time, even if the opposing party chooses not to listen or understand.

_____ **I have a high level of emotional self-control.** I can assert myself without resorting to screaming, harshness, sarcasm, or demeaning speech. If I lose control over my emotions, especially anger, I can apologize and repair, when appropriate. I can control feelings of rage so they do not infect the organization or alienate cooperation.

_____ **I can step back and get a wider perspective on a situation.** While it may be stressful or unpleasant to discipline someone or even terminate employment, I can hold a big picture in my mind of what is good for the organization.

_____ **I can take criticism.** While I may feel strong, unpleasant emotion during and after a disagreement, I can control my defensiveness and any instinct to retaliate against criticism. I know how to not take things too personally.

_____ **I possess self-confidence.** While I may have areas of doubt and need support, I am a self-confident person who can make tough decisions for the greater good.

_____ **I can bolster my decisions.** When I make a difficult decision, I know how to refrain from torturing myself with guilt, second-guessing, or shame. I can accept that the outcomes of some disagreements are unpleasant and may even lead to unexpected costs, but I operate in good faith and know how to live with my choices.

DISCUSSION PROMPTS

Dominating in a conflict, as we have repeatedly said, can easily be overused as a strategy. But the inability or unwillingness to ever use dominance is a big limitation. Discuss the following prompts with someone thoughtful and candid.

- Describe a situation in which I disagreed with someone too forcefully too soon. In other words, have you seen me use the dominance strategy prematurely or unnecessarily, to the point that it was not constructive?
- In what situation have I underutilized this strategy for navigating a disagreement? Was there a situation you can describe in which I was too soft, too patient, or too slow to confront or set limits? What actions can I take to make my power more clear and impactful in this organization, if I am underasserting my influence?
- Discuss a leader in our present or past who was skilled and judicious at winning during a conflict. He or she didn't do it too much or too little or in the wrong contexts, at least not very often. What do we know about that leader? How did he or she use power effectively for the good of the organization? How did he or she navigate power-unequal conflict?

7

Strategic Appeasement

PHIL JACKSON was a 6-foot-8-inch 220-pound NBA champion basketball player with the New York Knicks. He was large, impressive, and intimidating. Jackson had been a strong player and aggressive defender, but when he retired as a player and changed jobs, he needed to also change gears.

In 1989 he became the head coach of the struggling Chicago Bulls, and as the coach of some of professional basketball's greatest all-time star players (Michael Jordan, Scottie Pippen, and Dennis Rodman, to name a few) and largest all-time egos, he needed to make adjustments in how he managed conflicts with them and between them. Influenced by Eastern and Native American philosophy, Jackson earned the nickname "Zen Master," developing a coaching style that was quiet, respectful, and smart. Even when challenged by some of his most difficult and irrational players (such as Dennis Rodman), Jackson found a way to quietly address their concerns and manage them with a degree of deference. With Rodman, he found ways to tolerate and navigate the player's rebelliousness (missed practices, tardiness, off-color remarks to the press, and sexual escapades) and still keep Rodman in the game and performing at a high level. Jackson is today considered one of the greatest all-time coaches in the NBA, having won eleven championships (to date) and having the highest winning percentage of any NBA coach (.717).

This book is all about reaching your goals by navigating conflict — or by harnessing its power to increase honesty, creativity, and problem solving. Appeasement may seem like an unlikely strategy for achieving these ends. After all, appeasement means surrendering to the will of the powerful. It is the mindset of the oppressed victim.

However, appeasement can actually work as a strategy for achieving your goals. It may not be the most direct strategy, and it does not evoke the warm, positive feelings of the more straightforward strategies in this book. But in some ways it is the most ingenious, resourceful, and self-empowering of the seven strategies. A middle manager may be able to triumph in a disagreement with a direct report, but to achieve his goals with his own manager he may need to placate her at first, then use subtle influence methods to negotiate. A CEO may call the shots when she doesn't see eye to eye with her leadership team, but then acquiesce to a board member when necessary. Whenever you have less power than someone else who plays a demanding role in your relationship, and might even qualify as an SOB, appeasement may be exactly the right strategy.

Consider Christine, for example. She was the office manager, with HR- and financial-reporting responsibilities, for a 150-employee manufacturing site. Highly organized, knowledgeable about HR rules and industry-related laws, and precise with all budget and accounting tasks, she was skillful in her dual role. She was also popular with employees for standing up for them when necessary. As Marina, one of her direct reports and biggest fans put it, "She is a fair, strong manager; I think of her as a role model for me and the other women who work here."

But then Hank took over as the site leader, with his reputation preceding him. Like a character that stepped out of a bad World War II movie, he was known throughout the company (behind his back, of course) as "The Commandant." Hank was one of those always-hit-the-numbers-no-matter-what-it-takes guys. Decisive, contentious, demanding, and demeaning, he was a grueling can-do leader. And he loved to stir up conflict.

Hank rarely asked Christine for her opinion; he just told her what to do, and she seemed to put up with it. Her staff noticed right away.

"She used to be so assertive with the previous boss, but now she acts like a servant with Hank, just quietly taking orders," lamented Marina.

When Hank referred to Christine as "my bookkeeper," she responded with a polite smile. When he asked her to run out and get him a Caffè Latte from Starbucks, she did. When he rudely interrupted her in meetings, she did not complain. Her female colleagues struggled the most with her change in behavior.

"She must be afraid for her job," speculated one of her assistants. "But that's crazy. She has a great reputation in this company."

What happened to Christine? How did she go from a competent, assertive manager to an appeaser overnight?

The word *appeasement* is distasteful to most of us. It conjures up notions of submissiveness, weakness, and powerlessness. It makes us feel timid and pathetic. When you turn it into a noun, it gets worse: "Christine is an appeaser"—wimp, a coward, a weakling. But appeasement can be a powerful tool when we find ourselves stuck on the wrong end of a win-lose conflict. It often involves tolerating and placating an overbearing boss in order to avoid making matters worse. We appease to buy time or keep our job, appease until we can get the hell out. In the repertoire of savvy and adaptive leaders and team members, appeasement is necessary and can be employed strategically. While the tactic may not feel good, moving toward one's goals feels much better than being powerless.

The conflict situation in which the appeasement strategy fits is referred to as "unhappy tolerance," in which you find yourself in a purely win-lose conflict with a domineering superior and with no easy means of escape.

You may benefit from exercising strategic appeasement in conflict if

- you need to maintain your relationship with the other party to reach your goals;
- the other party is against you, not with you;
- the other party is much more powerful than you.

What Draws People to Appeasement?

Some of us are more inclined to appease during conflict with an authority figure. Bullies of all types — abusive parents, aggressive siblings, cruel peers, brutal bosses, hateful spouses, autocratic dictators — can engender this type of response. The longer we are exposed to such treatment, the more ingrained it becomes. People with low self-esteem or who hold a strong belief that their life is determined mostly by external forces will tend to accept their lot more often and so give in and appease others when in conflict.

The cultures in which we live and work also affect our inclination to appease. Organizations and institutions operating within steep hierarchies of authority, such as the U.S. military, the Catholic Church, sports teams, and even many corporations, often require and sanction appeasement behaviors from subordinates when addressing superiors. Anything else is insubordination. The same is true for some national cultures that value deference to authority and collectivism. When national and organizational cultures combine to foster appeasement from underlings, it is much more likely to become ingrained, automatic, and unquestioned.

But when appeasement becomes highly chronic, when it becomes our only choice, it becomes a problem. It has been found to be associated with negative health effects and can foster rage, rigidity, and hostility. This typically leads to poorer outcomes for the appeaser, the appeased, and the organization as a whole.

Self-Assessment: Are You an Appeaser?

To get a sense of how much you are drawn toward appeasement, apply the number that best describes your response to the statements below.

1 = Strongly disagree   4 = Agree
2 = Disagree   5 = Strongly agree
3 = Neutral

_____   **1.**   Over my lifetime, I've rarely or never disagreed with a boss.

_____   **2.**   Most people are just naturally more assertive than I am.

_____   **3.**   Most of the disappointing things in my life are due to bad luck.

_____   **4.**   Many times I feel I have little influence over the things that happen to me.

_____   **5.**   If I ever defy those in authority, I do it behind their back.

_____   **6.**   I have often found that what is going to happen will happen regardless of what I do.

_____   **7.**   Getting a good job depends mainly on being in the right place at the right time.

_____   **8.**   There are usually extreme costs to challenging or criticizing authority.

_____   **9.**   I can't stand conflict with someone who is in charge; I'd rather just go with the flow.

_____   **10.**   I like things stable and predictable, so I don't like to rock the boat.

_____   **11.**   When I don't like the way things are going where I work, I just put up with things until they get better.

_____   **12.**   I've always been known as an accommodator wherever I work.

_____   **13.**   The reason I have not achieved more is because of the hand I've been dealt.

_____   **14.**   The people who disagree with those in authority end up in worse circumstances than before they spoke up.

_____   **15.**   In most work situations, it's best to go along with things you don't like; speaking up doesn't help things or solve problems.

SCORING

The higher your score, the more you could be described as an appeaser. But the more important question is whether you apply appeasement *strategically* (as opposed to *automatically*). As we have said, the context of your organization and the particulars of your specific job determine how effectively appeasement can work for you.

Score	Meaning	Ask yourself . . .
<40	You are rarely, if ever, an appeaser.	Is it because the environment does not support this approach? Or are you underutilizing this strategy?
40–49	You are inclined toward this strategy.	Do you use it enough and in the right contexts?
50–59	You use this strategy quite a bit.	Do you use it too much or in the wrong contexts?
60+	You rely on this strategy in most circumstances.	You might be overusing it. Does the environment support appeasement as much as you use it? Are you using it effectively and in the right contexts? Do you need to improve your skills at discerning when to use other strategies for conflict?

Organizational Assessment: Do You Currently Work in an Appeasement World?

Next, complete the questionnaire below. It will give you a sense of the extent to which your current work environment invites the appeasement strategy. Rate your response to each of the following statements.

1 = Strongly disagree   4 = Agree
2 = Disagree   5 = Strongly agree
3 = Neutral

_____ 1. Where I work now, authority is seldom questioned.

_____ 2. Bosses do not consult their subordinates when making decisions.

_____ 3. We all know that in the end, management gets what they want, so we don't bother to disagree with them.

_____ 4. When you disagree with the boss here, it does not go well.

_____ 5. It's best to do what you're told where I work.

_____ 6. If you disagree with the boss, you get thrown under the bus; you get blamed or punished.

_____ 7. My boss is very dominant; he or she is not really interested in what the rest of us think.

_____ 8. At my job, people in positions of high power do not want their authority questioned.

_____ 9. Around here, subordinates rarely express disagreement with their superiors.

_____ 10. Bosses in my organization are very controlling.

_____ 11. My boss makes fun of you or gets harsh if you disagree with him or her in a meeting.

_____ 12. My boss tries to control everything.

_____ 13. Subordinates follow the instructions of their superiors without openly questioning anything.

_____ 14. We don't really cooperate where I work; we just do what we're told.

_____ 15. My boss doesn't like to talk about things and doesn't really want our opinions.

SCORING

Add up your score, which will fall between 15 and 75. The higher the score, the more it makes sense to use strategic appeasement in your organization. Now compare your self-assessment score to the organizational assessment you just completed.

_____ Self-assessment score from the previous questionnaire

_____ Organizational-assessment score from the most recent questionnaire

For the most part, similar scores mean that you are employing this strategy with good judgment according to the situations you face.

Six Good Reasons to Strategically Appease
Your Superiors in Conflict

1. **You're getting hazed.** You need to pass the dictator's test so you can join the club and get promoted. You suspect that management in this place tends to treat its newbies this way to test their mettle, but you believe it's only temporary. If you survive, things will change as you get accepted and move up in the ranks.

2. **You're planning the great escape.** You get dominated a lot these days but need to keep this job (and paycheck) until you find something better. This stinks, obviously, but not as much as being out of work. You just have to endure it bravely until you can get the hell out.

3. **You're playing a game called quid pro quo.** You need something specific: a raise, a transfer, a letter of recommendation, a good word. This is a short-term strategy that should have a worthwhile payoff.

4. **You're gaming the system.** You know how abusive bosses operate and what makes them tick, so you have decided to play this game better than them and make it work for you and ultimately to their demise.

5. **You're willing to pay tuition.** Some dominant and even horrible bosses have a lot to teach. Let them have their ego and their sense of power, and you can learn from them and then move on.

6. **You're up against the ropes.** Like a boxer, your opponent is getting the better of you and you don't see any options right now

other than to keep your head down and take the beating. If you had other options, you would take them, but you find yourself in a situation where appeasement is actually better than the alternatives.

The Consequences of Misusing Appeasement

British historian and politician Lord Acton warned, "All power tends to corrupt; absolute power corrupts absolutely." But the reverse is also true. Harvard Business School professor Rosabeth Moss Kanter reminds us that powerlessness corrupts as well, increasing "pessimism, learned helplessness, and passive aggression." She points out that when managers and employees feel they have high levels of responsibility but no influence over those with relatively more power, feelings of powerlessness set in and corrupt attitudes and motivation. At its extreme, powerlessness can produce a strong sense of latent resentment and rage, impairing the capacity to engage constructively in conflict. This often results in serious health problems, heightened rigidity, acting out, or an increased tendency to sabotage and undermine those in authority. Imagine the unseen costs to an organization. Appeasement, if it is not strategic and if it is prolonged, is a trap and a health hazard.

Even if it is not used chronically, appeasement can have negative effects. Some people use it out of context. They appease when they do not have to do so. They do not think that in a given situation they have other options. Or they miss the opportunity to use appeasement strategically. When it is misapplied, it wastes time and opportunities. Appeasement, like the other strategies in this book, is meant to be used in service of achieving your goals. It is thus important to apply appeasement strategically at the right time, in the right dose, and in the right conflict.

Furthermore, appeasement as a strategy is not to be confused with pernicious plotting to overthrow the boss or damage the organization. You have to have integrity to appease strategically for the good of your career, your reputation, and your colleagues. Shakespeare's Iago "appeased" Othello as part of a plot to destroy him; that did not end well for anyone.

What Does Effective Appeasement Look Like in Action?

Engaging strategic appeasement in conflict includes four main levers:

- Laying low and buying time
- Increasing the higher-power party's dependence on you
- Shifting the competitive nature of your shared goals toward cooperation
- Increasing one's own resources for power and influence over the high-power party

Your best bet with the vast majority of conflicts at work is to try to manage them effectively and steer them in a constructive direction. This becomes tricky, however, when you find yourself in a win-lose dispute with a domineering boss or superior who seems to enjoy crushing you and for whom supremacy is a way of life. Then it helps to redefine the idea of effectiveness and, if possible, think long-term. Swallowing the bitter pill of appeasement now and then is fine, more or less, until you find it becoming a habit or building resentment in you that could become damaging. Then devising and implementing a strategy can help relieve your resentment and regain a sense of control over the dreadful feeling of powerlessness.

Pure appeasement is at best a temporary solution; if overused, it will likely bring negative consequences. Remember that in work conflicts you almost always have a BATNA, or best alternative to a negotiated agreement, which is to quit and get out. This may be a bad or even painful alternative. But it is important to remember that if things get really bad, this *is* an option—you are never completely trapped.

Our appeasement strategy starts with facing the unpleasant fact that your boss is dominant and more powerful than you, and then, therefore, yielding to his or her superior position without challenge. This will buy some time while you figure out how to move things in a more constructive direction. Then, if your boss does not develop a more benevolent approach to disagreements, you need to slowly, incrementally turn up the heat and employ a series of tactics to bring pressure on him or her—but only in a manner that allows you to maintain deniability. Appeasement involves gradually changing the nature of the boss-subordinate relationship, so that you can eventually achieve your goals. Appeasement will fail as a strategy if you appear as an insubordinate subordinate.

Before Christine could effectively manage conflict with her dominant boss Hank, she needed to clarify her goals. Conflict for the sake of conflict has little constructive purpose. And she knew that Hank's controlling and dominant approach to disputes made it unlikely she could directly negotiate with him. So even before Hank arrived on the scene, she wrote down her long-term goals:

1. To continue working with this company
2. To get a promotion and higher pay
3. To relocate to my hometown

Christine knew she had a BATNA—she could probably change companies—but had already invested several years at this one. And she knew about the frying-pan-into-the-fire phenomenon; she had friends who had left a bad boss for another company, only to discover that dominant bosses exist in all organizations and that even good bosses can morph into bad. So she kept her BATNA in the back of her mind as a very last resort.

She also knew that her talents and her ability to market them within the company were not totally dependent on Hank's style. And she knew that the company had another site—a larger one with more opportunities for internal advancement—near the city where she grew up.

Thus, with her long-term goals clarified, she had a reason to strategically appease Hank. It is always easier to live through unpleasant circumstances if one has a higher purpose.

Ten Appeasement Tactics

1. PLACATE YOUR OPPRESSOR

Step out of the power struggle by temporarily yielding and giving in. Avoid all disagreements.

This one is simple: Suck it up and admit defeat. It's hard, but it can also be liberating.

One of the authors of this book worked for a time as a waiter in a busy Manhattan business lunch spot. Most of the other waiters working there when he was hired (all men) were aggressively competitive over tips, the best tables, knowledge of the menu, even sports talk and gambling. The place was brimming with conflict, hostility, and testosterone. When he first started, he found this off-putting and exhausting and thought about quitting. But then he stumbled onto a simple tactic that made life there easy. He acquiesced. When the other waiters fought over the best seating sections in the morning, he would simply claim the most remote area. The others would stop and look at him in disbelief. In truth, it made no difference what area he worked—the place was filled every day anyway. But simply winning mattered to the others. When the senior waiters bragged about their tips or their sexual conquests or the speed with which they could filet a Dover sole, he would say, "Yep, you are the king." Again, looks of astonishment. This tactic—giving in—was so odd, so unheard-of in this place, that it diffused the power strategy of the alpha waiters and changed the dynamic entirely. It wasn't always fun, but it worked well for a while, until a better job came along.

For Christine, this was step one with her boss Hank. She brought him coffee and lunches, she reformatted spreadsheets, she said yes to him when he seemed to want to hear the word. The tactic gave her time to consider more sophisticated approaches.

2. COZY UP TO THE BULLY

Make yourself more attractive to the more powerful parties in the dispute in order to prepare them for subsequent exploitation.

The effectiveness of this tactic depends entirely on how artfully it is delivered—and how much charm you can muster in the face of conflict. Ingratiation only works when the other person remains ignorant of your real intentions. Interestingly, the lower your relative power, the higher the likelihood that this tactic will be expected and seen as suspicious to the other party, and thus be less effective. So ingratiation may be more effectively used with those with moderate but not total authority over you. Or with those who are mostly oblivious to social-emotional cues— like Hank.

Christine ingratiated herself to Hank with a combination of flattery, exaggerating Hanks's good qualities and dismissing his weaknesses, ex- pressing agreement with his opinions, and doing favors for him.

Researchers at Arizona State University reviewed nearly a hundred studies on social influence and impression management, and concluded that men and women tend to use gender-stereotypical behaviors to influ- ence others in the workplace. Men are more likely to try self-promotion, to do favors, and to claim responsibility for positive outcomes. Women are more likely to use modesty, praise, and apologizing. The researchers concluded that gender-congruent behaviors (that is, actions and re- sponses your culture expects of you as either male or female) are more likely to help you achieve your goals than gender-incongruent behaviors. More specifically, researchers at the University of California at Berkeley and the London School of Economics collaborated on a series of exper- iments in which they had men and women negotiate in various situa- tions. Female negotiators were randomly assigned to either a "neutral style condition" (focus on the information) or a "feminine charm condi- tion" (make frequent eye contact, smile, laugh). The female negotiators who used "feminine charm" achieved better results overall, but the approach sometimes backfired when women appeared to be competing with their male counterparts.

Christine knew much of this intuitively, and began to refine her approach to strategic appeasement by watching others' successes and failures. She noticed her engineering coworker Niraj talking sports with Hank and boasting about the successes of the engineering department much more than he had ever talked about sports or boasted before. It seemed to work. Hank gradually favored Niraj's opinions and even tolerated some dissent. Christine also noticed her direct report, Marina, apparently flirting with Hank and receiving more praise and less harshness than others.

But Christine knew herself well and was thinking long-term. She was concerned that if anyone — Hank or other managers — perceived her as boasting or flirting to achieve her goals, or as competing with her boss, the approach would flop. So she selected her influence tactics carefully according to what she was relatively comfortable doing and how she wanted to be perceived. She found her own subtle ways to "cozy up" to Hank so he never knew she was doing it. She listened at length to his personal stories as if she were interested. She smiled when he attempted humor. She feigned empathy when he complained about people, the economy, and their company. Without Hank realizing it, she was preparing him for other appeasement tactics so she could achieve her goals.

3. TURN INVISIBLE TO AVOID SCRUTINY AND TO BUY TIME

Elicit less scrutiny by disappearing or appearing to be in complete compliance with demands.

Early under Hank's rule, Christine started experimenting with invisibility.

She made sure she was in the office on the days when Hank was traveling. She took her vacation days when she knew he would be around. She found as many legitimate reasons as possible to miss meetings, shorten conversations, stay in her office, and keep quiet. She gradually discovered which personnel situations could be managed with less involvement by Hank. She knew she could not completely avoid telling him some things, but she could change how she told him, when, and how much. Her goal was to elicit less scrutiny from Hank on challenging circumstances when they were likely to disagree—to stay off his dictatorial radar as much as possible—while all the time appearing to be in complete compliance with his demands.

Christine also tried changing the order in which she gave Hank certain information. If a topic was likely to evoke Hank's high need for control, she would introduce it later in a conversation. There were always too many things to discuss, so meetings were typically rushed near the end. If he followed up on the subject in a subsequent meeting, she could quickly report that the matter had been resolved.

This invisibility-and-avoidance tactic helped Christine manage Hank's perception of her as a loyal servant, leaving her a little more room for operating outside his hawk-eyed view. It also gave her more time to get to know Hank better, to try to understand where he was coming from, and to look for more constructive means to work with him. His defensiveness and curt manner made this challenging, but the longer she worked with him, the more transparent and predictable he became.

4. INCREASE THE DEPENDENCE OF THE DICTATOR

Build power by functioning as a primary gatekeeper.

Christine learned early in her career that many successful bosses were totally dependent on their assistants. Although the organizational chart (specifying who reports to whom) suggests that the boss will prevail in any *overt* conflict, she knew how assistants could influence decisions without ever uttering a word of dissent.

Christine applied this tactic to her work with Hank in several ways. Since she was the only person on site who fully understood some of the accounting procedures required by the company, Hank came to depend on her to make him look good. She was happy to do so. But occasionally, when Hank had been particularly tyrannical or nasty, Christine could send a message by delaying a report for ostensibly legitimate reasons, leaving Hank in a panic that he wouldn't meet a corporate deadline. Then she would step in at the last minute and let him know she had been able to pull things together, much to his relief and appreciation. Subtext: *Don't mess with me too much, Hank.*

Christine also noticed that Hank frequently took on far too many tasks and micromanaged too many people. This presented another opportunity for countercontrol. She began by doing him extra favors. She went the extra mile to keep him organized and offered to take minor tasks off his plate. Over time she and her staff took over his scheduling completely, becoming his primary gatekeeper. He was grateful for how Christine could manage his schedule. Consultants, salespeople, and even company executives could have a hard time getting to Hank, thanks to Christine and her staff.

Hank eventually encouraged Christine to knock on his door whenever she felt the need, because he had come to understand that he needed her to achieve his own goals. This made other managers dependent on Christine to get their needs known to Hank. While she rarely appeared to disagree with her boss, she could make things happen (or slow things down) in ways that made him gradually more motivated to loosen the reins on her.

5. DIMINISH YOUR PERCEIVED OPPOSITION BY SAYING YES

Create a high ratio of agreement to disagreement. Carefully select points of disagreement without appearing to contradict the boss.

Years ago Christine briefly considered a career in sales. While she ultimately decided to pursue management instead, she remembered a sales technique she learned early: the "Yes Set Close." The salesperson tries to elicit a set of yeses—usually a minimum set of three—so the prospect might say yes one more time at the close of the sale. Christine decided to try a variation of this on Hank. Instead of getting Hank to say yes, she would say yes to Hank as often as she could stand to do so, in hopes that when she eventually said no to him—by disagreeing with him or pushing back on a request—he would subconsciously give her credit for yeses already served.

It sometimes worked. When she privately disagreed with an opinion she knew he would never change, she responded to his brusque "Well, do you agree with me?" with "Yes, I do." When he proposed a course of action she thought was functional but somewhat inefficient, she said, "Yes, that will work. I'll get it started." She knew, however, that if she only said yes, even Hank would start to suspect that she was insincere. So, for purposes of credibility and influence, she would hold out for the opinion or proposal she thought was deleterious to the site or the company and then politely say, "Hank, I am concerned that what you are proposing will cost too much money" (he hated to waste money) or "This might not look right to upper management" (he was quite conscious of how he was perceived by those with more power than he had).

Using this variation on the Yes Set Close, and by avoiding the use of an outright no, Christine was occasionally able to influence Hank during a disagreement without incurring a tremendously dominant reaction.

6. ELICIT THEIR BETTER ANGELS

Present sensitive cases in a gentle and obsequious tone, appealing to the superior's compassion and management skills and self-interest.

When Poming, a hard-working member of Christine's staff, needed time off to help her aging mother—time beyond company policy and federal law—Christine went to Hank.

"Absolutely not!" he barked.

Christine nodded and calmly continued. "Remember, Hank, you have done several other very kind things for several staff members and their families. That's why people who work here respect you," she said convincingly. "And they care very much about Poming. This will not cost the company money, and my people will make sure the job gets done."

Hank knit his brow, uncomfortable with her appeal, but hesitant to dismiss her again.

"And," Christine added, "not that this is the main point, but I think upper management values the ability to be both tough and tender."

With that she excused herself.

Minutes later Hank's phone rang. It was an executive with whom Christine had briefly spoken of the matter. He told Hank he was just touching base to say he had been hearing great things about the work-site. Numbers were good, deliverables were all being met, and things generally looked great. The next step, he explained, would be the employee survey. He hoped that morale would be better than it was for Hank's predecessor and wished him luck.

This one-two punch paid off. The appeal to his values and self-interest might not have worked without encouragement from above, but it ultimately produced the intended results. Christine made sure, as she delivered the news, that her entire staff knew how very concerned Hank was about the staff member's mother.

Of course, this tactic requires that the superior have some semblance of decency and compassion. If you are dealing with a cold, calculating creep, read on.

7. SQUEEZE THE BOSS BY WORKING YOUR NETWORKS

Build networks by earning the respect of subordinates, peers, and company leadership that can create pressure and increase influence.

That was not the only time Christine reached out to her networks. Over the years she had worked for the company she had made many friends and earned great respect. She always knew that relationship building was the foundation of a successful and satisfying career. If she thought Hank was being too harsh or stubborn to other employees, she would enlist agents from her coalition to deliver feedback. These agents were always male, in positions of power, and respectful and protective of Christine. Their credibility in the eyes of Hank made them better messengers.

Because Christine continued to do great work and to gain the respect of other leaders in the company, there was more than one occasion on which Hank was reminded of what a great employee Christine was, how many times she had done notable things for the company, and how she was valued by the senior leadership team. This information may not have made Hank a fan of Christine, but it prevented him from pushing her too far. Hank was a control freak, but he had a nose for organizational politics. When Hank was at his best — decisive but cooperative and sane — Christine let certain power holders in the company know it.

8. RECONSTRUCT REALITY AND PRESENT NEW POSSIBILITIES

Change the power holder's understanding and perception of the situation.

This is a classic negotiation strategy of those in low power. The clothing salesperson uses this tactic when he or she tells you how good you look in an article of clothing. Political candidates use it when they try to get your vote by framing the issues in terms of your losses and gains. And your fifteen-year-old probably uses it when he or she is attempting to negotiate an early release from being grounded ("Just think of all the important educational experiences I am missing!"). A lower-power negotiator can alter the boss's goals and objectives in a conflict by convincing him that his desired outcome is more costly than he thinks or that a different outcome will be more valuable to him. This is a risky tactic because it can bring the conflict center stage and force the boss's hand, which is likely to result in further dominance. But a shrewd subordinate can sometimes persuade from under the veil of appeasement.

Christine used this tactic once.

Hank was preparing to terminate an employee Christine knew was going through personal struggles that had led to performance problems. Had she been the boss, she would have put the employee on a performance plan that also required outside counseling. But Hank was determined to fire him.

Christine could call corporate HR and at least slow down Hank's determination to terminate the employee. But she knew that if the conflict became institutional and bureaucratic, it would escalate. She decided to try to influence him rather than thwart him, telling him, "Hank, while I will implement whatever you tell me to do in this situation, I am concerned for you and how this will make you look to upper management. I'm concerned that without giving this employee time to straighten out his personal problems and his performance issues, instead of appearing results-oriented, you'll simply appear expedient. This is a well-liked, long-term employee with many friends here. Think of how people will think of you. But as I said, I'll put through the paperwork and do whatever you decide."

Hank silently recalculated the cost of the decision he was about to announce, and instead gave the employee ninety days to turn things around.

9. MAINTAIN PLAUSIBLE DENIABILITY

Develop passive-aggressive tactics for influencing superiors in a manner that maintains deniability and job security.

In a fascinating study conducted in Japan, executive secretaries who worked for callous or incompetent bosses were found to have developed an extensive array of passive-aggressive tactics for seeking revenge on their superiors in a manner that allowed them to maintain deniability and keep their jobs.[1] For example, female Japanese office workers, or "girls" as their male managers refer to them, would thwart the success of men in their organizations by compromising the men's reputations. When a man was kind and reasonable to his female secretaries, the word got around to all the women in the office. He was thus treated with respect, and the tasks he needed completed got done well and quickly. If, however, he was rude or too demanding, the entire female staff conspired against him. They would turn in his reports late and overlook glaring errors. If he complained to his boss about the "girls," he lost the respect of his superiors for not being able to manage women.

While Christine and Hank's situation was not identical, it was similar. Company leaders acknowledged Hank as very talented and results-oriented. But it was also known that he was too tough on people, a lousy listener, belligerent, and controlling in a conflict, and thus bad for morale. The employee survey stung him every year, no matter where he was transferred. Consultants and coaches were assigned to him from time to time, but to little avail. While everyone around him quickly learned to present an accommodating face, the rumors never failed to swirl. Like many rumors, these were neither all false nor all true. If he raised his voice in a meeting, the rumor would spread that he screamed at his team. When he got angry with a young female administrative assistant, rumors reached HQ that he made women cry "every week." So although Christine and the administrative staff had little formal authority or direct recourse to affect Hank's career, they did have the informal capacity to affect his reputation — even if only by *not* refuting such rumors.

10. "FORGET" TO ASK PERMISSION; REMEMBER TO APOLOGIZE

Do what you want to do and break rules, hoping that the system is so inefficient that no one notices; also prepare to apologize in case someone does.

Elias Chacour, a Palestinian archbishop in the Melkite Greek Catholic Church, recounts in a memoir that he once asked a convent if it could supply two nuns for a community literacy project. The mother superior said she would have to check with her bishop.

"The bishop was very clear in his refusal to allow two nuns," the mother superior told him later. "I cannot disobey him in that." She added: "I will send you *three* nuns!"

This tactic can work in the short term but may bring negative consequences and is not likely to work repeatedly. On very few occasions Christine preemptively made irreversible decisions she knew would lead to conflict with Hank (such as authorizing moderate expenditures or extending a deadline for a vendor), then apologized for misunderstanding his perspective. In each case, her apparent contriteness, along with her overall pattern of appeasement, limited the intensity and duration of his harsh disapproval.

How to Master Appeasement: The Building Blocks

When appeasement works as a strategy—when it is functional and helps a person achieve goals—it does so because of certain skills and attitudes. When it fails, it fails because of a lack of these skills and attitudes or because incompatible attitudes are at work.

Some of the basic attainable skills and attitudes associated with strategic appeasement include self-awareness, self-control, and resilience. Strategic thinking and networking will help you plan an escape from your current situation. It also helps to avoid victim, martyr, or entitlement thinking at work. It is so much more effective to appease from a place of strength, strategy, and self-respect.

Truly masterful appeasers will appear cooperative, earnest, and respectful to the dominator and at the same time win over the respect of colleagues. They may confide in some coworkers and even conspire with them to influence the dominator collectively.

Many control freaks claim they do not want to hear only yes during a discussion with different perspectives, but what they really mean is that they want to hear yes and believe it. Dysfunctional or unskilled appeasers fail to suspend their boss's disbelief and are thus likely to appear disengaged or passive-aggressive. Dysfunctional appeasement is not good for your career. If you are just trying to get through the day and vaguely hoping for a regime change or a lucky escape, raw appeasement will depend on chance to work. The very nature of strategic action is to minimize one's reliance on chance.

Christine had indeed become an appeaser—and an effective one at that. There was simply no other way at that time to achieve her goals without appeasing Hank. Had she applied the fighting spirit she was known for previously, she would have left the company as a noble martyr. Instead, she appeased. Strategically. After two years Christine was promoted, partly on the recommendation of Hank. She got to move to the city she preferred and received a substantial raise. Her strategic appeasement had a very impressive return on investment.

• STRATEGIC APPEASEMENT SUMMARY •

For Situations of Unhappy Tolerance: Here, you find yourself in low power, with purely or mostly competitive goals, and yet with a high need to remain in a relationship with the other disputant. People with less power in such conflicts are likely to feel anxious, annoyed, stressed, and angry during and afterward.

Strategy: To lay low and buy time while increasing the higher-power party's dependence on you and shifting the nature of your shared goals from competitive to cooperative in a manner and rate invisible to the power holder.

TACTICS

1. Placate your oppressor.
2. Cozy up to the bully.
3. Turn invisible to avoid scrutiny and to buy time.
4. Increase the dependence of the dictator.
5. Diminish your perceived opposition by saying yes.
6. Elicit their better angels.
7. Squeeze the boss by working your networks.
8. Reconstruct reality and present new possibilities.
9. Maintain plausible deniability.
10. "Forget" to ask permission; remember to apologize.

SKILL-DEVELOPMENT CHECKLIST

Check any skill you have already developed. Discuss your responses with someone you trust.

_____ **I can delay gratification; I have goals and can stay focused**

during stressful times. I think about the future and what I want long term, which keeps short-term compromises or struggles in perspective. When I appease someone with power, I can remind myself of why I do it and where I am going.

_____ **I can deal with someone else having more power and influence than I do.** I do not have to be in charge and can yield to authority when it fits my goals. I know when it benefits me to withhold an opinion or idea.

_____ **I build networks of supportive people within the organization.** I build relationships throughout my organization and get other people to like me and care about me. This attracts support to my situation, sometimes without asking, and I can reach for support without appearing to want to harm a dominant boss.

_____ **I have strong relationships outside the organization.** I have friends and other confidants to whom I can vent, seek advice, and get emotional support.

_____ **I know the rules and policies of my organization.** I can use this knowledge to influence others during a disagreement and sometimes to point out to someone in power that a request or suggestion is a violation of policy. My power in such conflicts does not come from me asserting my opinion so much as from the power of rules with which the power holder has to comply.

_____ **I know how to not take things too personally.** I can gain a larger perspective on the difficulties I sometimes have with my boss by thinking about the big picture, by consulting with others, and sometimes by tapping into my sense of humor. I may get my feelings hurt, but I can take care of myself so I do not stay hurt. When I am unjustly or harshly criticized by a dominant manager, I know how to work with myself so I do not take on the burden of perfectionism.

_____ **I can influence others using indirect methods.** When my goals do not align with someone in power, I have ways of influencing the situation without speaking in a straightforward manner as I would with a cooperative boss. I can influence timing, workflow, meeting preparation, scheduling, and other factors that camouflage the fact that I am not fully compliant or cooperative with a dominant authority figure.

_____ **I have a strong sense of ethics.** When I influence my boss through indirect methods, I refrain from doing anything that would harm the function or reputation of my organization.

_____ **I can think of things to do that make power holders need me.** I deliver value to my organization and my manager; I learn and do things that increase my value so that during a disagreement my boss still depends on me and thus cannot afford to totally dominate me or abuse me.

_____ **I keep my résumé polished and up-to-date.** I know that life is unpredictable and that organizations change, and I do not totally depend on this current job. I listen for opportunities in the job market so I have a backup plan.

DISCUSSION PROMPTS

Appeasement during a conflict with someone more powerful can be bad for your health if you do it too much or for too long. But it can also help you get something you want. Discuss the following prompts with someone thoughtful, candid, and trustworthy.

- What are your perceptions of me when I have to work with a dominant boss who does not apparently want my real opinions and ideas? Have you noticed ways in which I influence such a manager during a disagreement without appearing insubordinate? Be honest with me about missteps I have made in this area. Do you have any ideas for how I can more skillfully (and strategically) appease someone in power?
- Can you think of any situations in which I sabotaged my own goals by arguing or pushing too hard against a leader with a closed mind? Are there ways I can be more skillful at influencing someone more powerful when the direct approach does not work?

- Are there any individuals we both know who you think are masters of strategic appeasement? These would not be people who simply capitulate at the expense of their goals. They would be colleagues who can navigate various controlling authority figures and still achieve at least some of their goals. What do they do that works so well?

8

Selective Autonomy

QUIZ: What do Dirty Harry and Mary Poppins have in common?

1. They are both heavily armed.
2. They have the same goal: to make children laugh and help worka-
   holic parents appreciate their children.
3. Both argue with people in power.
4. Both act independently, pursuing their goals in a bleak urban landscape, for the most part ignoring the authority figures around
   them.

If you chose 1, you are incorrect. Harry Callahan carries a Smith &
Wesson model 29 revolver, chambered for a .44 magnum cartridge. Ms.
Poppins carries only a flying umbrella and a bottomless carpetbag.

If you chose 2, you are wrong. That's Mary's goal; Harry wants to
make punks pay.

If you chose 3, you made a mistake. Harry Callahan argues at length
with the DA, even calling him crazy. Ms. Poppins merely says to her employer, "I never explain anything."

The correct answer is 4. Both characters exemplify an approach to
conflict that is based less on team relationships than on the individual
pursuit of goals that happen to be good for the individual or organization,

even if the person is not fully engaged with it psychologically. Once Harry kills the last bad guy, he throws his badge into the water, then walks off into the distance. Once Mary transforms the Banks family, the wind carries her up and away to another "organization."

On January 28, 1986, the space shuttle *Challenger* exploded seventy-three seconds after liftoff, killing its entire crew. Determined to continue the shuttle program and repair NASA's image, the Reagan administration quickly called for an "independent commission" to investigate the tragedy. As journalist James Gleik reported, the commission ended up as a roster of NASA "insiders and figures chosen for their symbolic value," including Neil Armstrong, Chuck Yeager, and former secretary of state for Richard Nixon, William P. Rogers.[1] Richard Feynman was the one exception.

Feynman was a Nobel Prize–winning theoretical physicist with a strong independent streak. He was also dying of a terminal cancer at the time of the hearings. While the committee conducted a concerted campaign to protect NASA and the shuttle mission, Feynman's unilateral pursuit of the scientific and technical facts behind the disaster could not be silenced. In one memorable and dramatic moment during the commission's hearing, Feynman called for a glass of ice water and proceeded to demonstrate that the O-ring seals used on the *Challenger* would lose their resiliency at thirty-two degrees, the temperature at the launch site the morning of the disaster. Chairman Rogers was overheard in the men's room just prior to this demonstration telling Neil Armstrong, "Feynman is becoming a real pain in the ass."

Despite the physical evidence provided by Feynman and investigatory reporting by the *New York Times* suggesting that NASA knew of the risks of low temperatures on the O-rings, the committee's report largely cleared NASA of any wrongdoing. However, in his personal accounting of the procedures, Feynman wrote: "For a successful technology, reality must take precedence over public relations, for nature cannot be fooled." In the end, Feynman's concerns for scientific facts over politics led to a solution to the disaster—and to the protection of the lives of the many future many future astronauts.

Autonomy is not about running away from uncomfortable or scary conflicts. Sometimes it is the opposite.

This strategy flows from a strong focus on achieving your priority goals. If a conflict can help you reach your goal, by all means engage. But if it can't, or if the reward won't be worth the stress, you can either walk away or you can unilaterally achieve your goals despite the protests or concerns of others. Those who use the tactic of autonomy usually place less value on the relationship or on the specific incident surrounding the conflict than on achieving their ultimate goals through different means.

Ultimately, the choice to employ autonomy is based on whether you need to continue to relate to a particular person or group in order to achieve other goals. For Feynman, his pursuit of the scientific facts behind the crash and concerns over human safety trumped his interests in bolstering his reputation, relationships, or standing among his peers— particularly in light of his failing health. Autonomy is the power you experience when you don't need the other disputants to get what you need or want but they still need you. It is power apart from others.

Negotiators who can reduce their dependency on the opposite side in a negotiation tend to fare better. There are two main tactics for lessening dependency and increasing independence in conflict that lead to better outcomes in negotiations.[2] The first is to identify or develop an attractive BATNA. Having good options as alternatives to the ones offered by other negotiators gives you a sense of power and freedom in the dispute. The second tactic is to increase the other parties' dependence on you—to make them need you more than you need them.

You may benefit from exercising selective autonomy and disengaging from direct conflict altogether if:

- you *don't* need to maintain your relationship with the other party to reach your goals;

- the other party is against you, or
- it's hard to tell where you really stand with the other disputant.

If you're pursuing a strategy of autonomy, the relative power of the other party doesn't really matter.

What Draws People to Autonomy?

Some people prefer autonomy because they like to work by themselves and get their interpersonal needs met outside of a job. They tend to see themselves as individuals, not as group members or team players.[3] Many salespeople (but certainly not all) rely heavily on autonomy as a way of managing and avoiding confrontations.

Some people favor autonomy or resort to it quickly because they grew up in a family or culture where individualism and self-reliance were highly regarded. They likely had do-it-yourselfers as role models and learned to take pride in the ability to get the job done without help. They may even believe that it is noble to avoid depending on others most of the time, especially when it leads to struggle. Others inclined toward autonomy may simply be uncomfortable interacting with others and feel most comfortable working out their problems on their own. When autonomy is selectively chosen based on a specific state of affairs, it offers options for distance from struggles that are not worth the effort or are sticky or unproductive or are not related to your more important goals. The smart choice of this strategy, like all the strategies in this book, is based not on reflex or habit or personality or panic. It is grounded in a clear analysis of the probability of it helping achieve important goals with integrity.

But, as with all the other strategies, too much autonomy is rarely a good thing. Its overuse can alienate and infuriate others and lead to social or professional exclusion. It can make you seem selfish, self-focused, and standoffish. It earned Feynman a reputation as a "pain in the ass." So it is best to employ autonomy selectively.

Self-Assessment: Are You Chronically Autonomous?

The following questionnaire will help you get a sense of just how much you tend to use autonomous strategies in conflict. Indicate the number that best describes your response to the following statements.

1 = Strongly disagree   4 = Agree
2 = Disagree   5 = Strongly agree
3 = Neutral

_____ 1. If there is a conflict where I work, I always prefer to tolerate the immediate situation—and do nothing.

_____ 2. I tend to ignore conflict; it rarely matters much to me.

_____ 3. In work conflicts, I usually look for opportunities to separate myself from the situation and meet my needs elsewhere.

_____ 4. With most conflicts at work, I don't really do anything, because they rarely matter.

_____ 5. When I disagree with someone at work, I first try to find an independent way to get what I want or need before discussing it with the other person.

_____ 6. Acting as a unique individual is important to me.

_____ 7. I prefer to be self-reliant rather than dependent on others.

_____ 8. I take full responsibility for my own actions.

_____ 9. I enjoy being different from others.

_____ 10. I don't like depending on others for anything.

_____ 11. I act as an independent person, separate from others.

_____ 12. What happens to me is my own doing.

_____ 13. When I know a group decision is wrong, I don't support it.

_____ 14. I decide my future on my own.

_____ 15. If there is a conflict between my values and those of the groups of which I am a member, I follow my values.

SCORING

Add up your scores. Again, the context of your job matters the most. Study the table below. If you have a very high score, there is a good chance you are overusing this strategy. But a low score may also be cause for concern.

Score	Meaning	Ask yourself . . .
<40	You rarely, if ever, use autonomy in a conflict.	Is it because the environment does not require or support this approach? Or are you underutilizing this strategy?
40–49	You are inclined toward this strategy.	Do you use it enough and in the right contexts?
50–59	You use this strategy quite a bit.	Do you use it too much or in the wrong contexts?
60+	You rely on this strategy in most circumstances.	There is a high probability that you overuse the autonomy strategy. Does the environment really support this strategy as much as you use it? Are you using it effectively and in the right contexts? Do you need to improve your skills at discerning when to use other strategies for conflict?

Organizational Assessment: Do You Live in an Autonomy-Oriented World?

Next, complete the questionnaire below. It will give you a sense of the extent to which your current work environment invites the autonomy strategy. Rate your response to each of the statements below.

1 = Strongly disagree   4 = Agree

2 = Disagree   5 = Strongly agree

3 = Neutral

____ 1. At my job, each worker is encouraged to realize his or her own unique potential.

____ 2. People with good ideas make sure management knows the idea was theirs.

____ 3. Where I work, employees' ability to think for themselves is valued.

____ 4. Individuals who stand out in a high-performing group are recognized in my organization.

____ 5. Employees value independence in their job where I work.

____ 6. Each person's happiness is mostly unrelated to the well-being of their coworkers.

____ 7. The supervisors' opinions are not important influences in our decision making.

____ 8. I am never seen as responsible when one of my colleagues fails.

____ 9. Our coworkers' opinions never affect individual decision making.

____ 10. When my coworkers are successful, it does not really make me look better.

____ 11. Teamwork is not as important around here as individual contributions.

____ 12. You can be different, even a little weird, where I work.

____ 13. Most people here have an individualistic streak.

____ 14. Loyalty is not as important as creativity in my organization.

____ 15. A lot of us are sort of obsessive about our own independent goals.

SCORING

Add up your score, which will fall between 15 and 75. The higher the score, the more it makes sense to use the autonomy strategy in your organization. Now compare your self-assessment score to the organizational assessment you just completed.

_____ Self-assessment score from the previous questionnaire

_____ Organizational-assessment score from the most recent questionnaire.

Generally speaking, the more similar the scores, the more likely you are employing this strategy with discernment. Of course, the nuances of various conflict situations are such that you still have to distinguish when and with whom to use this strategy.

Six Good Reasons to Respond to Conflict with Selective Autonomy

1. **Your goal is more important than the relationship, at least for now.** Sometimes you want something so badly you are willing to strain a relationship or ignore a person or team. Go for the goal, not the hug.
2. **Some conflicts aren't worth the effort.** Conflict should not occur for its own sake. It should be part of a process through which one or all parties are seeking something valuable. But if the value of your goal is outweighed by the cost (time, money, hassle, dysfunction, abuse), it may serve you to find another way to achieve your goal outside the conflict.
3. **Your goals don't depend on the other party.** If you can reach your goal without dealing with someone else's resistance, especially if that someone is obstructive or more powerful, go for the goal alone.
4. **You are indifferent to the outcome of the conflict because it does not further your goal.** Don't waste time and emotion on the minuscule or pointless. Stay focused.
5. **You don't trust the motives or judgment of the other party.** If negotiations involve a lack of good faith, or you're dealing with a bad decision maker, it is easy for the risks to overshadow the rewards. Don't be a sucker. Find another way.

6. **If you start to negotiate, you have more to lose than win.** If the game is set up for you to lose, don't play.

The Consequences of Misusing Autonomy

Like all strategies, there are problems with extremes of autonomy. Colleagues who get stuck in autonomy may be seen as overly individualistic, selfish, narcissistic, conflict-avoidant, or generally unconcerned with their team or organization. Use autonomy too much and you run the risk of being branded not a team player.

Larry worked for a wholesale company and thought he would earn the promotion to sales manager by hitting the highest numbers each month. To achieve his individual sales goal, he skipped meetings, neglected schmoozing, and ignored tensions within the sales team. Had his only goal been to hit his numbers, it would have been fine. But since his other goal was management, he overlooked the relationship building that was necessary to win trust and cooperation. He was shocked when the promotion went to someone else with much lower numbers (who had spent much more time getting to know other members of the team, working through disagreements, and helping coworkers find common ground).

Disagreements and difficulties are not pleasant, but they can bring people together. People often get closer through the problem-solving and negotiation processes. When differences are worked through, the outcome often includes humor, bonding, and relief. If you refuse to engage in discussions in which issues get resolved, you could be seen as uninterested, uncaring, and unfriendly. A reputation for too much independence could also make you seem entitled or stuck up.

Finally, even if you don't use the autonomy strategy too often, you may use it in the wrong settings. This strategy is not about playing it safe or withdrawing out of weakness. If you are making that choice, you are not acting independently, you are acting scared.

What Does Selective Autonomy Look Like in Action?

Employing autonomy in conflicts effectively involves navigating artfully between your emphasis on your own needs in the situation and the need to not alienate important coworkers. It is useful when you do not depend on others (at least not very much) to reach a goal. Thus, power differences and conflict become less relevant to the situation and to your objectives.

When done well, autonomy can save you time and hassle. It can make you more efficient and effective at problem solving, and ideally it can have little negative impact on the relationships involved in the conflict that arose. It might even earn you a reputation as a can-do colleague who solves problems with little drama or fuss. But if used poorly, it can alienate your colleagues and cause new hassles down the road.

The primary focus of this strategy is on finding a way to meet your needs or interests in a conflict without engaging directly with the other disputant. There are many tactics that can be used to reduce dependency, but only a few that do so without aggravating others. Here are ten.

Ten Autonomy Tactics

1. DELIVER EXTRAORDINARY VALUE

If what you deliver to an organization is valuable enough to them, you can insulate yourself from interference from others.

In the film *Glengarry Glen Ross*, Ricky Roma (played by Al Pacino) is the top salesman in a real estate firm. He is usually only willing to initiate intense conflict if his goal (sales) is threatened. He doesn't need the cooperation of the other salesmen or the sales manager. He just needs the leads. He also happens to be a fairly despicable character, manipulating customers' insecurities and even lying to them to close a sale. But it's not his immorality that makes him autonomous, it's his focus. Because he creates extraordinary value for the firm, the sales manager overlooks his flaws.

As head of the cardiology department at a university hospital, Nadia was a team player, and a team leader. She knew that patient care and the implementation of new policies and practices required enormous cooperation from the many doctors and nurses who reported to her. While there were many aspects of leadership she did not care for, she gave it her all for years.

But her strongest passion by far is her research. "I want to get as many helpful heart drugs to market as I can before I die," she explained. Still, she is a strategic person and knew she could not step away from her leadership and clinical responsibilities unless she earned it.

After fifteen years of becoming one of the best heart surgeons in the country and working tirelessly to help achieve the medical center's goals, she went to her boss with a list of the seven major areas for which she was responsible. "I want to cross four of them off the list and reduce two more," she told him. "In six months—after our core grant is renewed—I want to focus mainly on research."

Nadia's boss pleaded with her to change her mind, but eventually approved her request. Within a year Nadia had expanded her research efforts. "People still try to pull me into all sorts of issues in the medical center. For the most part I pass those requests on to administrators, even if I don't think they'll be very effective. I want to obsess on my research."

Nadia doesn't avoid conflicts out of fear. She'll take on other doctors, administrators, and people with much more or much less power if some aspect of her research is compromised. Nadia's career strategy was selective autonomy, and her primary tactic was to be so valuable to the organization that she was buffered from other demands. She was fortunate that her organization was smart enough to let her stay and pursue her autonomous goals.

2. PRESENT YOURSELF AS A DETACHED EXPERT

Acquire specialized knowledge in areas that foster others' dependence on you. This enables you to preserve your detachment from an undesired fight that interferes with your goals.

Barry Veitel works as a technical analyst at ICAT, a ninety-employee firm providing insurance coverage to small businesses for catastrophes like earthquakes, tornadoes, floods, and hurricanes. He started as part of the general IT staff maintaining various systems. Over fifteen years, he evolved into a very autonomous subject-matter expert responsible for policy administration. He knows the database architecture and programming languages needed to maintain the documents required by state regulators. While not in management, Barry is the de facto authority on how policy administration IT is organized and executed; every single document the company distributes on a legal and contractual basis comes out of systems he maintains and operates. Nobody else directly supports what he does; nobody else fully understands it.

When managers need something, they don't tell Barry when they need it, they ask when they can get it. "I wouldn't have this much independence except for two things: I always deliver, and we have mutual trust. Leadership trusts my ability to execute, and I trust them to let me do it the way I know best — without interference."

His philosophy is simple: *know your job and do it exceptionally well.* The organization knows that if you stay out of Barry's way, you get more than you ask for.

A few years ago the chief information officer hired a director of information technology. She gave her new director the job of handling many of the day-to-day tasks of IT so she could focus on strategic innovation with the rest of the executive team. The new director certainly had a stellar résumé, but he tried to implement his directives and methodologies without understanding how the IT staff worked best. Instead of merging with the organization as expected, he disrupted it with what seemed like random team assignments and change for the sake of change. Barry didn't disagree with the director to his face, but when the CIO sensed tension and interviewed her staff as to the root cause, the new director was terminated.

The worst way to manage Barry is to manage him at all. He has a résumé that would land him another well-paid IT job in a week. His superiors know he's in the retirement window and doesn't really need this company the way they need him—at least for now.

If Barry had a different goal, such as the accumulation of power, he would do better to work his way up the management ladder and to weigh in on major decisions. The powerful tend to need others to achieve their goals, whether they fully realize it or not. But he's not interested in power. He wants freedom and independence.

3. NURTURE A NICHE AWAY FROM THE FRAY

Develop roles and opportunities that allow you to operate from the periphery and disengage from dissent.

Pete is not your stereotypical salesman. He's very reserved, even shy. But he works for a mechanical engineering company where he specializes in their most technical products. While other salespeople can sell most of the organization's line, Pete is the only one who can sell certain specialty products. He does it by staying meticulously organized, constantly studying, traveling to clients around the country for face-to-face discussions, and by avoiding the main office. He is willing to quietly disagree with a client who has misunderstood how to operate or repair a machine, because he wants to save the sale and add to it. He is willing to politely disagree with company policy if it prevents him from selling and helping customers. What he is not willing to engage in are personality conflicts, team squabbles, or office politics. And because clients and competitors frequently offer Pete good jobs, his company wants to keep him satisfied. His niche is his kingdom—far, far away from the fold. His employer does not want Pete to leave, so they leave him alone.

4. DELIVER A RESPECTFUL DECLARATION OF INDEPENDENCE

Without appearing competitive, apathetic, or disengaged, make clear to power holders and others that your greatest contribution is based on your independence.

Maria served as the director of night programs at a residential school for the emotionally disturbed. From 4:00 P.M. until midnight, she had responsibility for a small staff of five as well as the facilities and the students. Her boss, Nora, left at five, after which Maria independently ran the place until her relief showed up at midnight.

Maria had a clear goal that was valued by the organization: make the children feel wanted, significant, and loved, and help prepare them for a mainstream classroom. Twenty-five and suspicious of authority, she had a rebellious streak. Other staff members were objects in the environment to deal with or work around or ask for assistance. But she didn't think of "us" as a team. She pursued her individual goal of inducing positive feelings in the emotionally disturbed kids and teaching them how to behave. Parents and kids loved her; they nicknamed her the "Pied Piper."

She missed some of the late-afternoon team meetings, and looked distracted or bored at others. Discussions about how to improve the program or how to arrange a classroom or what the menu should be on family visitation day all left her disengaged. But if someone mentioned one of the kids to whom she was attached, she jumped in to defend the young person or argue or offer ideas for how to help.

For the children, she went above and beyond the requirements of the job. She wrote songs and played her guitar for them. She made up games. She spent extra time listening to and talked with young people whose emotional worlds were turbulent.

As the executive director, Nora would have preferred all of Maria's passion for the children plus a more emotional commitment to the team. If the director specifically asked Maria to do a task unrelated to her individual goals, it got done, imperfectly but acceptably. When Maria was asked to clean out some cluttered supply closets by Friday, she procrastinated all week but got it done.

At Maria's annual performance evaluation, Nora provided clear feedback that while Maria was valuable to the organization, "we need more of a team mentality." Then she told Maria that she was transferring her to the day shift so she could learn to cooperative better with the other staff.

Maria responded directly and respectfully. "I can commit to finishing assigned projects sooner, like the supply closets. But I am happiest and most committed to the school when I spend time with the kids in the later afternoon and evening. I like to make them feel better before they go to sleep. I'm pretty sure I would disappoint you if you put me on the day shift with twenty teachers when the kids are so busy at school. That's not why I'm here."

Nora realized, without Maria spelling it out, that she had a choice: independent Maria or no Maria.

5. DODGE OR DELAY ANYTHING THAT DOESN'T SERVE YOUR GOALS

Stay focused on your goals; let others do the details and squabble. Skip meetings, miss conference calls, and agree to small concessions that liberate you for more important pursuits.

When Malcolm was hired as an assistant professor of English at a large state university, he was thrilled. He now had a platform for expanding his research and writing about film as literature and developing a series of courses on the topic.

Soon after he arrived, a recently retired professor took him aside and said, "I tried very hard to be a team player during my three decades at this university. I have taken on many assignments, especially administrative ones, that didn't bring much in terms of status or material reward. My CV would have been much stronger had I not done so, in which case I would have made more money and quite possibly would have been offered more lucrative positions at other institutions." The man's remarks reminded Malcolm of some of the professors in his graduate program whom he had seen fritter time and energy on things that had nothing to do with their passion for writing and publishing. And some of them didn't even earn tenure. *That will not happen to me,* he pledged.

Getting involved in departmental or university politics can be time-consuming and exhausting. Many of Malcolm's new colleagues were shy, even socially inept, and would rather work in their offices with the door closed. Cooperation, even where it was available, was not likely to help him achieve his goals of tenure and a national reputation as a scholar. Malcolm decided to quietly chip away at his goals until he reached liberation through publication and tenure.

So Malcolm attended faculty meetings but stayed quiet during most debates and negotiations. He withheld his opinion during discussions unless it was a rare decision related to something he considered important, such as hiring a colleague or allocating budget resources.

Many departmental decisions seemed of little consequence to him. He would abstain, vote with the obvious majority, or simply state that he was neutral. Many of the debates heated up until they spilled into the hallways and simmered for days. But not for Malcolm. When the faculty meeting was finished, so was he. He chose instead to put his energy into receiving glowing teaching evaluations, publishing in prestigious journals, giving talks at national conferences to gain external credibility, and most of all working on his magnum opus. His goal was to build an indisputable portfolio upon which his tenure application would be judged and to dodge any controversy that would stand between him and his goals or that would waste precious time.

6. GET A GATEKEEPER

Conspire with someone who can keep others away while you pursue goals that are good for you and the organization.

Larson is the CEO of a medical technology startup. Most of the people he manages are self-professed geeks. Give them a lab and they're happy. Give them a business decision and they squirm. Still, they like to talk, analyze, and argue about some things. If he gets them too involved in decision making, he spends time that the CEO of a relatively small new company cannot afford.

So he recruited an operations manager, Debra, to serve as his gatekeeper. She has the patience to listen, inquire, validate, praise, and advise. When Larson is not around, which is quite often, she manages the staff and addresses most of their concerns, troubleshoots, and makes the decisions Larson does not want to think about. She gets things done and makes sure nobody feels overlooked. She handles the egos and the insecurities of engineers and scientists, and the day-to-day operations of the company, while Larson handles the external networking and negotiations upon which the company depends.

Once a month, Larson and Debra facilitate a meeting in which the group discusses certain decisions that need to be made. Debra collects the concerns and ideas of the team for discussion, and Larson adds other concerns he wanted the team to examine. Some of these deliberations are quite lively. The team weighs in on policies, practices, facility upgrades, scheduling, and other day-to-day matters.

Between meetings, Larson makes most of the big decisions about direction, strategic planning, major investments, and key costumers. He is a selectively autonomous CEO. He does not micromanage or dominate; he just makes most of the major decisions himself. His goal is to grow the company as efficiently as possible and not to sweat the small stuff.

Debra is the buffer that lets Larson function as a one-man strategic marketing department and big-picture leader.

His style wouldn't work in a larger company with several layers of professional management. Most people trained in leadership would want to feel more a part of the bigger decisions. But the engineers and biologists who work for him are satisfied with being consulted over site-related decisions—the matters they can see and hear and touch—and are fine with being detached from larger, more abstract matters like major contracts, financial analyses, and what the company will look like five years from now.

7. JUST DO IT

Don't ask for permission; don't wait around for encouragement. Carpe diem!

When Addie taught special education, she practiced autonomy. Her goal was to keep eighth graders with behavioral issues from dropping out of school. She knew that their BATNA was the street. She was determined to do anything to help them succeed.

Other teachers did not always share her goals. They were not trained in special ed; they found the kids difficult, even obnoxious. They didn't lose sleep when one of them dropped out of school or was expelled. They would rather put their extra attention into school committees and special events.

But Addie had one thing in mind: keep those kids in school. So she took several actions without asking for permission from the administration. She persuaded other teachers to give her students different kinds of homework they were more likely to complete. She got some of them to allow her students to share notes with the mainstream kids so they had better sources for studying. She convinced teachers to tell her ahead of time about topics and assignments in different classes so she could help prepare her students for new materials. She got the facilities manager to leave the gym open until 7:00 P.M. on Fridays so she could reward good behavior and completed homework with Friday basketball tournaments.

And while the other teachers were at first annoyed by her methods and her tenacity, within a year they saw the results and stopped pushing. The administration knew very little about this until Addie was voted Teacher of the Year by the rest of the faculty.

8. TAKE THE BYPASS WHEN THE TRAFFIC RUNS AGAINST YOUR GOALS

When a goal is more important than the feelings or opinions of the team, go around.

Bev is a nurse who thrives on teamwork. Unless, that is, teamwork gets in the way of her most important goal. Like most of us, she has several goals at work: get paid, do a good job, learn and grow, and more. But for Bev, one goal overshadowed all others: take great care of sick people.

When a healthy twenty-four-year-old construction worker was admitted to her unit after an appendectomy, she worked with her night-shift team to make sure he got the care he needed. For a few days, all was routine. But then Bev noticed something. He didn't look right. His color was slightly off. He was quieter than usual. She had a bad feeling.

She consulted with her team members. They were polite but disagreed. Bev asked the head nurse to call the doctor. "She is swamped today and there's no real reason to call her," her supervisor responded.

So she called the doctor herself. At one o'clock in the morning.

"Are his vital signs normal?" the doctor asked.

"Yes."

"Has his sleep changed?"

"No."

"Fever?"

"No."

"Problems with total parenteral nutrition?"

"No."

"Then I'll see him when I come in for rounds in the morning."

The next morning the doctor said the patient was recovering normally. She noted it in the chart.

The next night Bev had the same feeling. Her intuition wouldn't let her leave the situation alone. She awakened the patient in the wee hours to talk to him.

"Nurse," he mumbled. "I think I'm dying."

She was on the phone to the doctor in seconds.

"You are just not going to leave me alone, are you?" the doctor complained.

"Doctor, this patient is dying. I know it."

"Well, fine, then," the doctor grumbled. "Do a CT of the abdomen and pelvis."

The scan revealed a life-threatening abdominal leak, and an hour later the young man was in surgery.

Bev had sensed irritation from her team and unequivocal annoyance from the MD. But she didn't care. "I was doing my job. My goal was to take care of that young man. Most of the time I go with the team, but in that case I didn't care what they thought or what the doctor felt about me. Sometimes you have to go around the team."

9. GO OFF-ROAD

Embrace the iconoclastic approach. Get weird. Be yourself. Think outside the organizational chart.

An acting troupe that prided itself on teamwork was finally ready for opening night. After weeks of preparation, they felt eager to take the stage. Dan, who was always quirky and shy during rehearsals, had followed direction to create comic scenes that were funny, polished, and predictable. The director was pleased with the product and ready to watch audiences respond.

But the curtain went up and suddenly Dan morphed. He changed lines, added new shtick, and generally took over every scene. The other actors were thrown at first, until they heard the roar of the audience. Dan, like Jim Carrey or Amy Poehler, transformed himself in front of a live audience. Every scene was funnier than in rehearsal. By the end of the show, he even had won over the director.

Dan was not what actors call an ensemble performer. His goal was not to please or even get along with other actors or the director; his goal was simply to make a live audience laugh. Period. He didn't ruin the performance; he changed and improved it. And he did it differently every night. He's not a team player; he's just a wired and weird comic genius. The director decided to feature Dan for his independence rather than force him to conform.

Some autonomous individuals just can't stay between the lines of conformity drawn by social and organizational norms. They are so innovative they excel through iconoclasm. Hollywood rewards iconoclasts like Tina Fey and Andy Kaufman. Industries that thrive on rapid change elevate autonomous thinkers like Steve Jobs and Mark Zuckerberg.

10. GET OFF AT THE NEXT EXIT

When circumstances prevent you from the achievement of your goal, the ultimate form of autonomy is to exit the conflict or even the organization.

The autonomy strategy depends on two things more than anything else: a strong BATNA and quality results. Whether you are in sales, health care, management, education, engineering, HR, operations, finance, or any other niche or industry, extraordinary value and alternatives to an agreement are the keys to your full-time or selective autonomy.

Taking the next exit can manifest itself in different ways.

It's the team member who asks her manager to be taken off a project because she has another focus that is more valuable to the organization.

It's the salespeople who believe the ultimate form of job security and independence is an amazing résumé.

It's the nurse who transfers to a different hospital or clinic because her passion is patient care over revenue or bureaucracy.

It's the academic researcher who always finds a way to get external funding so she is less at the whim of her institution.

It's the executive who stays connected to everyone with whom he has ever worked so he has options if his company starts tying his hands as a leader.

It's the resourceful anybody who has other options and can always afford to say, "Take this job and shove it" (or at least think it while typing up a polite letter of resignation).

For many people, work is their community. For some, it is only a platform for chasing their goals. For most of us, it is some combination of both.

How to Master Autonomy: The Building Blocks

Dirty Harry and Mary Poppins didn't achieve their goals by accident. Like the nonfiction characters in this chapter, they were fore-thinkers rather than after-thinkers. If you are going to declare (or quietly advance) your independence in an organization, you need a few essential competencies.

First, you have to be realistic and creative about developing good BATNAs. If you are the toughest cop in San Francisco or the most supernatural nanny in London or your company's top salesperson or the hospital's top surgeon or one of the best teachers in the school, you've got options. Keep nurturing those options and don't assume they are static or everlasting. Autonomy takes maintenance and innovation.

Second, clarify your goals, again and again. Many people are quite happy to be assigned goals, at least some of the time. But having a sharp, indubitable clarity about your goals helps you decide when to fight, when to fold, and when to ignore disputes.

Third, if you want to be independent, at least in some of your work, you have to figure out how not to be dependent. The more the other party needs you and the less you need the other party, the better, assuming autonomy is something you value.

Finally, independence sometimes takes subtle influence tactics, indirect communication, and sometimes unusual behavior. The more comfortable you can get with being different, the more different you will be allowed to be.

• SELECTIVE AUTONOMY SUMMARY •

For Situations of Independence: You find you have little need to remain in the situation, conflict, or relationship with the other disputants. Thus, power or competing goals hold little significance.

Strategy: To decrease your dependency on the opposing party without creating an appearance of competition or alienation.

TACTICS

1. Deliver extraordinary value.
2. Present yourself as a detached expert.
3. Nurture a niche away from the fray.
4. Deliver a respectful declaration of independence.

5. Dodge or delay anything that doesn't achieve your goals.
6. Get a gatekeeper.
7. Just do it.
8. Take the bypass when the traffic runs counter to your goals.
9. Go off-road.
10. Get off at the next exit.

SKILL-DEVELOPMENT CHECKLIST

Check any skill you have already developed. Discuss your responses with someone you trust.

_____ **I am skilled at clarifying my goals.** I know how to set a direction for myself and know what I want to accomplish within the context of my organization. My goals are related to the needs of the organization and bring value to it, but they feel like _my_ goals.

_____ **I am very good at remaining focused.** I am skilled at resisting distractions that stand between my goals and me. No matter how many people or tasks try to grab my attention, I can filter out the nonessentials and keep going toward my goals.

_____ **I can distance myself from others.** When necessary, I can go my own way with little interaction with others. When I do interact with others, I keep it related to the goals I am working toward.

_____ **I am skilled at thinking for myself.** I listen to others' ideas and sometimes incorporate them, but I do not use others' ideas just to please them or compromise. I know what I want and I figure out for myself the best way to do something and how to get optimum results.

_____ **I feel okay ruffling feathers.** If my actions toward my goals bother some people, that is fine with me. My goals are more important than the feelings of the people around me. I don't need everyone to like me.

_____ **I can pursue goals with minimal amounts of praise and support.** I am self-confident and get tremendous satisfaction internally when I reach a goal. For this reason, a lack of praise from others is not a big problem for me.

_____ **I am skilled at operating outside of a team environment.** If a team helps me achieve my goals, I can work in one. If I do not need a team to get to the goal, or if a team stands in the way of a goal, I can do things myself.

_____ **I can ignore it when I know people are talking about me behind my back.** When I find out that some people do not like how independent I am and that they gossip about me or criticize me when I am not around, I don't let it bother me (much).

_____ **I am skilled at getting my job done with little or no supervision.** I deliver value to my organization, which often satisfies managers enough to leave me alone. I do not need someone else to tell me how to bring value as long as my goals are aligned with the organization's goals. I can deliver results without someone checking up on me or having to hold me accountable.

_____ **I am skilled at evaluating the importance of a debate or disagreement.** I engage in conflicts when it is necessary to achieve my goals, but I resist getting pulled into them without a clear purpose.

DISCUSSION PROMPTS

Operating independently, like all the conflict strategies in this book, has costs and benefits.

Discuss the following prompts with someone who will be very honest with you and who is insightful about your career and your organization.

- Am I too independent? In other words, are my goals or effectiveness decreased by how often and to what extent I strive for goals in a way that is not interdependent with others? Does my autonomy cost me something in terms of reputation, promotions, money, relationships, or something else that I value? Am I seen in a negative light by anyone who matters to me?

- Am I independent enough? Do I miss deadlines or opportunities or fail to achieve results because of unnecessarily depending on others? Do I sometimes pay more attention than is necessary to the relationships and personalities all around me, at the cost of achieving something?
- Are there any coworkers you or I know who get it right in terms of the degree and style with which they practice independence? Whether they are in positions of power or not, what are the keys to their effective goal completion?

9

Effective Adaptivity

IN 2008, THIRTY-EIGHT-YEAR-OLD Neil Barofsky left his dream job as a federal prosecutor in New York to become special inspector general of the Troubled Asset Relief Program (TARP) funds in Washington, D.C. He felt he had a moral obligation to help protect the American people against further bank fraud in the distribution of $700 billion of taxpayer money in the wake of the financial collapse of the previous year. But when he arrived in D.C., Barofsky discovered that his efforts at oversight would be obstructed and sabotaged by the Treasury Departments of both the outgoing Bush and incoming Obama administrations. Trained as a prosecutor, he had an approach to these obstacles that was smart, tenacious, direct, and confrontational. He knew he had both Congress and right on his side.

After several months on the job, he got nowhere.

But another thing Barofsky had learned as a prosecutor was how to learn. Ever persistent, he eventually figured out that he had to back off his righteous approach to pushing his agenda and make progress by leveraging every means at his disposal. He started framing his ongoing disputes with Treasury in light of their shared interest in the greater good. He used his ignorance of the Washington game to his advantage. (*You mean we can't refuse a request from the White House?*) He built trust and support with allies in the media by remaining consistently transparent with them. He turned to a strong network of former colleagues and Washington insiders for information and strategic guidance, and he ultimately relied on the members of Congress who had established his office to have his back when all else failed. His stint in D.C. was brief and locally unpopular and by many accounts, unusually effective.

Charles Darwin reportedly once said, "It is not the strongest of the species that survives, nor the most intelligent, but rather the one most responsive to change." Barofsky's experience and our research on conflict adaptivity support this. We have found that problems typically arise when people become fixated on any one approach to conflict (such as support or dominance) or when their chronic strategy fits poorly with the specific realities or demands of situations. From this perspective, flexibility and the ability to identify and respond to relevant changes in the environment are critical for effective conflict management, particularly over the long run.

Most people hold strong preferences for certain responses to conflict and find it emotionally distressing when situations require a very different approach. The strengths of these chronic preferences are shaped by combinations of individual personality and social factors but are ultimately determined by the degree and quality of people's direct and indirect experiences with each strategy. We know from neuroscience research that in our brains, the neurons that fire together become wired together. Repeated instances of associated neurons firing in particular patterns create pathways in the brain that become our neural "superhighways," relegating the untraveled "back roads" of unfamiliar neural pairings to increasingly less accessibility and use.[1] We literally become hardwired for habitual perceptions, communication patterns, and behaviors, despite their limitations and their associations with negative conflict outcomes.

But we are not the only problem. The rituals and expectations of our relationships at work also lock us into behavioral patterns. Even if power shifts in a relationship occur, expectations alone can be enough to maintain the original dynamic. This is a further challenge to adaptivity.

In this chapter, we break down conflict adaptivity, explaining the tendencies, competencies, conditions, and tactics that can help make it work for you.

Conflict Adaptivity: Adaptation + Integrity + Feedback

Adaptation is the developmental or evolutionary process by which a unit (amoeba, brain, person, group, organization, population, species, and so on) becomes better suited to its habitat or environment. In organizational terms, adaptation is defined as a change in behavior in response to salient cues, which leads to a functional outcome.[2] There are essentially two kinds of adaptation: proactive and reactive. *Proactive adaptation* occurs when the status quo doesn't change but you realize that your approach to the situation stinks and decide to adapt. *Reactive adaptation* occurs in reaction to change.

In the realm of conflict management, adaptation is the capacity to employ different strategies as they become necessary or useful in different situations. Although each of the strategies outlined in chapters 4 through 8 can be valuable and fitting in particular situations, they each have their associated costs and benefits. Too much dominance becomes oppressive and alienates. In the wrong context, benevolence seems passive and weak. Support feels needy and pathetic when misapplied. Chronic autonomy can appear selfish and disengaged. Chronic appeasement can be emotionally damaging. The key to conflict adaptation—proactive or reactive—is flexibility and the ability to identify and respond appropriately to relevant changes in the environment.

Despite the benefits of adaptation in conflict, too much or too little adaptation can be bad for you. Psychologists have found that too much change too fast in a person's orientation and approach to her or his environment can be destabilizing and create a tremendous sense of upheaval.[3] Being overly flexible can also give you a reputation for being a social chameleon, of weak character, or manipulative. When adapting to changing circumstances, people in conflict must also find a way to remain rooted internally to their sense of what is right, important, and necessary.

In our view, an adaptive approach to conflict management is composed of two somewhat opposing processes: adaptation and integrity. Adaptation, the capacity to change and fit in, is balanced by integrity, the capacity to hold on to a sense of consistency of values, worldview, goals, and aspirations. This orientation to conflicts allows for both flexibility in strategies *and* a sense of stability and capacity to achieve one's goals at a satisfactory rate. It provides the foundation for a more constructive, satisfying, and sustainable approach to conflict management. As others have proposed, adaptive individuals must be simultaneously principled and pragmatic,[4] firm with their goals but flexible with their means.[5] Sustainable adaptivity requires one more step: *reading feedback*. As Mary Parker Follett said when writing about work conflict in the 1920s, humans like to think of conflict as a static event and commonly make the error of viewing conflict as a momentary fixed entity. We see this all the time when managers attempt to unilaterally resolve a conflict and then say, "Okay, let's move on! This is fixed. Next!"

Conflict adaptivity is an ongoing process. It requires that before, during, and after conflict we remain situationally aware of the causes and consequences of both the conflict and the disputants' responses to it. This may sound exhausting and effortful, but effective managers learn to do this instinctually.

What Draws People to Adaptivity?

People who are more open, socially perceptive, emotionally and behaviorally complex, and self-aware are going to be more inclined toward adaptivity. But it's also a skill you develop over time, from many, diverse, repeated, and effective experiences with a variety of different types of conflict.

The social and cultural environments we were raised in, live in, and work in also affect our propensity for adaptivity. Research from our lab at Columbia University shows that when cultural groups have very simple (if X then Y) rules for negotiating with others ("When others deceive you, never trust them again"), they tend to have more contentious negotiations and come away less satisfied. But when groups have more-complex, nuanced rules for conflict negotiations ("When others deceive you, never trust them again . . . unless they were forced to deceive you or were unaware of their actions or generally meant well"), their dynamics tend to be more constructive and negotiations tend to go far more successfully.[6]

Research has shown that some work environments are more conducive to adaptability than others.[7] They include environments that require

- handling emergency or crisis situations;
- handling high levels of work stress;
- solving problems creatively;
- dealing with uncertain and unpredictable work situations;
- learning new work tasks, technologies, and procedures;
- demonstrating interpersonal adaptability;
- demonstrating cultural adaptability;
- responding to new physical challenges.

Subsequent research on team adaptation has suggested that there is one central factor that is key to these work conditions resulting in increased adaptivity of workers: *psychological safety*.[8] This concept comes from the seminal work of Edgar Schein and Warren Bennis, and refers to situations characterized by sufficient levels of interpersonal trust and mutual respect.[9] Without a psychologically safe work climate, the above eight conditions are more likely to result in failure or calcification than adaptivity.

Self-Assessment: Are You Naturally Adaptable?

To get a sense of how much you are inherently drawn toward adaptivity, rate your response to each of the following statements.

1 = Strongly disagree   4 = Agree
2 = Disagree   5 = Strongly agree
3 = Neutral

_____ 1. I will at times use conflict tactics that are uncharacteristic of me, because I know they can serve my long-term goals.

_____ 2. I believe there is not "one best way" to behave in order to resolve my conflicts.

_____ 3. I use many different tactics in conflict, because I feel they can help my long-term goals.

_____ 4. I rarely react impulsively to the current situation in conflict without considering the consequences.

_____ 5. I feel in control of my success in my career.

_____ 6. In different situations and with different people, I often act like a very different person.

_____ 7. I am good at making other people like me.

_____ 8. At times I adjust my opinions or the way I do things in order to please someone or win his or her favor.

_____ 9. I have little trouble changing my behavior to suit different people and different situations.

_____ 10. I can be very dominating in conflict when the work requires it.

_____ 11. I can appear vulnerable and dependent in conflict situations at work when I need to in order to reach my goals.

_____ 12. I can be confrontational and dominant in work conflict situations when necessary.

_____ **13.** I can handle work conflict situations that demand that I be subservient to others.

_____ **14.** I have experienced a wide range of emotions throughout my life.

_____ **15.** When I try, I generally succeed.

SCORING

Add up your scores and then refer to the table below. If you have a very high score, there is a chance you are overusing this strategy. But a low score may also be cause for concern.

Score	Meaning	Ask yourself . . .
<40	You rarely, if ever, use adaptivity in a conflict.	Is it because the environment does not require or support an adaptive approach? Or are you underutilizing this strategy?
40–49	You are inclined toward this strategy.	Do you use it enough and in the right contexts?
50–59	You use this strategy quite a bit.	Do you use it too much or in the wrong contexts?
60+	You rely on this strategy in most circumstances.	There is a high probability that you overuse the adaptivity strategy. Are you using it effectively and in the right contexts? Do you need to improve your skills at discerning when to use other strategies for conflict?

Organizational Assessment: Do You Work in an Adaptive Environment?

To get a sense of how much your current environment "pulls" you toward adaptivity, rate your response to each of the following statements.

1 = Strongly disagree   4 = Agree
2 = Disagree   5 = Strongly agree
3 = Neutral

_____ 1. Where I work, we are urged to be versatile across many different situations, including tense ones, rather than practice a rigidly consistent approach.

_____ 2. My work setting allows me to think clearly in times of urgency.

_____ 3. At work, we are often encouraged to learn about cultures other than our own.

_____ 4. Our work team seems to get energized when things become unpredictable.

_____ 5. Our organization provides broad principles and guidelines for our work rather than detailed instructions.

_____ 6. Our team excels when working in less-than-comfortable situations and surroundings.

_____ 7. We often find ourselves working on fresh and unfamiliar problems in my workplace.

_____ 8. Our team excels in unclear circumstances.

_____ 9. I have great respect for the majority of the people with whom I work.

_____ 10. I trust my coworkers to do the right thing.

_____ 11. My organization encourages taking action to correct work-performance deficiencies.

_____ 12. My work group is good at developing unique analyses for multifaceted problems.

_____ 13. Our work environment incentivizes being versatile in dealing with others.

_____ 14. My workplace provides us with a flexible sense of structure and rules.

_____ 15. We are encouraged to take risks in our work, even when outcomes are unpredictable.

SCORING

Add up your score, which will fall between 15 and 75. The higher the score, the more it makes sense to use the adaptive strategy in your organization. Now compare your self-assessment score to the organizational assessment you just completed.

_____ Self-assessment score from the previous questionnaire
_____ Organizational-assessment score from the most recent questionnaire

Generally speaking, the more similar the scores, the more likely you are employing this strategy with discernment. Of course, the nuances of various conflict situations are such that you still have to distinguish when and with whom to use this strategy.

Six Good Reasons to Be Adaptive in Conflict

1. **It works.** Case-based research on international negotiations found that parties tended to be more effective in negotiations when they were able to adjust their strategies and behavior to the relative (and relevant) power of the other side.[10] This was true for both weaker and more powerful parties alike. Other studies have found that effective negotiators rarely employ single conflict-handling styles; instead, they employ more blended or "conglomerated" approaches that utilize the beneficial components of a variety of tactics.[11] In fact, research with attorneys supports this, demonstrating that effective attorneys use a pattern of traits and behaviors in negotiations that do not neatly fit any one of the conflict-style categories.[12]

2. **It makes conflicts less painful.** One study found that participants who were asked to reflect on a positive conflict reported using more adaptive behaviors, which were more often in accordance

with the situational demands they faced, than did participants who reflected on negative conflicts.[13]

3. **We learn more.** Another study found that highly adaptive individuals reported learning more from and having more-global perspectives on conflict, and focusing more on both long-term *and* short-term goals in conflicts than less adaptive individuals did.[14]

4. **We like our adversaries more.** Higher levels of adaptivity are associated with higher levels of satisfaction with coworkers.

5. **We experience less stress on the job.** Higher levels of adaptivity are associated with lower levels of job stress.

6. **It makes us better leaders and managers.** Related research in organizations has found that executives high in behavioral complexity and social intelligence (the basic building blocks of adaptivity) are simply more effective in the long run.[15]

What Does Adaptivity Look Like in Action?

Adaptivity cuts across all seven conflict situations. This strategy is by its nature multisituational and may be useful in contexts of compassionate responsibility, command and control, cooperative dependence, unhappy tolerance, independence, partnership, and enemy territory. While not always advantageous (some ongoing conflicts call for a focus on only one or two of the strategies), over an extended period of time adaptivity is highly likely to lead to a more satisfying and effective work life.

The basic steps in adaptivity are quite simple:

1. Know what's really important to you in a conflict.
2. Know what type of situation you are in.
3. See the many strategies and tactics potentially available to you.
4. Pick the most fitting (and least problematic) option.
5. Implement it skillfully.
6. Learn.

That's it. Easy, right? Right, except when emotions, emotional reservoirs, chronic preferences, and other people are involved. Then it gets trickier. Here is a more comprehensive rendering of the main tactics that make up the adaptivity strategy.

Ten Tactics for Effective Adaptivity

1. MATCH AND MIX

Move from strategy to strategy and tactic to tactic as the conflict evolves.

Mike serves as a general manager for a $500-million-a-year manufacturing company. He can't get through a day without adaptivity. His boss, Walter, the CEO, is brilliant at business but awful with people. Often explosive, Walter both depends on Mike and abuses him.

Mike often uses strategic appeasement to reach his goals.

"Walter will go on a tirade for fifteen minutes to an hour," Mike says. "Sometimes his outbursts are about the decision or problem we are discussing, but other times they are just pure emotion, unrelated to what we're talking about. That's when I put up my invisible wall."

Mike's "wall" is conscious dissociation. He goes into his head, thinking about what he'll have for dinner or with whom he'll get together on the weekend. He'll nod occasionally and even look Walter in the eyes, or he'll pick up on a few words and repeat them as if he's actually listening.

Other times Mike combines strategic appeasement with cultivated support.

Walter sometimes rants when he disagrees with Mike about a specific decision. If the decisions are minor or a commitment isn't needed for a few weeks, Mike simply says, "Okay, let's do it your way." But when a few days go by and Walter is in a calmer state of mind, Mike brings it up again. Sometimes Walter reconsiders or negotiates. Mike observes, "We sometimes engage in a very cooperative conversation about our differences, and we can be very productive together."

Then there are the harangues about big, deadline-driven, irreversible decisions.

"That's when I don't put up my wall," Mike explains. That's when Mike is willing to stand up to abuse with constructive dominance, matching Walter's position of power with the power of facts, numbers, and his own assertiveness.

With his subordinates, Mike favors pragmatic benevolence during conflicts. He wants to make sure Walter's bombastic style doesn't trickle down and become a company culture. Mike practices a consensus approach most of the time with his team. When subordinates admit to a mistake or deliver bad news, Mike thanks them. When they disagree with him, he encourages them to say more. And while he emphasizes consensus, one out of ten times he listens but overrules a team decision. He makes sure meetings and social events are fun. When a team member was hospitalized for a week, Mike visited every day.

Finally, when there is an important goal that Mike feels is good for the business and he just doesn't want to deal with Walter's reaction, he just does it. Sometimes he encounters wrath for using selective autonomy, and sometimes he doesn't.

Mike is not in charge, but he is powerful. His power stems from his stellar results, which Walter's success depends upon, the loyalty he engenders in his subordinates and his boss, and his conflict adaptivity.

2. SHAKE IT UP

Capitalize on existing conditions that demand change or create new conditions that in fact destabilize the status quo. Initiate physical changes: movement, speaking with outsiders, traveling to new places in order to stimulate all parties to see, think, feel, and respond differently.

Shaking up the status quo can free you from the constraints of automatic processing and responses and help you develop and advance new strategies.

The conflict opportunities we face daily can get repetitive. When we have the same run-ins with the same petty tyrants over and over, it's tempting to employ the same response strategy every time. The challenge then is what the organizational theorist Gareth Morgan calls "opening the door to instability."[16]

One of our colleagues, Michelle LeBaron, tells a story of how in 1993, a group of diplomats from many parts of the world gathered near Dublin to generate new ideas for addressing the Israel-Palestine conflict. A primary challenge for the facilitators was to figure out how to move this group out of well-worn ruts when speaking about the conflict: positional statements, repetitive framings, and limiting assumptions that tended to dictate how they defined and responded to the troubles in the Middle East. For the first two days, the process followed a standard problem-solving format, and little of value transpired.

On the third day, the diplomats took a bus trip to Belfast. Jostled in the old school bus used for transport, the previously restrained participants began to experience each other differently. As they uncovered commonalities and shared passions, they began to relate more playfully. Several discussions with Northern Irish peacemakers and visits to bi-communal projects deepened the camaraderie within the group. As the bus headed back to Dublin following a group meal, participants sang together in the darkness. Professor LeBaron writes, "Only after this excursion did conversations enliven, originality emerge, and imaginative possibilities for shifting intractable conflict in Israel-Palestine begin to reveal themselves."[17]

The facilitators of the meeting were thrilled by the change in dynamics among the participants but struggled to understand what had happened. Then something struck them. LeBaron writes,

> An obvious, hidden-in-plain-sight truism occurred to us: everyone attending had real-life bodies with creative capabilities and a love of play and beauty. Why state these obvious facts? Because the workshop—like dozens of others—was designed as if everyone existed from the neck up. . . . Physical movement is a huge catalyst to attitude change in ways we are only beginning now to realize.[18]

Human beings are physical entities, so ignoring or denying this when we try to talk things out and negotiate is a mistake. Physical changes — movement, jostling, speaking with outsiders, traveling to new places — is one way to shake up and perhaps alter our programmed chronic responses to conflicts and thus allow and encourage us to see, think, feel, and respond differently.

Imagine the possibilities for your organization.

Companies shake it up when they take a team off-site, pushing them to encounter each other in a different way. Organizations shake it up when they take employees from different departments — who disagree because they do not understand each other's roles — and temporarily job-swap. Working directly with customers can change the perspective of someone who criticizes from the warehouse. Working physically in a hot warehouse under deadline pressure can change the way customer-service reps see what goes on behind the scenes to help them keep clients happy.

3. SEE THE SYSTEM

As conflicts and emotions are triggered and intensify, our thinking, feeling, and sense of our options shrink and simplify. A critical step for all parties is to try to view the conflict more holistically.

If you are like most *Homo sapiens,* when you find yourself in a conflict, you immediately focus on one thing — how wrong the other person is. This moves us into black-and-white, right-and-wrong, us-versus-them thinking, which consequently oversimplifies our sense of situations. This is a natural and logical protective response to threat. But it tends to limit our experience and our sense of the strategies available to us.

A critical step for disputants and mediators alike is to avoid premature oversimplification of problems and to identify the nature of the situation and the various strategic options available.

Jim was new to the position of division director in a U.S. government lab. His boss was asking how he would handle the revolt against Tom, a branch chief who "as of today is your headache." Jim asked for time to examine the conflict in context. He learned from previous experiences that some conflicts are not about individuals; they are more about systems. He wanted to understand the many forces at work.

He started by studying several different perspectives. He learned that Tom had met with the ten scientists who reported to him—only to bark at them. They barked back. The more Jim listened, the more he got an earful of rage. He learned the most from Tom himself. After hearing many complaints about other scientists and the job itself, Jim probed Tom about his interests. Tom had an understated passion for science, as well as two kids in college.

"I asked for this job," admitted Tom. "But now my research is stalled." Eventually Tom realized he wanted less management duty. A promotion that kept him from work he loved was no promotion at all. Jim let Tom return to research. Over the next year, Jim rotated different scientists through the branch chief position. The conflicts decreased as the group gained respect for the job. The fourth person in the job was good at it and settled in. Jim's advice about conflict: "Listen and ask questions first. Try to understand the whole thing, not just the first wave of complaints. The first solutions to problems that present themselves are usually suboptimal."

4. ADAPT TODAY WHILE LEANING TOWARD A MORE CONSTRUCTIVE TOMORROW

Adaptive individuals consider the appropriateness of their behavior in a given situation while never losing sight of the long-term goal of reconciling the conflict to benefit all parties.

In the short term, adaptation allows for a contingency-based approach to conflict. Such an approach helps manage the immediate demands of a situation, reducing the chances of escalation and fostering a more stable environment for constructive interaction. However, more cooperative approaches (such as benevolence, cooperation, and support) are more likely to lead to positive outcomes for all parties in the longer term.[19] Adaptive individuals consider the appropriateness of their behavior in any given situation while never losing sight of the goal of reconciling the conflict to benefit all parties involved.

What does this look like?

It's the manager at the nonprofit who adapts to the recently hired upstart, dominating in disagreements so the job gets done well and on time. But the manager sees talent behind the argumentativeness and establishes a basis to work more collaboratively with the new employee as she matures.

It's the leader who looks forward to building a team of competent professionals but is in the early stage of an entrepreneurial venture in which she has to do much of the work herself. She sets her own goals, goes after them, and uses her first few employees as assistants, ignoring most of their disagreements for now, knowing that this is the only way to reach goals in the beginning. But she also knows that her autonomous approach will limit her in the long run if she fails to build a strong team that knows how to work through their differences.

It's the corporate manager who has discovered that her new peer in another department is a controlling, political manipulator. So she watches her words and her back, thinking politically in every interaction with him, anticipating that the cooperative culture of the organization will eventually change her peer's behavior or force him out.

It's the school administrator who refuses to argue or negotiate with a young teacher who posts inappropriate material on Facebook after friending a student's parents. He uses his authority to decree a temporary policy so as to prevent more problems, but he plans to get more faculty involved in designing a longer-term set of rules for social media. His goal is a policy arrived at through reasoned negotiation by the group.

It's the experienced employee who can see that the new manager is overwhelmed and does not yet understand the business. He practices autonomy in the short run, sidestepping most of the chaotic disagreements in the department. From experience, he knows his goals and how to pursue them but hopes for the day that the manager develops the knowledge and cooperative leadership skills to set goals and implement business strategies together with his staff.

5. PRACTICE SHUTTLE DIPLOMACY

Go back and forth between the parties in conflict, employing different conflict-intelligence strategies at different stages. The goal is an outcome that is acceptable to all parties and the organization.

The phrase "shuttle diplomacy" was first used to label the efforts of U.S. Secretary of State Henry Kissinger to mediate conflicts subsequent to the Yom Kippur War.[20] It has since been used to describe the actions of mediators who meet alternately between disputants who refuse or are too upset to meet face-to-face.

Armand, an executive, sensed tension between Jane, his sales manager, and Ralph, his purchasing manager. Other managers saw the two avoiding each other, making sarcastic quips behind each other's back, and going around each other to get things done. So Armand brought them together in a three-way meeting. They clammed up at first, but as they answered Armand's questions, they eventually revealed their stubborn dislike for each other.

Armand decided to try shuttle diplomacy. He met with Jane and Ralph in turn, let them know his intentions and his goals, and carried messages between them hoping they'd eventually come together to manage their disagreements themselves.

He didn't need the two managers to like each other, but he wanted the hostility and avoidance to end. Their departments had to work together cooperatively for the organization, otherwise one or both of them would be reassigned or let go. He knew he had power, and he wanted to use it for the greater good.

First he met with them using a pragmatic-benevolence strategy, bringing out their differences of opinion and personality in the less emotional context of one-on-one discussions. He asked each what the other could do to facilitate more cooperation, and what behaviors, if any, each wanted less of from the other. Both, ironically, said they wanted more communication, quicker turnaround on requests for information, and for the other to be nicer. Each wanted less humor (they didn't find each other funny), an end to strident e-mails, and less complaining about each other's team. Armand saw these as very fixable matters, and he said so.

And so he went back and forth, carrying requests and telling each how he saw both of them in terms of contributions to the organization.

But before he concluded shuttle diplomacy, he added one meeting with each that could be characterized as constructive dominance. When they seemed ready to resume direct relations, he told each of them in private that he had to see change or he would take a different action in the future. He explained that he had engaged in this time-consuming diplomacy because both of them were very good at their jobs, but that being good at your job is not enough in their organization. He said he now expected them to get along, working through disagreements as they arose, even if they still didn't like each other.

Then he had a combined meeting with both of them in which he returned to his cooperative tone. He reviewed the shuttle meetings, how each of them was different, how each was valuable, and what each needed more of and less of from the other. And he put it in writing for them.

For two more years, Jane and Ralph improved their collaboration. While their relationship remained less than perfect, they ended their destructive behaviors (sarcasm, avoidance) and at least "made nice" in front of others, which was Armand's goal. When Ralph left for another job, all three were probably relieved. This conflict, like many, was never resolved, but it was well managed for two years.

6. EMBRACE THE ADAPTIVE WISDOM OF THE CROWD

We don't have to adapt alone. Our networks of friends, colleagues, allies, and even previous enemies can all serve to help us achieve our goals by applying in concert their various sources of influence and approaches to conflict management.

One of Antonio's leadership strengths is humility. He knows he needs help with conflict. By his own admission, he is chronically cooperative. Antonio relies on his network of conflict advisors to help him be adaptive. In order to face big, complex business decisions, he works for consensus, but he learned over the years that the sturdiest agreements come from a diverse network that can offer perspectives on how to manage a dispute, leaving fewer stones left unturned in the search for the most fitting resolution strategy.

For the really big decisions, he includes his father, who founded their successful import and wholesale distribution business. His father argues passionately to keep people employed, to keep costs down, and to give back to the community. Those were the secrets of his success, and he holds to them fervently. He tends to dominate in a disagreement, but because of his big heart he wouldn't be called a dictator.

The COO is all about the numbers. Conflicts are to be resolved through sound business logic and attention to the bottom line. "The data should be the judge when we can't agree on something." She's willing to compromise, but not until everyone has "faced the brutal facts."

Antonio's brother wants to know everyone's feelings. He works part-time for the business and has his own social work practice. He knows that as important as logic and tradition are in influencing disagreements, emotions have to be dealt with as well. Antonio knows he sometimes overlooks the latent emotions that flow through conflict, especially when subordinates don't want him to know they are anxious or angry. His brother brings those emotions to the surface so they can be acknowledged and their underlying concerns addressed.

Several years ago Antonio recruited an outside board, some of who had retired from Fortune 500 companies. The board brings the big-business perspective on how to manage conflict. The board members are more likely to ask questions during a dispute, like "What are the legal ramifications?" or "How will this look to the media?" or "How will the outcome of this conflict affect your ability to recruit and retain the best talent?"

And he listens to his employees, all the way down to the people who load trucks at the warehouse. When there was a disagreement about compensation, he not only wanted to know what they thought about the issue, he asked several of them how they thought he should approach the dispute. They told him he should allow them to elect a few representatives from among their ranks who would attend the executive meetings to discuss the situation.

And then there's the former board member who was asked to leave because he screamed at too many people. Antonio didn't speak to him for two years but decided to have coffee with him from time to time to seek his advice on how to handle specific disputes. "I'll tell you how to handle this conflict. You tell them you're the boss, and that's that," he preached in his tough Brooklyn accent. Antonio can't match the tough-guy voice, but sometimes he knows he needs to send one of his lieutenants into a situation that calls for such dominance.

Antonio would probably "resolve" conflicts quicker if he just told people how it was going to be or if he listened for a while and took a vote. But his group of advisors helps Antonio approach disputes in ways not always fitting with his personal comfort. The approach is complex, emotional, and time-consuming, but it's usually more effective.

7. WALK SOFTLY, BUT CARRY A BOTTOM LINE

Be creative, flexible, and integrative on certain issues, but be clear about your own bottom line on issues you see as nonnegotiable, and plan to shift into hardball tactics when necessary.

When John took over as manager of the department, his superiors told him to tighten things up. His predecessor was permissive and inefficient; John was directed to be firm and fair. John knew he was actually being sent a mixed message. The company's culture was not tolerant of dominant managers. He was expected to tighten things up without rocking any boats or making employees feel uncomfortable. Most of his new reports were excited by the change. They were talented and motivated and had felt frustrated by the previous manager.

But one employee, David, was not excited. He had been with the company for years and was only marginally productive. He had not mastered new software or other systems but nonetheless had several years of rubber-stamped evaluations rating him as "meets expectations." John knew that with such a record, it was impossible to get fired from this company.

So John negotiated up and down.

First he met with his boss and reached an agreement that if David was given ample time but was still unable to live up to increased expectations, John could transfer him to another department. Negotiations focused on the definition of "ample time" and where David might be transferred. They finally agreed that John could move David at the same site to an understaffed department that arranged special events, luncheons, and customer visits.

Then, without telling David about the possibility of a transfer, he negotiated new responsibilities for the longtime employee. He asked him to improve his performance on one software system and learn a second. David complained, saying he could not do both tasks at the same time. John compromised. Then John asked David to attend a series of training classes in another city. David said it was hard to be away from his family. John reduced the number of classes. Over a course of time, John negotiated with David, showing him that although he was not the permissive manager who preceded him, he was willing to accommodate.

When asked about his new manager, David described him as "a go-getter, but not unreasonable."

However, as David continued to demonstrate a reluctance to keep up with the inevitable changes in his job, John prepared to go from soft to hard. First he renewed the commitment from his superior. "Yes, if you just can't get David to change, you can transfer him," promised his boss. Then John went to David.

"David, I want you to succeed, but it looks like the changes we are making to the department are very stressful for you. I want you to consider a transfer to the special-events team."

David said he didn't think he would fit in there.

John insisted. "In thirty more days, if I do not see a turnaround in your attitude and productivity, I have support from my boss to transfer you." Negotiations were over.

Thirty-one days later, John transferred David.

8. COMBINE DIRECT WITH INDIRECT METHODS, STAYING FOCUSED ON THE GREATER GOOD

Adaptive conflict management across power differences sometimes requires a careful combination of straightforward persuasion and less direct influence. What differentiates this from manipulation or trickery is your integrity.

Dale grew up in West Texas, where roads are straight. You can drive fast and direct to wherever you want. To Dale, the people seemed that way, too. "You know where they're coming from and you can see where they're going."

But working in a global fertilizer and pesticide company was different. Some of the leaders he worked for over his career were managing a billion dollars in business; they were extremely results-driven and had immense power. If he took them on directly, he hit roadblocks. He had to find ways not so straight as the highways of West Texas.

During his years in the Canadian division of the company, he reported to the North America CEO, Chuck. Dale liked working for him. For the most part, when Chuck heard thoughtful and confident answers, he left decisions to Dale. Only rarely did he say, "Do it my way."

On one issue he left no room for discussion. He told Dale to move the company's Canadian headquarters from Toronto to Winnipeg.

"He told me to close the Toronto office after two decades and to convince all the right people to move fourteen hundred miles west to Winnipeg, which is a lot like Siberia," explained Dale. "Chuck grew up in Winnipeg, so he didn't have a problem with twenty-five below zero."

But Dale thought a lot about the company's long-term future and wanted to move HQ to Calgary, a vibrant, beautiful, cultural city. "Chuck and I totally agreed about getting out of the Toronto overhead. And we agreed that 80 percent of our business was in the West, so it really made sense to move."

Nevertheless, Winnipeg was an appalling idea, thought Dale. "But I didn't say so. I didn't want Chuck to think of this as a conflict between the two of us. I didn't want him to think it was about my feelings about the different cities." Dale knew he would be living and working back in the United States within a few years. He wanted a long-term solution that would work for the company and for the families that would be making the move.

"So I made it sound like he and I had the same problem: getting a bunch of snobby eastern Canadian professionals who had family ties and cultural prejudices to move west. I'm from Texas and he's from western Canada, so we both had feelings about condescending easterners."

This time it was Dale asking the challenging question: "How are we going to sell the easterners on moving west without simply forcing them?" Dale wanted to manage the conflict with the employees from the front end, rather than wait until they were angry about feeling bullied to relocate. And he wanted to prevent a toe-to-toe confrontation with Chuck. He knew the company would lose if it came to that.

Chuck saw the problem. He knew if he ordered the most talented and valuable people to move, they could afford to say no. In order to make people willing to move, but also to influence Chuck, Dale asked to create a process designed to find the best city for the business, and to attract and retain the best talent in the future. Chuck agreed, even though he thought Winnipeg was the obvious choice.

So Dale interviewed employees and consultants and took key staff to visit several cities. The consensus was that Winnipeg was not a good choice and that his secret preference, Calgary, was the best location. That's when Dale thought, *Chuck is going to squash my decision.* Chuck, as CEO, certainly had the power to do just that. But because the process was well thought out and was intended to solve "our" problem, Chuck did not veto the decision.

9. TEAM UP FOR ADAPTIVITY

One of the advanced tactics for employing adaptivity is through teams. As long as the team has similar goals, delegating the various strategies to individual team members when in conflict with other teams can be advantageous.

Nora is a branch chief at a federal agency that sponsors and directs research on disease and related behavior. One of her responsibilities is to influence scientists to work with her agency and with other research teams. That's not easy. Each research team tends to be passionate, even territorial about its particular research. Although most scientists share the grand purpose of understanding, preventing, and curing illness, from there they disagree on many things, such as research implementation, deadlines, methods, measurement techniques, interpretation of data, and recommendations.

When Nora kicks off a project, she sees it as a big jigsaw puzzle, each piece a different research group that she and her staff have to pull together into an integrated program. Some research teams are easy to deal with, some not. So she strategizes with her own team members to coordinate their strategies to more effectively deal with each research team, especially the difficult ones:

> I usually assume the dominant role, using my institutional power to set out the boundaries and parameters, the time frames, the expectations, and the rules for the program. I assert deadlines and regulations and explain that there are things that just have to happen a certain way at a certain time. Then I have a colleague who plays the role of the advocate. She tries to identify with the scientist's perspective and support it. And if a scientist is shy or inarticulate, she works to bring out their point of view. A third colleague is the benevolent mediator. She pushes for active dialogue and shared decision making, and tries to keep disagreements from being prematurely resolved. Sometimes we add a devil's advocate, sort of a

creative troublemaker, who stirs things up when we need some new ideas.

The result?

"It works very well. We tend to be very productive with the different research teams we encounter. We just kicked off a big project this week. We walked out of there with some new ideas we probably wouldn't otherwise have come up with, and everybody's next steps very clearly defined."

10. CREATE NEW ADAPTIVE HYBRIDS

You are surrounded by conflict, and you have many opportunities to observe, experiment, and learn from others. The nightly news is rich in lessons of conflicts managed well or poorly. Adaptivity includes the willingness to learn, combine, and synthesize, so your conflict management repertoire is constantly expanding.

This book presents seven prototypical strategies for conflict management, six of which are best suited to particular situation types. These strategies represent what we call *pure types* of responses. With practice, these types can be artfully combined to fit situations that are fuzzier and less typical of the pure situations presented here.

Scientists who study situations where disputants share critically important common and competing goals have identified a set of these hybrids. They include the following:

- Conditional assessment contingencies: This strategy employs both hardball and integrative win-win strategies at different times when situations demand or allow for one or the other, but parties remain aware of the fact that more contentious strategies typically lead to escalation, alienation, and other negative consequences.
- Tit-for-tat (reciprocal) strategy: When parties employ a strategy of reciprocity, copying whatever tactics their opponent employs, both parties often realize they are both ultimately better off when they

cooperate and work together toward joint solutions. (This strategy requires that the parties are of essentially equal power.)

- Overt/covert strategy: Used increasingly in international affairs, this is a strategy of employing one tactic publicly while using essentially the opposite approach in a clandestine manner. This can take the form of displaying a hard-line, contentious position publicly while secretly holding negotiations that attempt to find common solutions—or the reverse.

- Negotiation chains: Typically employed under conditions when leaders who are engaged in a contentious conflict need to hold a hard line and cannot be associated in any way with the other party, this tactic involves holding negotiations through a sequence of individuals in a manner that allows the leaders on both sides to maintain deniability of knowledge of the negotiations should they fail, backfire, or become public.

- Internal split strategy: There is a myth in the world of politics and negotiations that groups in conflict are most successful when they share one position within their group—the party line. However, research has shown that groups who contain internal splits—hawks and doves, hard-liners and conciliators—often fare better in negotiations. This is because the hard-liners make demands in the negotiations, while the more-flexible conciliators work to find integrative solutions that address the needs of all parties. This provides a more balanced approach and optimal solutions.

- Short-term/long-term strategy: Another approach attempted by more intrepid negotiators is to agree to enter typically contentious negotiations with a more cooperative, flexible orientation, but to resort to hardball tactics if their initial approach fails. This requires a high level of skill in integrative bargaining.

These are merely a few of the hybrid strategies you may employ as your agility and skill in navigating conflict grows. The mediation scholar Baruch Bush suggests that conflict is a "unique human crucible," which provides us with an exceptional opportunity to learn about ourselves and others.[21] The great news about conflict is that it is pervasive in our life, so we are presented with countless opportunities to practice our strategies and tactics.

• EFFECTIVE ADAPTIVITY SUMMARY •

Adaptivity Cuts Across All Seven Conflict Situations: This strategy is by its nature multisituational and may be useful in contexts of compassionate responsibility, command and control, cooperative dependence, unhappy tolerance, independence, partnership, and enemy territory — as they change over time.

Strategy: To read situations accurately and employ any of the strategies (benevolence, support, dominance, appeasement, autonomy, cooperation, competition, and possibly mini-revolutions) where they fit, in a manner and to a degree appropriate to the context. Then, to be capable of altering strategies and tactics as the situation morphs into another type altogether.

TACTICS

1. Match and mix.
2. Shake it up.
3. See the system.
4. Adapt today while leaning toward a more constructive tomorrow.
5. Practice shuttle diplomacy.
6. Embrace the wisdom of the adaptive crowd.
7. Walk softly, but carry a bottom line.
8. Combine direct with indirect methods, staying focused on the greater good.

9. Team up for adaptivity.
10. Create new adaptive hybrids.

SKILL-DEVELOPMENT CHECKLIST

Check any skill you have already developed. Discuss with someone you trust what other skills you might want to further develop to be more effective and successful.

_____ **I am flexible.** I can alter how I think about situations and how I approach various social circumstances. I rarely get stuck in my thinking or stubborn in my relationships.

_____ **I have a skill for staying focused.** I can discipline myself to keep my eye on a goal so I do not get distracted by a need to be right or smarter or superior.

_____ **I can see the positive.** One of my skills is to consciously look for the value in an unpleasant situation or uncomfortable conflict. I can think beyond my immediate negative feelings.

_____ **I can manage my emotions very well.** I can calm myself down, talk through my emotions, prevent escalation of hostility, and work within a reasonable degree of emotion so I do not over-respond to stress and make a conflict worse than it already is.

_____ **I am skilled at building a diverse set of trusted advisors.** I can seek advice and wisdom not only for the technical challenges of my work but also for how to approach difficult people and situations. I don't get input from just one or two people. I can even seek counsel from people I do not particularly like if it is good for my team, the organization, or me.

_____ **I reflect on events between meetings.** I take time to consider my actions before and after interactions or negotiations. I can make a plan, devise a strategy, and pick a tactic to apply to a challenging dispute. I have the ability to learn from my successes and failures.

_____ **I can see different perspectives.** In any disagreement, I'm not trapped by my point of view to the extent that I cannot even consider alternatives. I can willfully choose to open my mind.

_____ **I can alternate.** I can switch, as needed, between being very independent in my pursuit of goals, or very *inter*dependent. I have the ability to see what the situation calls for.

_____ **I have the ability to change.** Within my organization, I can be highly cooperative in some contexts and highly competitive in others. I can read the changing context.

_____ **I know who I am and what I stand for.** There are limits to my ability or willingness to adapt. I have a set of values, principles, and ethics that form the boundaries around my skills at adapting to some disagreements. I have integrity.

DISCUSSION PROMPTS

Discuss the following questions with someone you trust to help you develop your skills at leadership and conflict. Think about a complicated or ongoing disagreement at work, and discuss the following:

- Who has formal power in this situation? In other words, who carries the authority of a title? In addition to formal power, what informal power do I have to influence the outcomes of this disagreement?

- What is the history of this conflict? What are each person's or group's key interests? What is best for the organization? Does this differ from what is best for a group or individual involved? How can I frame this conflict as cooperatively as possible? How is the context changing? What has changed or is likely to change in the near future in terms of power or interests or the flow of events associated with this disagreement?

- What outcome do I want to see? Which of the seven strategies (or combination thereof) is most likely to bring about my desired outcome at this point in time?

10

Principled Rebellion

IN BEIJING, an American executive was held hostage in his medical-supply plant by one hundred workers angry about unpaid salary and demanding "fair or reasonable" compensation, following rumors their plant was being closed.

In Greece, half of the staff of Vio.Me, a company that made glue and tile-cleaning products before it went bankrupt, voted to take matters into their own hands and revamp the factory to produce environmentally friendly detergent and fabric softener.

In Appalachia, an employee for a nonprofit organization that administered Head Start programs to the poor was fired when he blew the whistle on his organization, which had responded to budget cuts by cutting programs like milk subsidies and speech therapy for disabled kids, while keeping the same staff on at high salaries.

In Palo Alto, California, in 1997, Steve Jobs, who had been ousted from Apple Computers a decade earlier, presented an ultimatum to the board of directors that they must all resign (with one exception) if he was to agree to return to the failing company and rehabilitate it. They did.

George Bernard Shaw said, "The reasonable man adapts himself to the world; the unreasonable one persists in trying to adapt the world to himself. Therefore all progress depends on the unreasonable man."

So let's be unreasonable.

This chapter describes what employees, managers, executives, and other leaders can do when adaptivity hits a wall. It describes those rare circumstances in which employing a conflict-management strategy that fits with the demands of a situation is ethically, morally, legally, or practically impossible (or simply wrong). It also explains the alternative strategies available for changing the game and lays out the conditions that make this more likely to happen.

Here are two stories — one tragic and one hopeful — in which the conditions for principled rebellion were present.

The oil rig Deepwater Horizon exploded at 9:47 P.M. on April 20, 2010. Earlier that day, at a safety meeting between managers and technicians, a conflict erupted and British Petroleum's top official on the rig pulled rank. Mike Williams, one of the last crew members to escape the explosion, told *60 Minutes*[1] that the BP manager ordered a faster drilling pace. A Transocean manager was explaining how they were going to close the well by following standard safety procedures, when a manager for BP interrupted. "I had the BP company man sitting directly beside me," explained Williams, "and he literally perked up and said, 'My process is different. And I think we're going to do it this way.'"

Another crew member, mechanic Douglas Brown, told a similar story. Brown told federal investigators that around noon on the day of the explosion, there was a "difference of opinion" and that "a skirmish" took place between "the company man" from BP and three Transocean employees. "The company man was basically saying, 'This is how it's going to be,'" and Transocean rig workers "reluctantly agreed."[2]

Despite obvious safety concerns, the highest-ranking manager on-site ordered a risky course of action, and his subordinates obeyed. Call it an abuse of power or call it a failure to stand up to power when the stakes could not be higher — either way, eleven people died, seventeen were injured, and 176 million gallons of oil flowed into the Gulf of Mexico.[3]

Before Marvin Miller was elected head of the Major League Baseball Players Association in 1966, the club owners controlled the money and thus the players' careers, and players did not complain. In major-league sports, money was power, and there was only so much to go around. But Miller had a different way of looking at power and money. He thought there was a way for everyone to get more of both. More for the players *and* more for the owners. First, he convinced the players of his day that baseball's reserve clause—a stipulation meaning the club owned the rights to the player forever—in effect rendered them as property, with no power to steer their careers. In 1974 he persuaded Andy Messersmith and Dave McNally to play a year without signing a contract. At the end of the year he had both players file grievance arbitration, and they were released from all legal obligations to their clubs. Free agency was born.

During his seventeen years as executive director of the Major League Baseball Players Association (1966–1983), Miller transformed it from a weak organization into one of the strongest unions in the United States and helped the average player's salary increase more than twelvefold, from $19,000 to $241,000 a year. Miller's vision and leadership increased the wealth of the entire game, including that of the owners. He professionalized Major League Baseball, expedited its evolution toward a major entertainment industry, and transformed poorly paid players into stars who would bring in more fans—and much more revenue. Baseball commissioner Bowie Kuhn, stuck in the mindset of fixed-pie power, predicted free agency would bankrupt Major League Baseball; instead it has become a $7 billion annual business. Because Miller transformed the economic model and power dynamics of the game, club owners make a lot more money than they did before his leadership, and so do the players.

Let's begin by defining our terms, as words like *rebellion* and *revolution* tend to scare most managers. Rebellions can range from minor protests to total upheaval. For our purposes, a *rebellion* is an active or deliberate choice to respond to a conflict in a nonfitting or disruptive manner. It is a direct attempt to challenge the rules of the game of conflict.

Revolution is different. It is associated with a fundamental change in power or organizational structure that takes place in a relatively short period of time. Most elections are not revolutions, even if they involve power shifts, because they take so long to happen and the change associated with them is rarely fundamental. Egypt experienced a revolution in 2011, when the thirty-year autocratic reign of Hosni Mubarak as president came to an end and was—at least temporarily—replaced by democratic elections. Steve Jobs's retaking of Apple in 1997 could be considered revolutionary because it caused a sudden, radical reorientation of power, people, and purpose at the company.

For our purposes, a rebellion is the choice to respond to a conflict in a disorderly manner, which may or may not lead to a revolutionary change in power relations and structures. Rebellion and revolution both tend to elicit anxiety and stress from all involved—albeit mostly from the powerful—because they disrupt the equilibrium of the status quo and can have severe consequences. They should be used sparingly and only then after thoughtful, strategic consideration. Nevertheless, both responses may become necessary at some point in your professional life and should therefore be seen as minor (rebellion) and major (revolution) "nuclear" options to keep handy in your conflict toolkit.

What Causes Rebellion?

Some people are born revolutionaries. In *Born to Rebel: Birth Order, Family Dynamics, and Creative Lives,* Berkeley professor Frank Sulloway argues that throughout history, later-born children are more likely than firstborns to challenge the status quo. His research suggests that the radical tendencies of siblings vary by birth order because they adopt different strategies in their attempts to win parental favor. Sulloway found that the eldest children tend to identify more with their parents and authority and occupy a place of relative privilege in the home, and therefore they support the status quo. In comparison, later-born children, who are relatively disadvantaged by traditional family hierarchies, more often rebel against it, leading to more radical anti-establishment tendencies in their later lives. His findings offer evidence to suggest that the family, not society, is the primary incubator for the great revolutionary advances that drive historical change.[4]

Nevertheless, the *perceived illegitimacy* of a leader's or a company's behavior has been found to be the primary driver of revolutionary responses to conflicts at work. Legitimate leaders and stable hierarchies are associated with higher levels of cooperation; the powerful lead and the less powerful follow.[5] But when those in low power see their leaders as illegitimate, they are less likely to accept directions from the powerful and more likely to attempt to change the situation unilaterally. Because illegitimacy signals instability and the possibility of change, the lower-power parties may also begin to focus on potential gains that may be achieved through conflict, whereas the powerful shift focus to avoiding losses.[6]

Imagine that you are a consultant called in to work with a company on the ongoing tensions and declining productivity of a previously top-functioning R & D team in the tech industry. After an initial investigation, you learn that the team has been run for years by a very efficient but brutal boss, who typically enjoys berating and publicly humiliating members of his team and staff. This is "business as usual" for the team and, to some degree, in the industry, and because they were functioning as one of the more effective R & D teams in the company, everyone went along with his style of leadership for years. This became the status quo of this team.

Then something happened. One of the new young interns reported being sexually harassed by the team leader. After this, it became clear that this type of behavior had been going on for years. The other women who had been harassed had simply been too fearful and concerned about losing their place on the team to go public with accusations. Once word got out about the intern, everything changed. Upper management came down on the boss, and the other members of the team began refusing to accept his hostility; in meetings, they started calling him out on his behavior. The climate of the team meetings became very contentious, and their productivity declined precipitously.

There are many ways to understand what happened at this company.

But from a psychological perspective, the leader crossed the boundaries of perceived legitimacy for the team. The entire team had grown accustomed to a destructive set of norms and expectations: abuse of power and fear at work that had become commonplace and seemingly tolerable for most. But this particular transgression—against a young intern—crossed a threshold, destabilized the system, and sent the team into free fall.

Research on something called relative deprivation suggests another condition conducive to revolution. *Relative deprivation* is defined as a perceived gap between what people have and what they feel entitled to. It refers to the discontent people feel when they compare their situations to others and realize that they have less than those around them, and it is generally thought to be one of the more major sources of interpersonal and intergroup conflict and violence.[7] When a whole group of people feel they are being deprived of what they deserve—especially when there are few legitimate channels of recourse open to them—they are much more likely to take more-extreme measures.[8]

Another facet of national and organizational culture that can affect rebelliousness is something the Dutch social psychologist Geert Hofstede labeled *power distance.* This is the extent to which the less powerful members of cultures, organizations, and institutions accept and expect that power is distributed unequally. It is an indicator of a nation's or organization's overall acceptance of inequality. The United States scores a 40 out of 100, compared to Arab countries, where the power distance is very high (80), and Austria, where it is very low (11). Employees working in lower-power-distance countries have been found to be more likely to speak out about their concerns over the actions of power holders and to justify their own deviant behavior.[9]

Self-Assessment: Are You Born to Rebel?

The following questionnaire may help you get a sense of just how naturally drawn you are toward rebellion. Rate your response to each of the following statements.

> 1 = Strongly disagree 4 = Agree
> 2 = Disagree 5 = Strongly agree
> 3 = Neutral

_____ 1. I excel at recognizing opportunities.

_____ 2. If I believe in an idea, no obstacle will prevent me from making it happen.

_____ 3. If I see something I don't like, I find a solution.

_____ 4. I am very comfortable speaking truth to power.

_____ 5. I am always prepared.

_____ 6. I continually look for innovative ways to improve my life.

_____ 7. I start conversations and get people thinking.

_____ 8. I notice a good opportunity long before others do.

_____ 9. I am always looking for improved ways to do things.

_____ 10. I pay attention to details.

_____ 11. No matter what the chances, if I believe in something, I will make it happen.

_____ 12. Wherever I have gone, I have been an influential force for constructive change.

_____ 13. I don't mind being the center of attention.

_____ 14. Nothing is more stimulating than turning my ideas into reality.

_____ 15. I love being a champion for my ideas, even against others' obstruction.

SCORING

Add up your scores and then refer to the table below. If you have a very high score, there is a chance you are overusing this strategy. But a low score may also be cause for concern.

Score	Meaning	Ask yourself . . .
<40	You rarely, if ever, rebel in a conflict.	Is it because the environment does not require or support rebelliousness? Or are you underutilizing this strategy?
40–49	You are inclined toward this strategy.	Do you use it enough and in the right contexts?
50–59	You use this strategy quite a bit.	Do you use it too much or in the wrong contexts?
60+	You rely on this strategy in most circumstances.	There is a high probability that you overuse the rebellion strategy. Are you using it effectively and in the right contexts? Do you need to improve your skills at discerning when to use other strategies for conflict?

Organizational Assessment: Does Your Organization Encourage Rebellion?

Respond to this questionnaire to gauge just how much your environment encourages or stimulates rebellion. Rate your response to each of the following questions.

1 = Strongly disagree 4 = Agree

2 = Disagree 5 = Strongly agree

3 = Neutral

_____ 1. In general, I have a negative opinion about where I work.

_____ 2. At my job, my coworkers and I are strongly discouraged from taking issue with management decisions.

_____ 3. At my job, it is customary for a manager to use the authority and power of his or her position forcefully when dealing with subordinates.

_____ **4.** The place where I work is not ethical.

_____ **5.** I don't feel I have a legitimate place to voice my concerns in my organization.

_____ **6.** At my job, managers are expected to make most decisions without discussing things with subordinates.

_____ **7.** In my opinion, companies like the one I work for are dishonest.

_____ **8.** I believe the organization where I work frequently does not follow government regulations.

_____ **9.** In the organization where I work, managers rarely ask for the perspectives of employees.

_____ **10.** Where I work, I believe that my superiors disregard most rules and policies.

_____ **11.** I feel like certain ethnic groups are treated more favorably where I work.

_____ **12.** Things are very unfair where I work.

_____ **13.** At work, managers hardly ever delegate important responsibilities.

_____ **14.** Corruption is widespread in my organization.

_____ **15.** Overall, the problems from my organization overshadow the positives.

SCORING

Add up your score, which will fall between 15 and 75. The higher the score, the more it makes sense to use the rebellion strategy in your organization. Now compare your self-assessment score to the organizational assessment you just completed.

_____ Self-assessment score from the previous questionnaire

_____ Organizational-assessment score from most recent questionnaire

Generally speaking, the more similar the scores, the more likely you are employing this strategy with discernment. Of course, the nuances of various conflict situations are such that you still have to distinguish when and with whom to use this strategy.

Six Good Reasons to Rebel at Work

There are many reasons why someone may choose to intentionally respond to a dispute with a superior at work in a manner that challenges the status quo, despite the consequences. Some of the more obvious include:

1. **They are cheats or crooks.** You have seen sufficient, repeated evidence of your boss or other superiors swindling people or breaking the law. You have come to see that you cannot trust what your superiors tell you. It is clearly not an anomaly.
2. **They harass you and/or others.** You find the way you or others are treated at work violates basic standards of human rights for dignity and respect. You have seen repeated instances of your superiors at work taking advantage of members of disadvantaged groups.
3. **They put workers or consumers unnecessarily at risk for injury.** You have seen too many instances in which you or others have been put in dangerous situations that exceed the agreed expectations of the job.
4. **They block all opportunities for fair recourse to express grievances.** When you and others do have legitimate concerns about policies, practices, or working conditions, you find that there are no suitable venues for sharing your concerns and for having them addressed in a timely fashion, such as an ombudsperson's office or mediation center.
5. **They encourage illegal or immoral activities.** Although you have not witnessed your superiors breaking the law, it is clear that

they encourage or incentivize employees to commit immoral or illegal acts.

6. **They cover up wrongdoing and/or ask you to do so.** The company seems to go too far in protecting its reputation or shielding itself from punitive measures of oversight agencies by hiding or destroying information.

In other words, these situations are ones in which responding appropriately feels inappropriate.

The Consequences of Misusing Rebellion

We all have stories of coworkers who were rebels without a cause — natural malcontents who were chronically critical and dissatisfied with their workplace (and often their lives in general). Such characters can play an important role at work. They often play devil's advocates and serve as a check on decision-making processes. However, they can also be a destructive force.

One of our faculty colleagues, Tomas, suffers from this syndrome — and shares the suffering. Ten years ago he held a high-level administrative position in a prestigious institute at Columbia University. However, when a new charismatic director was brought in to raise the profile of the institute, she cleaned house and replaced Tomas. As he was still a member of Columbia faculty, he stayed on, despite the rather public embarrassment of being replaced. He clearly felt wronged and humiliated.

Tomas's bitterness was immediately apparent. At meetings of the faculty and various subcommittees, he has become a hypercritical voice. He often raises multiple concerns on pending decisions and actions before the faculty. He is frequently correct in his assessments, but because of his high level of cynicism and obvious contempt for the leadership of the institute, his views are usually met with indifference or ignored altogether. In his tireless campaign to expose the failings of the leadership and display his own competence, he mostly serves to alienate other faculty and further isolate himself. He is a rebel without a following.

What Does Effective Rebellion Look Like in Action?

Choosing to rebel in response to a work conflict should be carefully considered and strategic. Of all the strategies discussed in this book, this one is the most dangerous and consequential. Most managers frown on deviance and defiance, and most organizations prefer order to disorder. So choosing to rebel at work is likely to have costs, especially the lower you are on the totem pole.

Fortunately, the world of community organizing and political activism has given this strategy some serious thought. Classic writings like Saul Alinsky's *Rules for Radicals*; Gene Sharp's *The Politics of Nonviolent Action, Part Two*; Rinku Sen's *Stir it Up*; and Morton Deutsch's "Framework for Thinking About Oppression and Its Change" have broken down the many tactics of this approach for us. Many of the methods cited in these works could be effective in the context of an organizational or industrial conflict. Here are a few of the more workplace-relevant tactics in further detail.

A Ten-Point Sequence for Rebellion and Revolution

1. PERSUASION TACTIC #1: APPEAL TO SELF-INTERESTS

When you hit a moral, ethical, or legal wall at work, your first step should be to appeal to the self-interest of the other parties involved. It's possible they are unaware of the implications of what they are demanding. So questioning their positions or demands, framing them in terms of the potential costs and implications *for them,* is a way to test the waters. This is also a way to signal your discomfort with their proposal and to give them a way to quietly withdraw their demands without losing face.

When a salesman for a small company that imported pesticide discovered that he had unknowingly sold more than a million gallons of defective product to major distributors, he went to his boss.

"At first he thought we should walk away from it. The supply chain is so long," the salesman said, "from multiple Chinese producers, to our company, to multiple U.S. distributors, to several regional distributers, to hundreds of farmers. He said we could plausibly deny responsibility; we could spread the blame."

But the salesman disagreed with his boss, strongly. "That's a gamble. If you lose, we'll never sell another product."

"It will cost millions to take back that product," warned his boss.

"You're right. But it will cost us more in the long run if we don't. We'll lose our credibility. Nobody will ever trust us again."

Eventually he convinced his boss that, ethics aside, they had to solve the problem down to every warehouse and every farmer, or they were risking business suicide.

His boss, a tough-minded pragmatist, reluctantly agreed.

When your boss is not amenable to appeals to self-interest, move on to persuasion tactic #2.

2. PERSUASION TACTIC #2: APPEAL TO MORAL VALUES

Most of us prefer to hold a positive self-image and like to believe that we are essentially decent people. We dislike the dissonance we feel when we become aware of the fact that our behavior is inconsistent with our own positive image of ourselves. Emphasizing the more fair, decent, and humane aspects of people, particularly in the context of a conflict where they may be evidencing more banal or despicable intentions or behaviors, can help to highlight this gap and increase their dissonance.

On April 24, 2013, the eight-story Rana Plaza collapsed in Bangladesh, killing more than a thousand people, most of them young women working in the garment factories inside.[10] On the other side of the planet, Darren worked as a manager in a clothing import company, an organization small enough to avoid the media scrutiny faced by Benetton, Walmart, and Bonmarché. Since he was often teased for being the company liberal, he anticipated endless debates if he talked to his colleagues one at a time. So he waited a few days and brought up the matter at a management meeting attended by the CEO. He wanted to raise the issue quietly and when it would have the strongest effect.

"Has anyone looked at the business we're conducting in Bangladesh? Are we in any way connected to the Rana Plaza?" asked Darren.

The quality manager assured him they were not.

"Good. Then we don't have to worry about PR. But based on the news reports, it sounds like the overall environment in Bangladesh is ripe for another such event. Are we planning to take any additional steps to ensure our suppliers are acting responsibly, or to remove ourselves from Bangladesh entirely?"

The CEO sat quietly, listening.

The quality and supply-chain managers explained that they were taking a closer look to make sure no orders were being subcontracted to Bangladeshi factories for which the company had not done social audits."

"Thank you. Because if we don't monitor our suppliers carefully, we are essentially complicit, without really knowing it up front."

Finally, the CEO spoke. "I want us to look more closely at everyone with whom we do business. I want the lives of factory workers on the other side of the world to be just as important as anyone's in this room."

Of course, not everyone is as open-minded as that CEO. In some cases this tactic might just serve to make the other parties angry or defensive. They may simply feel you are being manipulative and self-righteous, or that you are exaggerating the negativity of their actions. In this case, move on to tactic 3.

3. JUST SAY NO

If you are asked or expected to respond to a conflict in a manner that you just can't justify to yourself, and if your attempts at explaining the consequences of meeting these expectations falls on deaf ears, then it is best to simply refuse. If what you are being asked to do is illegal or immoral or unethical, then your refusal to acquiesce and your subsequent silence may be enough to worry or intimidate the other disputants into backing off and reconsidering their demands.

Imagine a salesperson asked to lie to a customer, or an accounting clerk being told by her manager to enter false numbers into a spreadsheet, or a technician in a research lab instructed to falsify data, or a manufacturing associate commanded to ignore safety rules. In any of these cases, a simple and firm no might send a message to the person in power that they are putting themselves and others in jeopardy.

4. JUST SAY NO LOUDER

When saying no doesn't work, it's time to turn the volume up. If your attempts to sway the other disputant on your own have not gotten traction, bring in others. This can start locally, by speaking with friends and colleagues about the conflict and getting their advice and counsel. It might even be possible for you to recruit colleagues to your cause.

If this is not feasible without putting other people's jobs in jeopardy, then it might be time to blow the inside whistle. This might entail speaking to your supervisor, or if the dispute is with him or her, speaking to that person's superiors. Alternatively, it could entail speaking with an ombudsperson, if your organization has such a dispute-resolution mechanism, or with other organizational neutrals within human resources that might be able to offer advice. The idea at this stage is to mobilize others in the organization to do the right thing and put an end to the dispute. This tactic tends to work best within more bureaucratic organizations, but only if formal mechanisms exist to encourage internal whistle-blowing.[12] In general, as a whistle-blower, you should be aware that isolated expressions of grievances or acts of resistance are often ignored or simply quashed, so you should be prepared for repeated action over the long run. Being prepared to provide evidence and establish your own credibility will enhance your chances of success. You should also realize that formal grievance channels seldom work, so you should always have an alternative plan.[13]

Toya worked as a nurse in a suburban hospital. Her unit clerk, Meredith, was in charge of coordinating services on the unit. Meredith told orderlies and nurses when a patient needed restroom assistance, medication, or other help.

The main conflict on the unit was Meredith herself. She was a bully. If Meredith decided it was your turn to be her target, she overworked you, harshly criticized you, and made fun of you. The unit manager was a wimp: likable, cooperative, but scared of Meredith himself. Occasionally he said he would talk to Meredith about her "style," but nothing ever came of it.

When Toya's turn for Meredith's abuse came up, she wasn't confident enough to stand up to her. She hated conflict. She tried to placate and avoid Meredith, but it only made it worse. She had decided to quit the job she otherwise loved, when a friend gave her a fourth option. "Meredith's behavior isn't just mean," the friend said, "it's unethical. You should go to the ethics and compliance department."

Now Toya didn't have to be tough, she just had to be honest. After several meetings with the ethics and compliance department, and repeated documentation, Toya's unit manager sheepishly told her he was transferring Meredith to another unit. But the other unit manager was not a wimp. Two weeks later Meredith got a call from HR and was terminated.

5. BROADCAST NO

When tactics 1–4 don't work, it is time to consider blowing the outside whistle. This is a big deal and is likely to have more severe negative consequences for you and others, no matter how it plays out. Scholars at Indiana and Ohio State Universities outlined conditions that are more conducive to effective whistle-blowing.[14] They concluded that whistle-blowers are more likely to succeed if they have high credibility or status within the organization (particularly in contrast to the wrongdoer), if they forgo anonymity and identify themselves at the outset of the proceedings, if the complaint recipients have high enough power or credibility to respond (and support the whistle-blower), if the organization is not highly dependent on the wrongs being enacted, and if the evidence that the wrongdoing has occurred is convincing and the acts clearly illegal and unambiguous.

Of course, it would be rare for any work situation to have all these conditions. But the more you can check off the list, the better your chances. And those elements that you have more control over—identifying yourself early on, bringing the complaint to someone with sufficient authority to act, and providing strong and unambiguous evidence of wrongdoing—should be heeded.

When the local owners of a Pizza Hut franchise in Elkhart, Indiana, told the store's manager, Tony Rohr, he had to open on Thanksgiving, he said, "Look, we have to talk about this Thanksgiving thing. It isn't right. I'm not going to make everyone work."[15] His bosses told him they could not afford to close because the competition would be open. Tony pushed back: "Can't we be the company that says we care about our employees and they can have the day off?" So he was instructed by the owners to write a resignation letter. Instead, he refused to go quietly and wrote a letter explaining why the store should not open on Thanksgiving. When a local CNN affiliate caught wind of it, they interviewed Tony. He told the station he thought people should have the day off to spend with their families.[16] Eventually Pizza Hut's corporate office admitted the franchise owners "made a serious error in judgment," and the owners agreed to hire Tony back.[17]

6. POWER TACTIC #1: GATHER YOUR OWN POWER

Another tactic that can be engaged in tandem with many of the previous ones is to attempt to change the power dynamic between yourself and the other disputant by enhancing or consolidating your own power.

Nelson Mandela provided an excellent example of this while serving in prison on Robben Island for twenty-seven years. Mandela, a trained boxer, awoke at 4:30 A.M. every morning—an hour before the guards would awaken the prisoners—to train. He believed that keeping fit and maintaining control of his own fitness regimen were critical to his own sense of power and control in prison. In addition, Mandela studied the rules and regulations of the prison carefully, so that he had full knowledge of his rights and privileges established by the rules—as well as the constraints and limitations of his captors—so that he could use them when necessary. He also held strongly to his own self-concept of morality and decency and refused to submit to the derogatory self-image the prison guards tried to impose on him. Through these acts, he was able to maintain and bolster his own physical, procedural, and psychological power, even under dire circumstances.

7. POWER TACTIC #2: GATHER YOUR FRIENDS

When it comes to rebellions and revolutions, allies matter. Again, Mandela and the leaders of the African National Congress made a considerable and concerted effort during their struggle against apartheid to recruit and cultivate relationships with international associations and other key members of the international community. The economic, legal, and moral forms of pressure that these members of the international community were able to bring to bear on the South African Afrikaner government was paramount to the government's ultimate willingness to release Mandela from prison and negotiate with the ANC. Without this mighty network of allies, apartheid might very well be alive and well in South Africa today.

Workplace examples of this tactic can range from several people from a department going to a manager together to complain about conditions or treatment, to something as massive as workers from Walmart organizing labor demonstrations and strikes in twenty-eight stores across twelve states to protest the company's retaliation against workers who speak out.[18]

8. POWER TACTIC #3: PRACTICE JUJITSU

As the illustrious community organizer Saul Alinsky once wrote, "Since the Haves publicly pose as the custodians of responsibility, morality, law and justice (which are frequently strangers to each other), they can be constantly pushed to live up to their own book of morality and regulations. No organization, including religion, can live up to the letter of its own book."[19] In other words, sometimes the oppressed can use the rules, policies, and power of the oppressor to oppress the oppressor.

In fact, Alinksy goes on in his book *Rules for Radicals* to outline a variety of tactics in which the red tape of bureaucratic organizations is used by members of communities to entangle the organization in their own rules and regulations. For example, he cites examples of entire neighborhoods showing up at local banks accused of discriminatory lending practices to open savings accounts with one dollar and then returning to the back of the line to close the same account. Similar tactics have been employed to tie up bathrooms of public facilities such as airports and train stations as a form of protest. All of these acts fall within the purview of the policies of the organizations but can be used to introduce chaos within their ranks.

When Penn State University notified its nonunion employees about an initiative that obligated them to "complete an online wellness profile" and undergo a "preventative physical exam," Professor Matthew Woessner objected.[20] He felt the hundred-dollar-a-month deduction for failing to comply was coercive, given that it applied to some of the lowest paid employees at the institution and that it was a violation of privacy to require men to disclose online whether they carry out "a monthly testicular exam" or if women perform "regular breast exams." So he advocated jujitsu in an open letter to all employees. He encouraged employees go online and fill the mandatory health survey with bogus information. "For example," he explained, "I'm 3 feet 8 inches tall, I weigh 50 pounds [the minimum values permitted by the website], and my last cholesterol test was performed when I was six months old." He verified with the university's HR department that there was no method of verifying the accuracy of information entered into the web survey. The university required compliance but could not punish respondents for ludicrous information. In response to this and other protest actions, and to adverse national publicity,[21] President Rodney Erickson announced a few months later the suspension of the deduction and that nobody would be penalized for noncompliance.[22]

9. POWER TACTIC #4: REDUCE THE POWER HOLDER'S POWER THROUGH ORGANIZED NONCOOPERATION

When Carol Harnett was twelve years old, her parochial school class performed an act of civil disobedience. As this human resources expert explained it,[23] she had an extraordinary teacher, Mrs. Costello, who introduced the young students to Gandhi and King and encouraged independent thinking. She also gave her students the choice of how to arrange their classroom and to influence the curriculum. The students rejected straight rows of desks in favor of a more creative arrangement, until the principal, Sister Bernadette, discovered the change and told Mrs. Costello to put the desks back in rows and stop being so permissive.

That night, in a flurry of phone calls, the class activists convinced everyone to follow the inspiration of Martin Luther King.

The next day the entire class began a week of silence. The principal scolded them: "It's time you learned to do as you are told." But the class stood fast, and Sister Bernadette eventually negotiated.

We are not used to thinking of civil disobedience as occurring inside organizations. Such actions are usually thought of as citizens protesting immoral laws, like the civil rights movement in the United States, or the women of Saudi Arabia disregarding a ban on female drivers.[24] But if seventh graders can do it, so can adult workers, and they do.

Like the librarians in Victoria, British Columbia, who stopped collecting late fines to protest the inequity between their compensation and that of other municipal workers.[25] And the Walmart workers who were arrested at Yahoo! headquarters for protesting what they claimed were unfair terminations of other workers and demanding to meet with Yahoo! CEO Marissa Mayer, who joined Walmart's board the previous year.[26] And the teachers in a Seattle high school who called a press conference to announce they were not going to cooperate with standardized testing. The action spread to other schools in the city.[27]

Noncooperation is a form of nonviolent protest or resistance. To be done effectively, it must be conducted strategically. Tactics of noncooperation are very likely to backfire unless a full strategy has been developed and is implemented with an eye to adaptivity. Our history texts are full of examples in which nonviolent protests resulted in catastrophes for the protesters. But the same texts also feature brilliant illustrations of protests and social movements that were greatly advanced through the use of noncooperation.

10. POWER TACTIC #5: TAKE POWER

If all else fails, it may be time to take over through direct action. This is what befell the American executive who was held hostage in his medical-supply plant by angry workers in Beijing. It is what transpired at Vio.Me in Greece, when half the company took over the facility and revamped it to produce environmentally friendly detergent and fabric softener. It is what Steve Jobs did when he presented his ultimatum to Apple's board of directors. Imagine what would have happened differently if the engineers on the Deepwater Horizon had revolted.

This tactic, obviously, is the most risky. But it should always be considered a last-stand BATNA, a backup plan should all else fail.

How to Master Rebellion: The Building Blocks

Rebellion and revolution are risky, and they involve much more than making noise. They require a high level of moral and ethical thinking. When the ethical violations are severe enough, training in nonviolence strategies and tactics is essential. "Revolutionaries" in the workplace need to expect and tolerate high levels of conflict, sometimes prolonged. Assertiveness and cooperation with fellow revolutionaries is also critical. With these building blocks, and a lot of tenacity, conflicts can sometimes be resolved without the use of benevolence, support, dominance, appeasement, autonomy, or adaptivity.

• PRINCIPLED REBELLION SUMMARY •

For Situations of Unhappy Tolerance That Have Become Intolerable: Here, you find yourself in low power and can no longer tolerate a violation of your conscience. Despite the risks and the costs, you have to take some action to interfere with corruption, injustice, or immorality.

Strategy: To name, shame, and, if necessary, defame your opponents in order to bring them back in line with what is legal, fair, ethical, and right. This strategy is likely to be utilized when there is extreme injustice or a highly toxic work environment.

COMPETENCIES REQUIRED

- High moral and ethical development
- Skill in nonviolence strategies and tactics
- Tolerance for high levels of conflict
- Assertiveness

TACTICS

1. Appeal to self-interests.
2. Appeal to moral values.
3. Just say no.
4. Just say no louder.

5. Broadcast no.
6. Gather your own power.
7. Gather your friends.
8. Practice Jujitsu.
9. Reduce the power holder's power through organized noncooperation.
10. Take power.

SKILL-DEVELOPMENT CHECKLIST

Check any skill you have already developed. Discuss your responses with someone.

_____ **I have the ability to question authority.** I can bring up ethical considerations and am willing to ask questions to get people thinking. I have the ability to push others to consider fairness.

_____ **I consciously practice discernment.** I realize that many situations come in shades of gray or even multiple colors, rather than simply black or white, and I am able to give such circumstances thoughtful consideration so as not to overrespond. I know how to make room for nuance and complexity. Some unpleasant or even unfair things are not worth protesting. And some are.

_____ **I think through actions.** Before I take action that will stir up controversy, I consider the purpose of my actions, the methods that are most likely to effect change, and the risks I face. I do not simply react from emotion or self-righteousness; I have a meaningful goal and a sound plan.

_____ **I have the ability to take a stand.** I can take an unpopular position when I have thought through my actions and believe it is important enough. I have courage to ask tough questions when I think something is wrong.

_____ **I know how to speak up and remain standing.** Beyond taking a stand, I can make myself heard, I can make noise, and I can stand the scrutiny and the potential backlash that comes with pushing against authority.

_____ **I am skilled at measuring my emotions.** I can express myself with passion when doing so is persuasive and effective; I can downshift the intensity of my emotion when the situation calls for it.

_____ **I am good at facing high levels of conflict.** I can stand the emotional intensity that can come with confronting authority or speaking out against a person, group, or policy. I can deal with people getting mad at me.

_____ **I can gather support.** I know how to reach out to supportive people when conflict is ongoing and intense. I can ask for advice, emotional support, and feedback. I can also ask people to join me in my protest. I know better than to go it alone or isolate myself.

_____ **I am resilient.** I bounce back from adversity. I am skilled at dealing with setbacks. When I try to change something and do not succeed, I still manage to enjoy other aspects of my work and my life.

_____ **I am tenacious.** If it is important enough, I don't give up. I keep trying. I come back for more. If something is worth fighting for, it's worth fighting again and again.

DISCUSSION PROMPTS

Discuss these questions with someone who can thoughtfully and confidentially help you evaluate your organization and your own ability to speak up when something is not right. Remember, rebellion and revolution bring the highest risk of the seven strategies. They take a lot of thought and consultation to have an effect on those in authority.

- What are the values of my organization that people live by? What are the values that leadership not only endorses but reinforces? What are the most positive ethical attributes of my organization?

- Where, if at all, does my organization fall short of its own "constitution," its own declared set of values and principles? If the organization or any of its members does fall short, is it within reasonable parameters of human fallibility, or does it significantly hurt or mistreat people? Are there violations of basic human fairness that hurt the organization itself in terms of reputation or probability of success?

- Who is a role model for standing up for fairness, safety, equality, and the other values I expect my organization to live by? What is it about this person, specifically, that makes him or her admirable? (Challenge yourself to look beyond the famous cultural heroes, and describe an actual person you know or have known in real life.)

CONCLUSION

THIS BOOK HAS offered you seven strategies, seventy tactics, and lots of science on making conflict work up and down the ladders of power in organizations.

So now what? What are the next steps for increasing your conflict intelligence and, as a result, your satisfaction with conflict and relationships at work?

In this concluding chapter we lay it out for you in a set of straightforward steps and activities that you can use for managing conflict in almost any situation.

Step 1: Get to Know Yourself Better in Conflict

Practice reflecting on your feelings, thoughts, and behavioral reactions soon after experiencing your next few conflicts in order to become more aware of your common tendencies, traps, and emotional hot buttons.[1] You can do this by simply reflecting and journaling on your own, through conversations with friends and trusted coworkers, or by attending workshops and coaching sessions on conflict management. Completing the series of short questionnaires provided in each of the strategy chapters in this book will give you some preliminary sense of your preferred, go-to strategies in conflict.

Which of the following do you tend to fall into?

a. Emotional reservoirs of high negativity to positivity ratios
b. The traps of high-power disputants in conflict, including ignoring power analyses, feeling bulletproof, breaking the rules, always dominating, and going too far
c. The traps of low-power disputants, such as having needlessly low aspirations in negotiations, being trapped by low expectations and rage, or becoming acutely concerned with maintaining your status in disputants with peers

How do you generally respond?

a. Taking up responsibility in a collaborative and supportive way
b. Seeking help and support from powerful others
c. Commanding and controlling others to win
d. Sucking it up—saying nothing and tolerating it
e. Moving away from others and getting it done by yourself
f. Competing doggedly against the others to win at all costs
g. Striving to find common ground and framing the conflict as a mutual challenge
h. Revolting and fighting the power
i. All of the above, depending on the situation

If you would prefer a more rigorous assessment of your chronic mindsets and capacities for adaptivity in conflict, we encourage you to go to our website, MakingConflictWork.com, where you will find a link and a set of simple instructions for completing our Conflict Intelligence Assessment (CIA). Once you complete it, we will send you an individualized feedback profile that will walk you through the results of your assessment and provide a comparison of your scores to those of the multitude of other employees, managers, and executives who have completed the survey.

The CIA was developed by our team at Columbia University to assess tendencies for navigating different types of conflicts across situations at work. It presents fifteen different work-conflict scenarios and asks participants to tell us how they would typically respond to each situation. The choice options reflect the primary strategies to conflict across power differences. It is based on years of original research. The feedback profile will provide you with some baseline information in order to give you a sense of your strengths and areas to work on to improve your *conflict intelligence quotient* (CIQ) and then provide you with a specific set of exercises for enhancing it.

Because most of us tend to change our preferences and tendencies for conflict management over the course of our careers, usually in response to the different circumstances and experiences we have with conflict, we recommend that you return to the website and take the assessment every year or two and use it as an opportunity to reflect further on your challenges and areas of growth in your conflict-management competencies.

For example, let's return briefly to the story of Christine from chapter 7 on strategic appeasement. Her new job with the same company in her hometown was enjoyable at first. She had achieved her goals. She reported to a benevolent manager who wanted to hear her ideas and opinions. But when the company replaced the benevolent boss with a micromanager who dominated every disagreement — even more than her former boss Hank did — Christine swung back into strategic appeasement mode. This time it took more of a toll; one day she let the new dictator know how angry she felt. That resulted in a ninety-day Performance Improvement Plan, which she survived, but her new goal is to appease strategically until she can find new employment elsewhere.

Step 2: Enhance Your Competencies
for Reading Conflict Situations

The next step for increasing your conflict intelligence is to enhance your competencies for accurately reading critical aspects of the relationships and situations in which you experience conflict. Sometimes we simply find ourselves in the middle of a conflict, without forewarning. In this case, we need to practice taking the time to ask ourselves: *Do I need to engage in this conflict and relationship? Are the others with or against me or both? Who has more power?* And then act accordingly.

Other times, we have some sense that we are heading into a dispute. Either we are intending to initiate it, have a gut feeling that something is about to escalate, have been called to an office of a supervisor or HR official where a conflict is likely to follow, or know that a formal negotiation is scheduled to discuss something such as our salary or position expectations. For these situations, we have provided you with our Conflict Intelligence Goal-Setting and Conflict-Planning Questionnaire (see the appendix), designed for pre-negotiation or pre-conflict management planning. It walks you through a pre-conflict/negotiation planning process, helping you identify key factors and appropriate strategies for addressing the anticipated situation of conflict at hand. It will help you explore the nature of your emotional history with the other disputants and whether you share high or low positivity–negativity ratios. It can help you identify the nature and conditions of the situation you are facing.

This planning format is currently employed in the courses and workshops we offer on conflict intelligence and will help you develop a preliminary assessment of the situation type and strategies and tactics available to you in any conflict.

Of course, your analysis of a pending dispute may be incorrect or different than how the other disputants see it, or the conflict might change as the discussion unfolds. Nevertheless, it is valuable to conduct a pre-conflict analysis when possible as, if nothing else, it will refresh your sense of the various strategies and tactics available to you and thereby ready you to be more adaptive if necessary.

Step 3: Practice the Strategies and Tactics

Become mindful of which strategies and tactics are feasible and available to you in different situations. Ask:

- How skilled am I in implementing each of the different strategies effectively?
- What levers are available to me for moving the conflict toward lower intensity, more cooperative, or more overt processes?
- How are my competencies and skills at employing power in this situation?

Fortunately, life tends to provide us with ample opportunities to experience conflict and practice new strategies. Both the online Conflict Intelligence Assessment and the Planning Worksheet provide you with a working understanding of your levels of competency and skill with each of the strategies.

Step 4: Enhance Your Capacities to Reflect on the Consequences of Your Choices

In conflicts, try to take the time to consider how the scene will play out over time. What are likely to be the short-term effects and consequences of your chosen actions? What might the long-term consequences be? Remember that constructive strategies (pragmatic benevolence, cooperation, and cultivated support) are usually *less* costly in the long run and *more* likely to result in satisfied outcomes for all involved.

Step 5: Always Know Your Bottom Line

Ultimately, it is critical that you consider your bottom line in conflict. Know when you need to move from more cooperative and conciliatory strategies into more competitive or contentious ones. Know when to respond to conflict in a manner that "fits" the situation, but also when *not* to. Know what it looks like when the other disputants cross lines that you refuse to cross. Know when it is time to rebel or revolt.

The many conflicts you face in your daily life present you with both traps and possibilities. They present opportunities to learn about yourself and others, to grow, and to feel empowered. They offer prospects to fix what is broken, to change your relationships and your world, to innovate, and to make things better and more just. They can introduce rare occasions to better understand the human condition—to have others really listen to you and recognize what is important to you, and for you to genuinely see and hear others as they struggle through the challenges posed by their lives. In a way, each conflict provides you with a renewed chance to be your best self and to connect—to be human.

Of course, the opposite is also true.

Ultimately, the choice is yours.

ACKNOWLEDGMENTS

IT TAKES a village to write a book. We offer special thanks to our siblings (Bob, Cookie, Michelle, Patrick, Genine, Scott, Bonnie, Laurie, Lynn, and Brian), who offered our first lessons in power and conflict; to our parents (Adelyn, Bob, Harvey, and Marilyn), who were our first benevolent/dominant bosses and intermediaries; to our spouses (Leah and Sandy), who supported (and put up with) the writing of this book; and to our children (Cam, Ella, Hannah, and Adlai), who continue to tutor us on conflict and adaptivity, as they grow into extraordinary adults.

We thank our colleague Katharina Kugler, whose research acumen provided the backbone for this book. We also appreciate our many colleagues and friends who shared ideas, stories (sometimes painful ones), conversations, feedback, and trust, and our students — particularly Kyong Mazzaro and Regina Kim, who offered editorial support. And we thank our literary agent, Jessica Papin, for championing us, and our extraordinary editor, Courtney Young, for *Making Conflict Work* work.

Finally, we acknowledge the life and legacy of Nelson Mandela, who set the bar for conflict intelligence. Remember, as President Obama said after Mandela's passing, *"For nothing he achieved was inevitable."*[1]

APPENDIX

Conflict Intelligence Goal-Setting and Conflict-Planning Questionnaire

1. **What is my goal in this conflict?** (for example, disagreement, difference of opinion, alternative perspective, and so on)

   Short-term goal: _____

   _____

   _____

   Longer-term goal: _____

   _____

   _____

2. **How important is my preferred outcome?**
   _____ Slightly important
   _____ Very important
   _____ Highly important
   _____ Extremely important

3. **Why is the outcome important to me?**

   _____

   _____

   _____

4. **What are the obstacles to my goal?**

_____

_____

_____

5. **With whom am I in conflict?**

An individual: _____

_____

A group: _____

_____

6. **To what extent do I need this relationship to reach my goals?**
   _____ Not at all
   _____ Slightly
   _____ Significantly
   _____ Very much so
   _____ Extremely so

7. **Is the other party with me or against me?**
   _____ With me (pointing to a cooperative win-win solution to our differences)
   _____ Against me (pointing to a competitive win-lose solution to our differences)
   _____ Mixed (pointing to a combination cooperative-competitive solution to our differences, which is quite common)

8. **Is the other party more or less powerful than me (in the sense of formal authority)?**
   _____ More
   _____ Less

9. **Do I have methods or resources for using informal power to influence the outcome of this disagreement?** Informal power includes methods other than formal authority or position power or an official title, such as those listed here. For additional information, review the skill-development checklists at the end of each strategy chapter.

- **Listening** (to de-escalate negative emotion)
- **Seeing different perspectives** (so you do not come off as rigid or stubborn and thus increase competitive aspects of the disagreement)
- **Appealing to others' interests** (so they have a reason to appeal to yours)
- **Cooperating** (thus motivating others to engage in give-and-take with you)
- **Consulting** (earnestly suggesting how others can reach their goals, eliciting their motivation to help you in return)
- **Creating positivity** (creating positive emotions and likability that in turn motivate others to work things out with you)
- **Fostering reciprocity** (doing things for others so that the natural human tendency to reciprocate is activated, even during a dispute)
- **Persuading rationally** (without sounding like a know-it-all)
- **Building networks and coalitions** (attracting supportive people within your organization who are willing to support and advocate for you when you need it)
- **Creating dependence** (through expertise or niches that make others need you and thus motivate them to negotiate rather than fight or dominate)
- **Invoking conformity** (influencing the other party in a disagreement by invoking group norms or organizational culture)
- **Knowing rules and policies** (which you can sometimes use to resolve a conflict by invoking the other person's power and legitimacy)

10. **If I cannot fully achieve my goal, what are sufficient or best alternatives to a negotiated agreement?**

_____ Settle for less. Describe:

_____

_____

_____ Wait for a better opportunity; this is not urgent. Describe:

_____

_____

_____ I have a creative alternative that might appeal to the other party's interests and get me some of what I want. Describe:

_____

_____

_____ I can achieve my goal through other means and other relationships or by myself. Describe how:

_____

_____

_____ I can afford to stop relating to the other party and reach my goals through other means. Describe:

_____

_____

_____ I can afford to leave the team or the entire organization if I do not achieve my goal or a sufficient alternative. Describe:

_____

_____

11. **Accordingly, which one (or combination) of these strategies is most likely to achieve the outcome I want?**

_____ Pragmatic benevolence

_____ Cultivated support

_____ Constructive dominance

_____ Strategic appeasement

_____ Selective autonomy

_____ Cooperation

_____ Competition

_____ Effective adaptivity

_____ Principled rebellion

NOTES

INTRODUCTION

1. E. K. Wayne, "It Pays to Find the Hidden but High Costs of Conflict," *Washington Business Journal,* afternoon edition newsletter, May 9, 2005.
2. I. W. Zartman and J. Z. Rubin, *Power and Negotiation* (Ann Arbor, MI: University of Michigan Press, 2002); J. C. Magee and A. D. Galinsky, "Social Hierarchy: The Self-Reinforcing Nature of Power and Status," *Academy of Management Annals* 2, no. 1 (2008): 351–98; J. C. Magee, A. D. Galinsky, and D. H. Gruenfeld, "Power, Propensity to Negotiate, and Moving First in Competitive Interactions," *Personality and Social Psychology Bulletin* 33, no. 2 (2007): 200–212; J Z. Rubin and B. R. Brown, *The Social Psychology of Bargaining and Negotiation* (New York): Academic Press, 1975.
3. D. Tjosvold, "Unequal Power Relationships Within a Cooperative or Competitive Context," *Journal of Applied Social Psychology* 11 (1981): 137–50; D. Tjosvold, "Power and Social Context in Superior-Subordinate Interaction," *Organizational Behavior and Human Decision Processes* 35 (1985a): 281–93; D. Tjosvold, "Effects of Attribution and Social Context on Superiors' Influence and Interaction with Low-Performing Subordinates," *Personnel Psychology* 38 (1985b): 361–76; D. Tjosvold, "Interdependence and Power Between Managers and Employees: A Study of the Leadership Relationship," *Journal of Management* 15 (1989): 49–64; D. Tjosvold, *The Conflict Positive Organization* (Reading, MA: Addison-Wesley, 1991); D. Tjosvold, "The Leadership Relationship in Hong Kong: Power, Interdependence, and Controversy," in *Progress in Asian Social Psychology,* ed. K. Leung, U. Kim, S. Yamaguchi, and Y. Kashima, vol. 1 (New York: Wiley, 1997); D. Tjosvold and B. Wisse, *Power and Interdependence in Organizations* (New York: Cambridge University Press, 2009).

1. THE NATURE OF CONFLICT AND POWER

1. C. K. W. De Dreu and M. J. Gelfand, "Conflict in the Workplace: Sources, Dynamics and Functions Across Multiple Levels of Analysis," in *The Psychology of Conflict and Conflict Management in Organizations,* ed. C. K. W. De Dreu and M. J. Gelfand (New York: Lawrence Earlbaum, 2008).

2. T. Parker-Pope, "Is Marriage Good for Your Health?" *New York Times Magazine,* April 4, 2010.

3. M. P. Follett, "Power," in *Dynamic Administration: The Collected Papers of Mary Parker Follett,* ed. E. M. Fox and L. Urwick (London: Pitman, 1973); original work published in 1925.

4. M. Losada, "The Complex Dynamics of High Performance Teams," *Mathematical and Computer Modeling* 30, no. 9–10 (1999): 179–192; M. Losada and E. Heaphy, "The Role of Positivity and Connectivity in the Performance of Business Teams: A Nonlinear Dynamics Model," *American Behavioral Scientist* 47, no. 6 (2004): 740–765.

5. J. M. Gottman, "The Roles of Conflict Engagement, Escalation, and Avoidance in Marital Interaction: A Longitudinal View of Five Types of Couples," *Journal of Consulting and Clinical Psychology,* 61, no. 1 (1993): 6–15; J. M. Gottman, et al., *The Mathematics of Marriage: Dynamic Nonlinear Models* (Cambridge, MA: MIT Press, 2002).

6. D. Tjosvold, *The Conflict-Positive Organization* (Reading, MA: Addison-Wesley, 1991).

7. D. Tjosvold, "The Leadership Relationship in Hong Kong: Power, Interdependence, and Controversy, in *Progress in Asian Social Psychology,* ed. K. Leung, U. Kim, S. Yamaguchi, and Y. Kashima, vol. 1 (New York: Wiley, 1997).

8. For an extensive discussion of the pathologies of cooperation, see M. Deutsch, *Distributive Justice: A Social-Psychological Perspective* (New Haven, CT: Yale University Press, 1985).

9. R. M. Emerson, "Power-Dependence Relations," *American Sociological Review* 27, no. 1 (1962): 31–41.

10. The BATNA concept was developed by Roger Fisher and William Ury of the Harvard Program on Negotiation, authors of *Getting to Yes* (Boston: Houghton Mifflin, 1981).

11. R. L. Pinkley, M. A. Neale, and R. J. Bennett, "The Impact of Alternatives to Settlement in Dyadic Negotiation," *Organizational Behavior and Human Decision Making Processes* 57, no. 1 (1994): 97–116; P. H. Kim, "Strategic Timing in Group Negotiations: The Implications of Forced Entry and Forced Exit for Negotiators with Unequal Power," *Organizational and Human Behavior Processes* 71, no. 3 (1997): 263–86; P. H. Kim and A. R. Fragale, "Choosing the Path to Bargaining Power: An Empirical Comparison of BATNAs and Contributions in Negotiations," *Journal of Applied Psychology* 90, no. 2 (2005): 373–81; P. H. Kim, R. L. Pinkley, and A. R. Fragale, "Power Dynamics in Negotiation," *Academy of Management Review* 30, no. 4 (2005): 799–822; E. A. Mannix, "The Influence of Power, Distribution Norms, and Task Meeting Structure on Resource Allocation in Small Group Negotiation," *International Journal of Conflict Management* 4, no. 1 (1993): 5–23.

12. See D. C. McClelland, *Power: The Inner Experience* (New York: Irvington, 1975).

13. M. Sashkin, "Participative Management Is an Ethical Imperative," *Organizational Dynamics* 12, no. 4 (1984): 5–22; R. M. Kanter, "Some Effects of Proportions on Group Life: Skewed Sex Ratios and Responses to Token Women," *American Journal of Sociology* 82, no. 5 (1977): 965–83.

14. J. S. Nye, Jr., "Soft Power," *Foreign Policy* 80 (1990): 153–71.

15. Ibid.

16. C. A. Crocker, F. O. Hampson, and P. R. Aall, *Leashing the Dogs of War: Conflict Management in a Divided World* (Washington, DC: US Institute of Peace Press, 2007), 13.

17. P. T. Coleman and M. Voronov, "Power in Groups and Organizations," in *The International Handbook of Organizational Teamwork and Cooperative Working,* ed. M. West, D. Tjosvold, and K. G. Smith, pp. 229–54 (New York: John Wiley & Sons, 2003).

18. M. Deutsch, *The Resolution of Conflict: Constructive and Destructive Processes* (New Haven, CT: Yale University Press, 1973).

2. POWER-CONFLICT TRAPS

1. J. R. Curhan, H. Anger Elfenbein, and H. Xu, "What Do People Value When They Negotiate? Mapping the Domain of Subjective Value in Negotiation," *Journal of Personality and Social Psychology* 91, no. 3 (2007), 493–512.

2. B. E. Wexler, *Brain and Culture: Neurobiology, Ideology, and Social Change* (Boston: MIT Press/Bradford, 2008).

3. A. Bechara, "The Role of Emotion in Decision-Making: Evidence from Neurological Patients with Orbitofrontal Damage," *Brain and Cognition* 55 (2004), 30–40.

4. J. C. Magee, A. D. Galinsky, and D. H. Gruenfeld, "Power, Propensity to Negotiate, and Moving First in Competitive Interactions," *Personality and Social Psychology Bulletin* 33, no. 2 (2007): 200–212.

5. Andy J. Yap, Malia F. Mason, and Daniel R. Ames, "The Powerful Size Others Down: The Link Between Power and Estimates of Others' Size," *Journal of Experimental Social Psychology* 49, no. 3 (May 2013): 591–94.

6. S. T. Fiske and J. Berdahl, "Social power," in *Social Psychology: Handbook of Basic Principles*, ed. A. W. Kruglanski and E. T. Higgins, 2nd ed. (New York: Guilford, 2007).

7. Ibid.

8. I. W. Zartman and J. Z. Rubin, *Power and Negotiation* (Ann Arbor. MI: University of Michigan Press, 2002).

9. P. K. Piff, D. M. Stancato, S. Côté, R. Mendoza-Denton, and D. Keltner, "Higher Social Class Predicts Increased Unethical Behavior," *Proceedings of the National Academy of Sciences* 109 (2012), 4086–91.

10. P. Brown and S. C. Levinson, *Politeness: Some universals in language usage* (New York: Cambridge University Press, 1987); B. M. DePaulo and H. S. Friedman, "Nonverbal communication," in *The Handbook of Social Psychology*, ed. D. T. Gilbert, S. T. Fiske, and L. Gardner, 4th ed., vol. 2, pp. 3–40 (New York: McGraw-Hill, 1998).

11. C. Anderson and J. L. Berdahl, "The Experience of Power: Examining the Effects of Power on Approach and Inhibition Tendencies," *Journal of Personality and Social Psychology* 83 (2002), 1362–77.

12. Zartman and Rubin, *Power and Negotiation*.

13. C. Anderson and A. D. Galinsky, "Power, Optimism, and the Proclivity for Risk," *European Journal of Social Psychology* 36 (2006): 511–36; J. K. Maner, M. T. Gailliot, D. Butz, and B. M. Peruche, "Power, Risk, and the Status Quo: Does Power Promote Riskier or More Conservative Decision-Making? *Personality and Social Psychology Bulletin* 33 (2007), 451–62.

14. Magee and Galinsky, "Social Hierarchy."

15. Ibid.

16. L. Babcock and S. Laschever, *Women Don't Ask: Negotiation and the Gender Divide* (Princeton, NJ: Princeton University Press, 2003).

17. R. Rosenthal and L. Jacobson, *Pygmalion in the Classroom* (New York: Holt, Rinehart and Winston, 1968).

18. R. Humphrey, "How Work Roles Influence Perception: Structural-Cognitive Processes and Organizational Behavior," *American Sociological Review* 50 (1985), 242–52.

19. P. G. Zimbardo, *The Lucifer Effect: Understanding How Good People Turn Evil* (New York: Random House, 2007).

20. R. M. Kanter, "Powerlessness Corrupts" *Harvard Business Review*, 2009.

21. N. Mandela, *Long Walk to Freedom* (Dubuque, IA: Little Brown, 1995).

22. Magee and Galinsky, "Social Hierarchy."

23. C. K. W. De Dreu, "Coercive Power and Concession Making in Bilateral Negotiation," *Journal of Conflict Resolution* 39, no. 4 (1995): 646–70.
24. Zartman and Rubin, *Power and Negotiation.*
25. Ibid.
26. Ibid.

3. CONFLICT INTELLIGENCE

1. R. Kim, P. T. Coleman, C. Chung, and K. Kugler, "Culture and Conflict Landscapes in Organizations," working paper.
2. M. Deutsch, *The Resolution of Conflict: Constructive and Destructive Processes* (New Haven, CT: Yale University Press, 1973).
3. R. Fisher and W. Ury, *Getting to Yes* (Boston: Houghton Mifflin, 1981); W. Ury, *Getting Past No* (New York: Bantam Books, 1991).
4. T. C. Schelling, *The Strategy of Conflict* (Cambridge, MA: Harvard University Press, 1960).
5. See also R. J. Lewicki, B. Barry, D. M. Saunders, and J. W. Minton, *Negotiation,* 4th ed. (New York: McGraw Hill, 2003).

4. PRAGMATIC BENEVOLENCE

1. G. L. Graham, "If You Want Honesty, Break Some Rules," *Harvard Business Review,* repr. R0204B (2002): 42–47.
2. See M. P. Follett, "Power," in *Dynamic Administration: The Collected Papers of Mary Parker Follett,* ed. E. M. Fox and L. Urwick (London: Pitman, 1973), original work published in 1925.
3. R. M. Kanter, preface to *Mary Parker Follett — Prophet of Management: A Celebration of Writings from the 1920s,* ed. Pauline Graham (London: Pitman, 1973).
4. D. W. Johnson and R. T. Johnson, *Cooperation and Competition: Theory and Research* (Edina, MN: Interaction Books (1989); D. W. Johnson, and R. T. Johnson, "New Developments in Social Interdependence Theory," *Psychology Monograph* 131, no. 4 (2005): 285–360.
5. F. Karakas and E. Sarigollu, "Benevolent Leadership: Conceptualization and Construct Development," *Journal of Business Ethics* 108, no. 4 (2011): 537–53.
6. V. H. Vroom and A. G. Jago, "The Role of the Situation in Leadership," *American Psychologist* 62, no. 1 (Jan. 2007): 17–24.
7. S. H. Appelbaum, D. Hebert, and S. Leroux, "Empowerment: Power, Culture and Leadership—A Strategy or Fad for the Millennium?" *Journal of Workplace Learning: Employee Counseling Today* 11, no. 7 (1999): 233–54; M. Beirne, *Empowerment and Innovation: Managers, Principles and Reflective Practice* (Northampton, MA: Edward Elgar Publishing, 2006).
8. W. C. Bogner, "Robert H. Waterman, Jr., on Being Smart and Lucky," *Academy of Management Executive* 16, no. 1 (2002): 45–50; J. O'Toole, *Leading Change* (San Francisco: Jossey-Bass, 1995).
9. D. Tjosvold, *The Conflict Positive Organization* (Reading, MA: Addison-Wesley, 1991); D. Tjosvold, "The Leadership Relationship in Hong Kong: Power, Interdependence, and Controversy," in *Progress in Asian Social Psychology,* ed. K. Leung, U. Kim, S. Yamaguchi, and Y. Kashima, vol. 1 (New York: Wiley, 1997).
10. Karakas and Sarigollu, "Benevolent Leadership."
11. D. C. McClelland, *Power: The Inner Experience* (New York: Irvington, 1975), p. 20.

12. Vroom and Jago, "The Role of the Situation in Leadership," *American Psychologist* 62 (2007).

13. These were the findings of a meta-analysis of research done by Johnson and Johnson in 1989 of 750 studies conducted since 1898.

14. Karakas and Sarigollu, "Benevolent Leadership."

15. In one study, 90 percent of exceptionally successful executives were depicted as concerned for the careers of their subordinates as much as or more than their own. Only 4 percent were seen as mostly focused on their own careers. Ibid., 537–53. Another study of 686 supervisor-subordinate dyads collected from a manufacturing company in China found benevolent leadership to be positively and strongly related to successful work outcomes. D. Tjosvold, "The Leadership Relationship in Hong Kong: Power, Interdependence, and Controversy," in *Progress in Asian Social Psychology,* ed. K. Leung, U. Kim, S. Yamaguchi, and Y. Kashima, vol. 1 (New York: Wiley, 1997).

16. Karakas and Sarigollu, "Benevolent Leadership."

17. Ibid.

18. D. Kearns Goodwin, *Team of Rivals: The Political Genius of Abraham Lincoln* (New York: Simon and Schuster, 2005).

19. Ibid.

20. Vroom and Jago, "Role of the Situation in Leadership."

21. Ibid.

22. Ibid.

23. F. Karakas and E. Sarigollu, "The Role of Leadership in Creating Virtuous and Compassionate Organizations: Narratives of Benevolent Leadership in an Anatolian Tiger," *Journal of Business Ethics* 113, no. 4 (2013): 663–78.

24. L. W. Fry, "Toward a Theory of Spiritual Leadership," *Leadership Quarterly* 14 (2003): 693–727; L. W. Fry and M. S. Nisiewicz, *Maximizing the Triple Bottom Line Through Spiritual Leadership* (Stanford, CA: Stanford University Press, 2013).

5. CULTIVATED SUPPORT

1. B. Thomas, *Building a Company: Roy O. Disney and the Creation of an Entertainment Empire* (New York: Hyperion, 1998), p. 3.

2. Ibid., p. 2.

3. Ibid., p. 3.

4. I. W. Zartman and J. Z. Rubin, *Power and Negotiation* (Ann Arbor, MI: University of Michigan Press, 2002), p. 277.

5. M. D. Ainsworth, *Infancy in Uganda* (Baltimore, MD: Johns Hopkins Press, 1967; J. Mercer, *Understanding Attachment: Parenting, Child Care, and Emotional Development* (Westport, CT: Praeger Publishers, 2006).

6. M. Losada and E. Heaphy, "The Role of Positivity and Connectivity in the Performance of Business Teams: A Nonlinear Dynamics Model," *American Behavioral Scientist* 47 (2004): 740–65.

7. J. M. Gottman and N. Silver, *The Seven Principles for Making Marriage Work* (New York: Three Rivers Press, 1999); J. M. Gottman, C. Swanson, and K. Swanson, "A General Systems Theory of Marriage: Nonlinear Difference Equation Modeling of Marital Interaction," *Personality and Social Psychology Review* 6, no. 4 (2002): 326–40.

8. Gottman and Silver, *Seven Principles;* Losada and Heaphy, "Role of Positivity and Connectivity."

9. See M. E Turner and A. R. Pratkanis, "Twenty-Five Years of Groupthink Theory and Research: Lessons from the Evaluation of a Theory," *Organizational Behavior and Human*

Decision Processes 73 (1998): 105–15; D. W. Johnson, R. T. Johnson, and D. Tjosvold, "Constructive Controversy: The Value of Intellectual Opposition," in *The Handbook of Conflict Resolution: Theory and Practice*, ed. P. T. Coleman, M. Deutsch, and E. C. Marcus, 3rd ed. (San Francisco: Jossey-Bass, 2014).

10. D. Tjosvold, *The Conflict Positive Organization* (Reading, MA: Addison-Wesley, 1991).

11. D. Tjosvold, "The Leadership Relationship in Hong Kong: Power, Interdependence, and Controversy," in *Progress in Asian Social Psychology*, ed. K. Leung, U. Kim, S. Yamaguchi, and Y. Kashima, vol. 1 (New York: Wiley, 1997); D. Tjosvold and B. Wisse, *Power and Interdependence in Organizations* (New York: Cambridge University Press, 2009).

12. This is known as Deutsch's Crude Law of Social Relations; see M. Deutsch, *The Resolution of Conflict* (New Haven, CT: Yale University Press, 1973).

6. CONSTRUCTIVE DOMINANCE

1. M. Siebert and A. L. Ball, *Changing the Rules: Adventures of a Wall Street Maverick* (New York: Free Press, 2002).

2. http://www.seniorwomen.com/articles/mchugh/articlesMcHughIntSiebert.html.

3. M. H. Bazerman and M. A. Neale, *Negotiating Rationally* (New York: Free Press, 1992); L. Thompson and R. Hastie, "Judgment Tasks and Biases in Negotiations," in *Research in Negotiation in Organizations*, ed. B. H. Sheppard, M. H. Bazerman, and R. J. Lewicki, vol. 2, pp. 31–54 (Greenwich, CT: JAI Press, 1990).

4. D. R. Carney, A. J. C. Cuddy, and A. J. Yap, "Power Posing: Brief Nonverbal Displays Affect Neuroendocrine Levels and Risk Tolerance," *Psychological Science* (2011), 1363–68.

5. J. Hogan, H. Hogan, and R. B. Kaiser, "Management Derailment: Personality Assessment and Mitigation," chap. 15 of *APA Handbook of Industrial and Organizational Psychology*, vol. 3 (Washington, DC: American Psychological Association, 2010).

6. K. Lewin, R. Lippitt, and R. White, "Patterns of Aggressive Behaviour in Experimentally Created 'Social Climates,'" *Journal of Social Psychology* 10, no. 2 (1939): 271–99.

7. http://www.businessweek.com/stories/2006-11-26/mistakes-made-on-the-road-to-innovation.

8. Ibid.

9. D. Reina and M. Reina, *Trust and Betrayal in the Workplace: Building Effective Relationships in Your Organization* (San Francisco: Barrett-Koehler Publishers, 2006).

10. W. Isaacson, *Steve Jobs* (New York: Simon & Schuster, 2011).

11. Ibid., p. 359.

12. Ibid., pp. 119, 122, 123, 146, 178.

13. See D. G. Pruitt and S. H. Kim, *Social Conflict: Escalation, Stalemate, and Settlement,* 3rd ed. (New York: McGraw-Hill, 2004).

7. STRATEGIC APPEASEMENT

1. Y. Ogasawara, *Office Ladies and Salaried Men: Power, Gender, and Work in Japanese Companies* (Los Angeles: University of California Press, 1998).

8. SELECTIVE AUTONOMY

1. J. Gleick, *Genius: The Life and Science of Richard Feynman* (New York: Pantheon Books, 1992).

2. R. L. Pinkley, M A. Neale, and R. J. Bennett, "The Impact of Alternatives to Settlement in

Dyadic Negotiation," *Organizational Behavior and Human Decision Making Processes* 57, no. 1 (1994): 97–116; P. H. Kim, "Strategic Timing in Group Negotiations: The Implications of Forced Entry and Forced Exit for Negotiators with Unequal Power," *Organizational and Human Behavior Processes* 71, no. 3 (1997): 263–86; P. H. Kim and A. R. Fragale, "Choosing the Path to Bargaining Power: An Empirical Comparison of BATNAs and Contributions in Negotiations," *Journal of Applied Psychology* 90, no. 2 (2005): 373–81; E. A. Mannix, "The Influence of Power, Distribution Norms, and Task Meeting Structure on Resource Allocation in Small Group Negotiation," *International Journal of Conflict Management* 4, no. 1 (1993): 5–23.

3. H. R. Markus, and S. Kitayama, "Culture, Self, and the Reality of the Social," *Psychological Inquiry* 14, no. 3 (2003): 277–83.

9. EFFECTIVE ADAPTIVITY

1. N. Doidge, *The Brain That Changes Itself: Stories of Personal Triumph from the Frontiers of Brain Science* (New York: Penguin Books, 2007); A. Pascual-Leone, N. Dang, L. G. Cohen, J. P. Brasil-Neto, A. Cammarota, and M. Hallett, "Modulation of Muscle Responses Evoked by Transcranial Magnetic Stimulation During the Acquisition of New Fine Motor Skills," *Journal of Neurophysiology* 74 (1995): 1037–45.

2. C. S. Burke, K. C. Stagl, E. Salas, L. Pierce, and D. Kendall, "Understanding Team Adaptation: A Conceptual Analysis and Model," *Journal of Applied Psychology* 91 (2006): 1189–1207.

3. D. Hicks, "How Functional Aspects of Identity Become Dysfunctional in Protracted Conflict" (paper presented at the Annual Conference of the International Association for Conflict Management, San Sebastian, Spain, July 1999); R. Kegan, *In Over Our Heads: The Mental Demands of Modern Life* (Cambridge, MA: Harvard University Press, 1995); J. Piaget, *The Construction of Reality in the Child* (New York: Ballantine, 1937); E. H. Schein, "How Can Organizations Learn Faster? The Challenge of Entering the Green Room," *Sloan Management Review* 34 (1993): 85–92.

4. D. Druckman and C. Mitchell, "Flexibility in Negotiation and Mediation," *The ANNALS of the American Academy of Political and Social Science* 542, no. 1 (1995): 10–23; S. M. Farmer and J. Roth, "Conflict handling behavior in work groups: Effects of group structure, decision processes, and time," *Small Group Research* 29 (1998): 669–713; R. Fisher and W. Ury, *Getting to Yes: Negotiating Agreement Without Giving In* (Boston: Houghton Mifflin, 1981).

5. D. G. Pruitt and J. Z. Rubin, *Social Conflict: Escalation, Stalemate, and Settlement* (New York: Random House, 1986); E. Van de Vliert, M. C. Euwema, and S. E. Huismans, "Managing Conflict with a Subordinate or a Superior: Effectiveness of Conglomerated Behavior," *Journal of Applied Psychology* 80, no. 2 (1995): 271–81; E. Van de Vliert, A. Nauta, M. C. Euwema, and O. Janssen, "The Effectiveness of Mixing Problem Solving and Forcing," in *Using Conflict in Organizations,* ed. C. K. W. De Dreu and E. Van de Vliert, pp. 38–52 (London: SAGE Publications, 1997).

6. C. Chung, P. T. Coleman, and M. Gelfand, "Conflict, Culture and Complexity: The Effects of Simple Versus Complex Rules in Negotiation" (working paper, Columbia University, 2014).

7. R. E. Ployhart and P. D. Bliese, "Individual Adaptability Theory," in *Understanding Adaptability,* ed. S. Burke, L. Pierce, and E. Salas, pp. 3–39 (Oxford: Elsevier, 2006).

8. C. S. Burke, K. C. Stagl, E. Salas, L. Pierce, and D. Kendall, "Understanding Team Adaptation: A Conceptual Analysis and Model," *Journal of Applied Psychology* 91 (2006): 1189–1207.

9. E. H. Schein and W. Bennis, *Personal and Organizational Change Through Group Methods* (New York: Wiley, 1965).

10. See I. W. Zartman and J. Z. Rubin, *Power and Negotiation* (Ann Arbor. MI: University of Michigan Press, 2002).

11. Van de Vliert, Euwema, and Huismans, "Managing Conflict"; Van de Vliert, Nauta, Euwema, and Janssen, "Effectiveness of Mixing Problem Solving and Forcing."

12. G. R. Williams, *Legal Negotiation and Settlement* (St. Paul, MN: West, 1983); G. R. Williams, "Style and Effectiveness in Negotiation," in *Negotiation: Strategies for Mutual Gain*, ed. L. Hall, pp. 151–74 (Newbury Park, CA: SAGE, 1993).

13. P. T. Coleman and K. G. Kugler, "Tracking Adaptivity: Introducing a Dynamic Measure of Adaptive Conflict Orientations in Organizations" (working paper).

14. Ibid.

15. R. Hooijberg and M. Schneider, "Behavioral Complexity and Social Intelligence: How Executive Leaders Use Stakeholders to Form a Systems Perspective," in *The Nature of Organizational Leadership*, ed. S. Zaccaro and R. J. Klimoski (San Francisco, CA: Jossey-Bass, 2001); R. Hooijberg and R. E. Quinn, "Behavioral Complexity and the Development of Effective Managerial Leaders," in *Strategic Management*, ed. R. L. Phillips and J. G. Hunt (New York: Quorum Books/Greenwood Publishing, 1992).

16. G. Morgan, *Images of Organization* (Thousand Oaks, CA: SAGE Publications, 1997).

17. M. LeBaron, "The Alchemy of Change: Cultural Fluency in Conflict Resolution," in *The Handbook of Conflict Resolution: Theory and Practice*, ed. P. Coleman, M. Deutsch, and C. Marcus (San Francisco: Jossey-Bass, 2014).

18. Ibid.

19. K. W. Thomas, "Conflict and Conflict Management: Reflections and Update," *Journal of Organizational Behavior* 13, no. 3 (1992): 265–74.

20. G. Lenczowski, *American Presidents and the Middle East* (Durham, NC: Duke University Press, 1990), p. 131.

21. B. Bush and J. Folger, *The Promise of Mediation* (San Francisco: Jossey-Bass, 1994).

10. PRINCIPLED REBELLION

1. "Blowout: The Deepwater Horizon Disaster," *60 Minutes*, CBS News, May 16, 2010.

2. MSNBC: http://www.msnbc.msn.com/id/37363106/#.

3. E. K. Wilson, "Oil Spill's Size Swells," *Chemical and Engineering News* 88, no. 39 (Sept. 27, 2010), http://pubs.acs.org/cen/news/88/i39/8839notw7.html; http://articles.latimes.com/2010/aug/03/nation/la-na-oil-spill-20100803; and http://hosted.ap.org/dynamic/stories/U/US_GULF_OIL_SPILL?SITE=FLTAM&SECTION=HOME.

4. F. Sulloway, *Born to Rebel: Birth Order, Family Dynamics, and Creative Lives* (New York: Vintage Books, 1997).

5. J. Lammers, A. D. Galinsky, E. H. Gordijn, and S. Otten, "Illegitimacy Moderates the Effects of Power on Approach," *Psychological Science* 19 (2008): 558–64.

6. Ibid.

7. R. K. Merton, "Social Structure and Anomie," *American Sociological Review* 3 (1938): 672–82; T. R. Gurr, *Why Men Rebel* (Princeton, NJ: Princeton University Press, 1970).

8. I. Walker and H. J. Smith, *Relative Deprivation: Specification, Development, and Integration* (Cambridge, UK: Cambridge University Press, 2001).

9. G. Hofstede, *Culture's Consequences: International Differences in Work-Related Values*, 2nd ed. (Beverly Hills CA: SAGE Publications, 1984).; G. Hofstede, G. J. Hofstede, and M. Minkov, *Cultures and Organizations: Software of the Mind*, 3rd ed. (New York: McGraw-Hill, 2010).

10. http://theworldoutline.com/2013/05/the-rana-plaza-collapse-while-death-toll-rises-pressure-on-western-retailers-and-bangladeshi-government-grows/.

11. A social audit is a formal review of a company's endeavors in social responsibility. A social audit looks at factors such as a company's record of charitable giving, volunteer activity, energy use, transparency, work environment, and worker pay and benefits to evaluate what kind of social and environmental impact a company is having in the locations where it operates. Social audits are optional: companies can choose whether to perform them and whether to release the results publicly or only use them internally (www.investopedia.com).

12. J. P. Near and M. P. Miceli, "Effective Whistle-Blowing," *Academy of Management Review* 20, no. 3 (July 1995): 679–708.

13. Ibid.

14. Ibid.

15. http://www.nydailynews.com/news/national/pizza-hut-manager-refuses-open-thanks giving-forced-resign-article-1.1531530?.

16. http://www.ibtimes.com/pizza-hut-manager-tony-rohr-fired-refusing-open-restaurant-thanksgiving-day-1488698.

17. http://www.cnn.com/2013/11/28/us/pizza-store-thanksgiving-firing/.

18. http://truth-out.org/video/item/12066-wal-mart-workers-in-12-states-stage-historic-strikes-protests-against-workplace-retaliation.

19. Alinsky, S. *Rules for Radicals,* 1971, p. 152.

20. http://pa-aaup.com/2013/07/30/the-penn-state-healthcare-mandate-and-a-call-for-civil-disobedience/.

21. http://blogs.hbr.org/2013/08/attention-human-resources-exec/; http://www.npr.org/blogs/health/2013/08/02/208167230/penn-state-to-penalize-workers-who-refuse-health-screenings.

22. http://gantdaily.com/2013/09/19/penn-state-suspends-fee-for-employees-who-dont-take-health-care-survey/.

23. C. Harnett, personal interview, November 18, 2013.

24. http://www.cnn.com/2013/10/26/world/meast/saudi-arabia-women-drivers/.

25. http://www.canada.com/vancouversun/news/story.html?id=c40c507f-19a0-4bbd-a465-48245151076d&k=3577.

26. http://www.thenation.com/blog/174964/fired-walmart-workers-arrested-protest-yahoo-headquarters#.

27. http://www.good.is/posts/how-mass-civil-disobedience-at-a-seattle-high-school-catalyzed-the-education-spring.

CONCLUSION

1. For a list and discussion of "hot buttons," see C. Runde and T. Flanagan, *Building Conflict Competent Teams* (San Francisco: Jossey-Bass, 2008).

ACKNOWLEDGMENTS

1. http://www.cbsnews.com/news/obama-mandelas-struggle-woke-me-up-to-my-responsibilities.

INDEX